TELLING
SCOTLAND'S
STORY

IAN STEWART

THE SCOTSMAN
200 Years

ACKNOWLEDGEMENTS

I would like to thank Donald Walker for his great generosity in sharing his expertise and knowledge, and would also like to thank Tina Evans, Denise Brydon and Kerry Black for their invaluable help in making this book a reality.

Great Northern Books Limited
PO Box 1380, Bradford, BD5 5FB
www.greatnorthernbooks.co.uk

ISBN: 978-1-912101-65-8

Design and layout: David Burrill

Cover illustration: Gavin Munro

CIP Data
A catalogue for this book is available from the British Library

Contents

Introduction   9

Chapter

one: **Good sense and courage**   11

two: **True crime**   21

three: **The Scotsman's biggest scoop**   27

four: **Boldly going**   33

five: **The death of Queen Victoria**   44

six: **Scott of the Antarctic**   48

seven: **The Great War**   50

eight: **The tragedies continue**   62

nine: **World War II**   67

ten: **The birth of the world's greatest arts festival**   78

eleven: **The coronation of Queen Elizabeth II**   97

twelve: **The modern world**   103

thirteen: **Delivering the news**   112

fourteen: **Books and writers**   134

fifteen: **Independence and a' that**   138

Subscriber list   158

Ready to hit the road, delivery vans line up outside *The Scotsman* building on Market Street.

The Scotsman offices in Cockburn Street, Edinburgh.

The Scotsman offices on North Bridge.

Introduction

News reports are the first draft of history, unpolished, often incomplete, and all the more fascinating for that. As Scotland's national newspaper marks its 200th year it is possible to get a fresh perspective on those years by looking back in *The Scotsman's* archives and seeing how it covered the great events of its time.

The reports not only take us through history but also chart the changes in language and journalism as newspapers have evolved and developed. In many cases knowing now the fuller context of the events described gives an even more meaningful insight. I defy anyone not to be moved by the first-hand reports of soldiers' stoicism during the Battle of the Somme in 1916 knowing as we do now the full horror and tragedy of what happened on that bloody field.

But although newspapers have changed greatly over the years, one striking and perhaps surprising message from the archives is just how the principles and values of the founders of the paper are still the bedrock of good journalism today. It was then, as it still is now, about having the integrity to do the right thing and hold the powerful to account. Even many of the techniques used by the journalists at the very birth of their craft are very much recognisable to today's journalists living in the digital world.

From the trial of Old Town murderers Burke and Hare to the bitter political divisions of the 2014 Scottish independence referendum this book is about looking at how the story of Scotland was told through the pages of the newspaper, and how the story of the world was told to the people of Scotland.

Of course any selection from the archives is hugely subjective, given just how many stories have been told. Some select themselves, but I have picked out others for a great variety of reasons, some personal, and sometimes just because they are wonderful pieces of writing.

I believe *The Scotsman* has a very special place in the fabric of our nation, and that place has been hard-earned by many thousands of dedicated souls over two hundred years. I hope this book gives some insight as to how that came about.

Ian Stewart
Editor, 2012 - 2017

THE SCOTSMAN,

OR

EDINBURGH POLITICAL AND LITERARY JOURNAL.

This is not the cause of faction, or of party, or of any individual, but the common interest of every man in Britain.——Junius.

No. 1. SATURDAY, JANUARY 25. 1817. Price 10d.

"What! can ye lull the winged winds asleep,
"Arrest the rolling world, or chain the deep?"

Campbell.

Before proceeding to the ordinary business of our paper, we beg to observe, that we have not chosen the name of Scotsman to preserve an invidious distinction, but with the view of rescuing it from the odium of servility. With that stain removed, a Scotsman may well claim brotherhood with an Englishman, and there ought now to be no rivalry between them, but in the cause of regulated freedom. In that cause it is our ambition to labour; but we must remind our more sanguine friends, that it is impossible in a first number to develope all our principles. Time and change of circumstances afford the only sure tests of human conduct. And it is of much more consequence that we redeem our pledge, as occasions offer, for firmness, impartiality, and independence, than that we should surprise by temporary brilliancy. Of those who expected much we solicit an exercise of the patient virtues: we make the same request of those who shall think we go too far in the outset: in time we hope to please both. We shall not, we assure our readers, remain unconcerned spectators of what passes around us. Public occurrences have already made us feel both regret and indignation; but whether we shall in future have to feel regret for the errors of the people, or indignation at the folly or crimes of the minister, we shall endeavour to preserve that temperance of judgment, which most becomes those who are in the habit of addressing the public.

We commence our labours at a period which many circumstances combine to render peculiarly interesting. We have but lately reached the termination of a war, long, bloody and expensive beyond example. The peace that has opened upon us, though hailed with rapture by all nations, has not brought the usual fruits of peace in its train. Instead of healing the wounds which the war had inflicted, it has exasperated every evil in our condition; and rich as the war has been in wonders, the peace promises to surpass it, by exhibiting the singular spectacle, of a nation that had supported the expence of immense armaments by sea and land, and subsidized its numerous allies during a period of twenty years,—sinking at length under the diminished pressure of a peace establishment.

War is a state of preternatural exertion, kept up by a degree of excitement which may be compared to intoxication. Men are not then in a state to reason calmly on the consequences of their conduct. But a period of intense action is naturally followed by a period of reflection, and this period we hope is now arrived. It is time to draw the moral of that great drama, in which we have acted so conspicuous a part. Of the causes from which the war originated, and the spirit in which it was conducted, we are now able to judge with considerable certainty, because alternate failure and success have proved the principles, and disclosed the views of all the parties concerned in it. Of its immediate effects too, we know something by experience; but its ultimate consequences, we think, are likely to be no less singular than its causes, and the events to which it promises to give birth, not less surprising than any that have marked its progress. That war, it appears to us, was an effect of the sudden development of principles, which, before its commencement, had scarcely manifested their influence in the scene of European politics. These principles were less or more connected with most of the great changes that took place in the course of hostilities; they have survived the great contest they occasioned; they are still operating with undiminished force, and cannot fail to produce effects which may render the peace even more eventful and interesting than the war that preceded it. They furnish the key, in fact, by which the great moral phenomena of the age are to be explained, and we therefore think, that a short view of their progress and development on the Continent of Europe, may form a suitable introduction to our future speculations.

The principles of civil liberty have been so long familiar to our own thoughts, that we are apt to forget how recent their origin is among our neighbours. In truth, half a century has scarcely elapsed since the continental nations first formed any conception of political rights. It may surprise us, that the many signal advantages we enjoy under a free constitution, should have so long escaped their notice. But we must recollect, that notwithstanding the infinite efforts we have made to bring our neighbours into better acquaintance with us, by intermeddling in their affairs, we were, and perhaps still are, considered on the Continent as a singular people, separated from the rest of the world, as much by our peculiar humours, as by our insular situation. Our institutions, therefore, although admitted to be excellent, were not considered as models for their imitation; since, in this respect, we were classed with the small republics in Europe, which, like us, nourished the principles of freedom, but were supposed to want such points of resemblance with the great monarchies, as to render the example of the one applicable to the other. The rapid advancement of knowledge, however, could not fail to turn men's thoughts to political subjects, and to bring their paramount importance into view. Montesquieu was the first able writer that treated political topics in a popular style; and as he drew many of his ideas from the British government, his work extended the knowledge of our constitution among foreigners. He was followed by Rousseau, Raynal, and others, who, though tinctured with the rashness of speculation, unquestionably did much to rouse men to a sense of their rights, and to generate a strong desire for political change.

If the origin of great changes is to be sought only in general causes, it is no less true that accidental events furnish the occasions that call latent causes into action. The war between Britain and her American Colonies, which was accidental with reference to the continental nations, hastened the development of those principles which had now taken root. That great contest is distinguished from the ordinary wars of ambition, vanity, or national jealousy, by this circumstance, that it was undertaken to establish a political principle. The Americans had differences with the mother country on matters of minor importance, but the fundamental point upon which they appealed to arms was, that taxation without representation is tyranny. It was singular to see Great Britain, whose free constitution was her boast, waging a war for the extinction of the principles on which that constitution was founded. But, perhaps, it is not correct to say, that the British nation went to issue with the Colonists on the point: it was a Tory faction who had entrenched themselves in the Court, and who were probably well pleased to have a plausible pretext for putting down those doctrines abroad, by which they were continually annoyed at home. Men of enlarged views saw how much our success would have ultimately injured our own constitution;—they saw that the war involved principles of universal interest, and they were alarmed, when a cause affecting civilized society so deeply was staked upon such an unequal contest. The Americans, however, maintained the conflict, till assistance came from a quarter whence it was least to be expected,—from three of the principal continental nations of Europe, who were moved to take this step, partly by a jealousy of Britain, and partly, perhaps, by a secret sympathy with the Colonists. The parties engaged in the war seemed now to have exchanged characters; for, as Britain was in arms to maintain the principles of arbitrary governments, so the despotic rulers of the Continent were become the champions of freedom. The continental nations had hitherto been mere spectators of the war; but, from the time that France, Spain, and Holland joined in it, the cause of the Americans was brought home to the people in these countries, and through them, to the other nations of Europe. A general interest was excited in the progress of the revolution; and from Cadiz to Archangel, questions respecting the principles of representation and the right of resistance were agitated, and uniformly decided, both by the people and their governors, in favour of liberty. This was a great step gained; and the success which happily attended the American arms, crowned the doctrines with double authority. The independence of America came then to be considered by discerning men, not as a prosperous event affecting the fortunes of one particular state, but as a great question settled in favour of the dearest rights of mankind.

The new political spirit was now silently gaining ground every where, and from the close of the American war in 1782, to the commencement of the French Revolution, innumerable indications appeared of its increasing force in the opinions of mankind. It was not confined to the closets of the speculative; it found its way into the tribunals of justice, the courts and cabinets of princes, and even the cells of the Inquisition. Many of the leading men in the French Court were almost open professors of the new political philosophy: in Italy, in Germany, and even in Spain, it had many abettors, and it may be said to have mounted the throne in the person of the Emperor Joseph. This prince, although he conducted his reforms in a despotic spirit, certainly contributed much to lessen men's reverence for ancient abuses, and to prepare the way for useful changes. Without entering into particulars, it may be sufficient to mention, his new penal code; his edicts in favour of the liberty of the press; for enlarging the privileges of the Jews, and for suppressing convents. Of the same nature were the innovations of his brother, the Grand Duke of Tuscany,—the limitation of the powers of the Inquisition in Spain,—the adoption of a more liberal system by that power towards her colonies,—the abolition of torture, and the extending of religious toleration in many countries. To these we may add the efforts made by the States of Holland in 1787, to abridge the powers of the Stadtholder, which were defeated chiefly by the treacherous interference of Prussia with a military force. In short, the eight or ten years preceding the French Revolution, were distinguished by a great number of useful reforms, effected without commotion, and by the prevalence of a liberal spirit that gave the promise of many more.

Men's ideas, however, on political subjects advanced so fast, that these reforms fell far short of what the friends of liberty judged necessary, and, indeed, the distance between such subordinate alterations, and the establishment of a free constitution, the grand remedy for all disorders, is so great, that the one could scarcely be considered as a step towards the attainment of the other. But an unexpected combination of circumstances suddenly presented the means of realising this great advantage in France, the state most likely to lead the others by her power and her example. The revolution in that country broke out in 1789, and till it occurred, no adequate idea was entertained of the deep hold which the principles of civil liberty had taken, and of the new power they had raised up in society. Public opinion advanced with such rapidity that the government was overthrown, not so much from resisting its force, as from yielding too slowly to its pressure. The early part of that revolution certainly presented a gratifying spectacle to the friends of humanity, that of a great nation united by one ennobling sentiment, and effecting, without bloodshed, a great improvement in their social condition. Unfortunately, however, the habits necessary to establish and support a free constitution can only be formed under it: those who first make the attempt are exposed to many dangers, and must gain wisdom from innumerable mistakes and failures. It was not to be expected that men who had been brought up in a state of slavish subjection, should at once sustain the part of free citizens with perfect moderation. The excesses they committed when so suddenly emancipated, ought in justice to be charged upon the system that had debased them. If, in the first intoxication of their zeal, they abolished royalty, it should be recollected that they saw in it only the image of chains and of degradation. The destruction of the privileged orders was the natural consequence of the slavery in which these had held the people. Their outrageous infidelity, the worst feature in their conduct, is accounted for, though not excused,

Chapter one

Good sense and courage

It is entirely fitting that the birth of *The Scotsman* newspaper was about a story, and a drive to tell that story to reveal a scandal and to hold the powerful to account.

William Ritchie was a native of Lundin Mill in Fife, just over the river Forth from the capital, and was a successful lawyer working in the Supreme courts in Edinburgh. This was at a time when the establishment retained a deathgrip on Scottish civic life, maintaining its own power and influence and suffocating any challenge or insubordination.

Ritchie had penned an article laying out an account of mismanagement at the Royal Infirmary in Edinburgh at the request of friends and some clients.

But the newspapers of the day refused to print it, and then they refused to take cash and print it as an advertisement. Ritchie was incensed that the press were closing ranks with the powers-that-be to keep the public in the dark. It was described as "the unblushing subserviency of the Edinburgh press of the day to the powers that were" and it was believed "an unfortunate estrangement has taken place between the people and those who held power over them".

This came at a time when Scotland was still in the throes of momentous social change. At the beginning of the 18th century nine out of ten Scots lived in the country and the vast majority eked out a living by subsistence farming. But by the end of the century almost a third of the population had moved to the rapidly expanding cities and the cities were not equipped to deal with this massive and traumatic surge. The infrastructure needed to deal with this was simply not in place leading to the inevitable social and health problems that ensued.

The growing populations were housed in cramped conditions, it was common for families to live in one room or two, and inadequate sanitation meant contaminated water supplies and human waste piled in streets. It was the perfect breeding ground for disease. Typhus appeared regularly in Scotland between 1817 and 1837, and a cholera plague in 1831-32 claimed 10,000 lives.

But even without disease it was a hard life especially for the poor. Infant mortality rates were high with 18% of babies not seeing their first birthday. Adults could expect to die in their late thirties (Robert Burns died aged 37 in 1796).

And it was a time of great civil unrest with riots common throughout Scotland and could be sparked by new taxes, food shortages or even celebrations getting out of hand.

The first *Scotsman*
25 January 1817.

But by the middle of the 18th century Edinburgh was a city undergoing a massive transformation. The Enlightenment had seen a growth in the professional and merchant classes of Edinburgh and they were finding the excessively cramped and smelly Old Town unsuited to their desires. The decision was taken to build a New Town to the North of the city, and this meant draining the cess pool that was the Nor' Loch and building a new, elegant, spacious quarter. Although James Craig's plan was first drawn up in 1766 it took many years for the New Town to be built, Charlotte Square not being completed until 1820, three years after the first *Scotsman* newspaper took to the streets.

William Ritchie, co-founder of *The Scotsman* newspaper.

To give some idea of the pace of change in the early lives of the founders of *The Scotsman*, Charles Maclaren, one of the two major initial founders, was born in 1782, the same year that saw the repeal of the Proscription Act, allowing again the wearing of tartan in Scotland and the carrying of weapons, banned after the Jacobite uprisings.

As a young boy he may well have been taken to the public hanging of notorious Edinburgh figure Deacon Brodie, the respectable cabinet-maker and city councillor by day and burglar by night. He was hanged at the Old Tolbooth in the High Street on 1 October 1788, before a crowd of 40,000.

The end of the 18th century and the beginning of the 19th were also a period of great change in Scottish culture and literature. There was a new framing of a Scottish identity in literature, probably begun by James Macpherson who published what he claimed were the long-lost works of an ancient Celtic poet Ossian which celebrated great martial victories. And of course there was the poetry of Robert Burns, who rose to fame after the publication of his work in 1786. And Sir Walter Scott, who would become the pre-eminent man of letters of his generation and commonly accused of creating the tartan-and-misty-

Charles Maclaren.

Robert Burns.

Walter Scott.

George II.

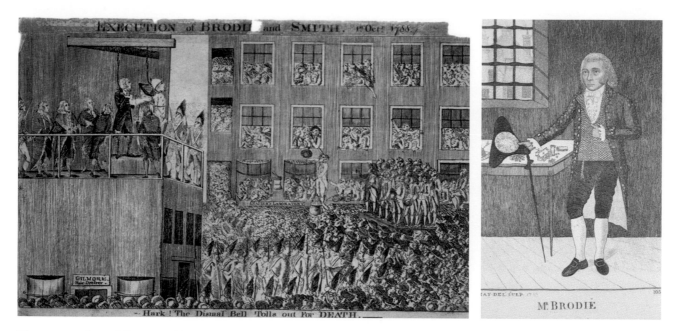

The execution of Deacon Brodie in the Grassmarket in 1788.

Deacon Brodie.

glen romanticised image of Scotland, published his first novel Waverley in 1814, albeit anonymously.

Robert Burns was very important to the founders of the *The Scotsman*, as they saw in him a fellow rebel against the establishment and shared interest in a new view of Scottishness and Scottish culture.

They picked his "symbol dear" of the nation, the thistle, and used it for their masthead, as it still is today, and they picked Burns night in 1817 for the launch of *The Scotsman's* first edition.

But back to the story that started it all. The expansion of the Royal Infirmary in Edinburgh was one of many huge projects underway in the bustling city, and another one which seemed to embody the twin prevailing attitudes of scientific discovery and improving the lot of the human race and the less well off in particular.

The infirmary was very important to Edinburgh particularly as a growing centre of medical excellence and research, a reputation that continued to grow and would soon play a major part in one of the most enduring horror stories of the century and one that would see *The Scotsman* and other Edinburgh newspapers play a vital role.

The very first Edinburgh Infirmary opened in August 1729. It was paid for by public funds, after an appeal was launched by the Royal College of Physicians of Edinburgh. The use of public funds and funding from Edinburgh's concerned philanthropists would continue to play a large part in the life of the hospital.

The first hospital was tiny, with only four beds and this rapidly proved inadequate, but in 1736, a Royal Charter was granted by King George II. A new building was opened in Infirmary Street in 1741 with a huge 228 beds. But demand for medical services and Edinburgh's growing reputation as a centre of medical innovation and research saw the infirmary gradually expand its territory in Edinburgh's Old Town.

But all was not right in this flagship city institution. Reports had come to William Ritchie from friends and clients about conditions in the hospital he felt needed to be exposed as they were of the greatest interest to the public.

His concern centred around what he called alleged abuses "not in the medical practice, but in the domestic management of the institution." He understood that patients were not being fed enough and that hygiene standards were not being met.

At this time Edinburgh was not short of newspapers. The well established *Edinburgh Evening Courant* was published three times a week and was a supporter of the ruling Tory party and was rarely critical of the establishment, and the *Caledonian Mercury*, which favoured the Whigs broadly followed the same non-critical path, and there was the *Edinburgh Star* among others.

But the editors of these newspapers were not willing to publish Ritchie's article. He was incensed. Their refusal simply reinforced his existing view that the existing press were spineless and doing a disservice to the public.

Around twelve years earlier, he had met Charles Maclaren, a farmer's son born at Ormiston in East Lothian, as they were both members of a number of debating societies. They also knew other, like-minded people.

The idea of founding their own newspaper to make good this social wrong and to provide a newspaper they saw fit for purpose was not that of Ritchie, but was an idea cooked up by Maclaren and an Edinburgh bookseller John Robertson.

Maclaren later revealed the idea was run past Ritchie "before it was two days old. After a little reflection he entered in to it warmly. He assisted in forming the plan, suggested the title, drew up the prospectus and by his exertions and influence contributed more than any other individual to establish the paper".

They brought others on board. The men that started *The Scotsman* were not rich or powerful but driven by a shared desire for social justice. They were, along with Ritchie, Maclaren and Robertson, Ritchie's brother John, a haberdasher in Nicolson Street, John McDonald a silk manufacturer, A Abernethy who was a printer and John McDiarmid of the commercial bank.

It was an undertaking not without some financial risk. The price of the paper was set at 10d, a hefty sum at the time, but that included the 4d government tax on every copy. The government was keen to dissuade as many as possible from starting up newspapers which they feared would reveal what they wished to be kept from the public and provide a voice to challenge the establishment.

Because the founders of *The Scotsman* fully intended to be as big a thorn in the side of the establishment as they could they were also realistic about their prospects of advertising revenues from established names, companies and institutions. Advertising was a bit scarce for all newspapers anyway as the government also levied a tax of 3s6d on every one. The founders did not expect to make much from advertising and therefore were relying heavily on the cover price.

To raise money and seek backing the founders published a prospectus on St Andrews Day 1816 laying out their reasons for taking the action they intended and exactly what they planned to do.

It is worth repeating in full because it is wonderfully written with passion and candour, and because it is staggering how much of it is as relevant today as it was then.

Long observation has impressed the Projectors of this Work with a belief that nothing of a very spirited or liberal nature can find its way through the Edinburgh daily or weekly press; that many political matters and transactions in Scotland are thus never generally known; and that the Conductors of the Edinburgh Prints act, editorially, as if they dreaded nothing so much as the idea of being thought independent.

How far this is correct, and whether it proceeds from an erroneous calculation of interest, or the fear of incurring ridicule, need not be determined. The more material fact is not to be denied, that, contrasted with the London, or many even of the Provincial Newspapers, those of Edinburgh are cold, unvaried, and spiritless.

If the Projectors could have persuaded themselves that the existing Prints reflected truly and fully the Spirit and Manners of the Times, and represented all classes in the Metropolis of Scotland, by exhibiting their various feelings and opinions, *The Scotsman* would never have been offered to the public. But although it was thus to remedy an evil, tending in its consequences to extinguish Public Spirit, that the present publication was thought of; the Conductors do not mean to confine their Journal to the discussion of politics.

They shall endeavour also, by making it a reflector of morals and literature, to multiply the sources of rational amusement, without neglecting any proper opportunities for affording instruction. No promise, however, is given to gratify fastidiousness of taste; no pretensions are made to fine writing or profound speculation; but the Conductors pledge themselves for impartiality, firmness, and independence.

As the name implies, Scottish affairs and interests will meet with peculiar attention; but no principle of exclusion will be allowed to operate; and the pages of *The Scotsman* will be open to all who shall, without personal abuse or libellous matter, bring forward a case which, politically, morally, or religiously, is deserving of general consideration. News, Foreign and Domestic, which bear upon any great interests or questions, or which are in themselves extraordinary or surprising, will be faithfully given, and occasionally commented on. Discoveries in Science, Inventions and Improvements in the Arts, will be carefully communicated. Literary Works of merit will be introduced to the notice of the readers, with specimens and criticisms. Manners and Amusements, particularly those of the Theatre, will receive attention. And, in short, by uniting liberal discussion with judicious notices of what is passing in the Political, Literary, Fashionable, and Busy World, the Conductors of *The Scotsman* will endeavour to "hold the mirror up to nature," and exhibit, as much as possible, "the very shape and pressure of the times."

For accomplishing such a varied and difficult task, there are obviously many facilities in Edinburgh, which are not to be found in any other part of Scotland; and though no similar undertaking has been attempted hitherto on this side of the Tweed, the Editor and his friends are not discouraged, since it is pretty manifest that the great requisites for the task are only good sense, courage, and industry.

The Editor and his immediate supporters are lovers of their country.—They are attached to its manners, its scenery, and its literature; but they are still more strongly attached to that regulated freedom, which they enjoy as Scotsmen through their birth right as Britons. This constitutional liberty they wish to preserve equally from the encroachments of power, and the distractions of anarchy.— At present, they conceive there are dangers to be apprehended from both; for an unfortunate estrangement, they fear, has taken place between the people and those who hold office over them. This renders the task of every Editor more delicate and important; and it seems also to call for explanation of the Political Principles on which any intended work is to be conducted. The Projectors of *The Scotsman*, then, hold with Mr Burke, that "although government is certainly an institution of divine authority, yet its forms, and the persons who administer it, all originate from the people;"— that "no power is given for the sake of the holder, but that King, Lords, and Judges, are trustees for the people, as well as the commons;"—that "a vigilant and jealous eye over executory and judiciary magistracy, an anxious care of public money, an openness approaching towards facility to public complaint, are the characteristics of a House of Commons;"— that "public duty demands and requires, that what is right should not only be made known, but be made prevalent; that what is evil should not only be detected, but defeated."

With a living Author, whose genius and knowledge of political truths they conceive to be greater still than those of Burke, they also hold, that "there is nothing else, but a free government, by which men can be secured from those arbitrary invasions of their persons and properties,—those cruel persecutions, oppressive imprisonments, and lawless exactions, which no laws can prevent an absolute monarch from regarding as part of his prerogative;—and, above all, from those provincial exactions and oppressions, and those universal insults, and contumelies, and indignities, by which the inferior minions of power spread miscry and degradation among the whole mass of every people which has no political independence.

With the same Author they are of opinion, that "the dissensions of a free people are the preventives, not the indications of radical disorder; and the noises which make the weak-hearted tremble, are but the natural murmurs of those mighty and mingling currents of public opinion, which are destined to fertilize and unite the country, and can never become dangerous till an attempt is made to dam them up, or to disturb their level."

This creed of the Projectors will not be considered less sound, because it is expressed in the language of departed and living genius. Authority is thus superadded to reason; and when the highest species of both are united, he must be very sceptical, or possessed of a most perverse intellect, who can resist their force. In the present instance, the Projectors are only anxious that their faith may not be discountenanced by their practice. Their first desire is to be honest, the second to be useful.

The fulfilment of both depends less perhaps on themselves than on the Public. Virtues, like manufactures, thrive only where there is a demand for them. When an undertaking is formed, and to be supported on public grounds, gain should not, and cannot be the object of the Projectors; but those concerned here are at the same time desirous to avoid loss; and they must see a prospect of being secured against it, in a number of Subscribers, before they throw off their first paper. Fame can hardly be looked for from their labours; and prudence imposes limits on the degree in which private fortune ought to be injured for the sake of public good. The Public, they conceive, are deeply interested in supporting a publication, which is to be, not in profession only, but in reality, a servant of their own.

To the honest, the liberal and the well-meaning, *The Scotsman* will be faithful in his services. It remains, therefore, with them to shew whether they can estimate the value of what is to be done for them. Encouragement withheld, like hope deferred, withers the powers that deserve it. And, without a figure, the call for subscriptions to this work will afford one test of the public temper and feeling. It will in some degree fix the amount of legitimate patriotism, which is to be found in the country. That it may be great, is desired by the Projectors, more anxiously for the country's sake than their own. Conscious of the purity of their motives, and the sincerity of their professions, they are neither ashamed nor afraid of making a frank appeal; and their anticipations certainly are, that it will not be made in vain.

As they said, all they needed for the task was "good sense, courage and industry". Oh and money, which they got to a bit later on.

They said: "When an undertaking is formed, and to be supported on public grounds, gain should not and cannot be the object of the projectors."

Now there is a message that has been somewhat lost over the centuries.

So the backing must have been forthcoming, because on January 25, 1817, the first edition of *The Scotsman* rolled off the printing press of Messrs Abernethy and Walker, Old Bank Close, Lawnmarket, and in to the hands of the public.

The founders had calculated that they needed to sell 300 copies of each edition to make the paper pay. They were in business. *The Scotsman* was born.

And what happened to the story that sparked its creation? In modern day newsroom terminology, the fight to improve the Royal Infirmary became a *Scotsman* campaign, and one that brought them a great degree of success.

It was a story that was to feature many times in its pages in the coming months, using many of the techniques that would be familiar to journalists and editors today. They investigated practices at the hospital:

"By Royal Charter dated the 25th of August 1736…two of the Managers are to visit the hospital at least once in the month and to write down and subscribe a report of what they observe in a book to be kept for that purpose, which book is to be laid before the Managers monthly. This has not been attended to."

And it took criticism for carrying on its crusade for better conditions: "We are quite aware that our labours under this head (Royal Infirmary) have been greatly, we think rather purposely, misrepresented."

And it told its readers why the powerful needed to be held to account: "The Managers of the infirmary…have clung for a series of years to a system of self election; they have entrenched themselves behind a charter which enables them to perpetuate their own power in management."

And this sparked more information coming in: "We received a communication from a medical gentleman who had recently been an attendant in the infirmary stating abuses of the very same description."

They went in to great detail to report the alleged abuses at the hospital.

10 NOVEMBER, 1817
The New Infirmary

It appears that the average daily number of patients for last year was between 200 and 210 and that the family of Clerks, Nurses &C averaged from 45 to 46. From the table No 11 on page 119 it appears that the whole beef purchased last year was 1241 stones of 14 lbs per stone, or in all 17,374lbs. from this must be deducted a suitable allowance for the family of robust servants each of whom will consume ¼ pound of meat per day which to 45 persons is, in a year, 10,418 and ¾ pounds, leaving as a year's allowance for the patients only 6055 and ¼lbs for patients, a quantity which would hardly make the beef tea required by patients averaging 210 a day for the entire year. And thus, although the allowance to the family was considerably overrated it is obvious from the account of what was paid for that the broth for the patients could not have been half so rich as they should have been and that the quantity of meat to each patient on full diet could only have been the mockery of a meal to most surgical and convalescent patients.

The patients spoke to the same effect that the meat was generally bad and in small quantity.

But let us look now at the meal account. It seems impossible therefore that the patients could get porridge at once in sufficient quantity and of a proper consistency.

As a security against the spreading of contagion, as well as for the sake of cleanliness a pair of clean blankets and sheets should be given to each patient. This is done uniformly at the Glasgow Infirmary: at Edinburgh it could not in possibility be done as to blankets; for during the last year the number of patients admitted exclusive of those remaining in the house at the commencement of the year was 2250 while the pairs of blankets washed in all were only 1791, from which a deduction must be made for the family of 45 persons, and also for the changes to those patients who remain for a long period in the hospital, or who are affected by diseases that require frequent changes. As to the sheets again deducting 522 pairs for the family, the remainder of 3375 pairs got washed would afford a change to each person averaging 209 daily once in the 27 days only; but when it is considered that many patients do not remain 27 days and that many require changes of sheets almost daily, that after giving a clean pair to each patient on admission there were not enough behind for securing cleanliness.

And *The Scotsman* kept on campaigning. "We cannot devote much of each week's paper to this subject (The Royal Infirmary) but, as it is one of the greatest local and perhaps we might say national importance we shall not soon lose sight of it."

And their perseverance and courage was rewarded with success: "From the notices to our correspondents our readers will readily conceive something of the pleasure which we feel in being now able to announce that a Committee has been appointed by the last Court of Contributors to examine the affairs of "The Edinburgh Royal Infirmary" generally and in particular to investigate the facts respecting certain alleged abuses, not in the medial practice, but in the domestic management of the institution."

So the paper stayed true to its values and stated ideals, and strove to do what it considered was the best for the people of Edinburgh, and it made itself a thorn in the side of the establishment wherever it could.

But it would be wrong to mention the early days of *The Scotsman's* history without detailing one of the most bizarre and unusual events; rival editors fighting a duel.

And it wasn't even the more excitable Ritchie, but the dour and dependable Maclaren who took to settling the dispute with pistols.

Maclaren had for some time been having a war of words with the editor of the rival *Caledonian Mercury* Dr James Browne. The Mercury took the traditional Whig view of life, and *The Scotsman's* radical liberalism were bound to bring the two papers in to conflict.

But the conflict became very personal name-calling in the pages of their respective organs, with the *Mercury* saying of *The Scotsman*: "Why is *the Scotsman* petulant, we thought him good-humoured instead he must be a vinegar cruet."

Although that would probably not raise an eyebrow on Twitter today it was trolling 19th century style and Maclaren complained of "wanton and obscene libels" by the *Mercury*.

So on November 12 1829 the two men with seconds and surgeons met at Ravelston to the north west of the city, now a leafy suburb for the well-heeled, and faced each other. It was out of character for Maclaren, in fact it has been described as: "the ridiculous spectacle of a man of Maclaren's sense and intellect taking part in a meeting of this sort".

But to give Maclaren his due as a journalist he recognised the newsworthiness of the encounter, and published an account from the seconds in *The Scotsman*.

Dr Browne, attended by Mr Peterkin and Mr Liston surgeon, and Mr Maclaren attended by Mr L Macdonald and Mr Syme surgeon, met precisely at the hour appointed at a fixed point on the Ravelston road, near Bell's Mill. They went to a field adjacent to the road and before taking the ground Mr Peterkin asked Mr Macdonald if he had any proposal to offer relative to the conference of the preceding evening. Mr Macdonald said he has none. Upon which, having proposed to proceed, Mr Peterkin measured the distance at Mr Macdonald's request, twelve paces.

They then successively loaded, in each other's presence, a brace of pistols each, and the principals took their ground. It having previously fallen to Mr Peterkin's lot to give the word, a pistol was given to each party, and on the word 'fire' the parties fired almost on the same instant, without effect.

Mr Macdonald then came up to Mr Peterkin and asked what further was to be done. Mr Peterkin inquired if he was authorised by Mr Maclaren to offer any apology. Mr Macdonald replied that he was not. Mr Macdonald said: "Do you consider it necessary to proceed further?"

A brief conference then took place in which it seemed to be their mutual impression that nothing further was necessary…Mr Macdonald asked if Mr Peterkin thought the gentlemen should shake hands, Mr Peterkin replied that they had both conducted themselves with calmness and courage and like gentlemen, and, that being the case, he acquiesced in Mr Macdonald's view that nothing further was necessary… Mr Peterkin intimated aloud his opinion that the parties had conducted themselves in a gentleman-like manner but that no apologies or pledges were given on either side. Mr Peterkin then advanced and shook hands with Dr Browne and the parties left the field.

It may be proper to state that Mr Ritchie (William, associate editor to Mr Maclaren) appeared at a short distance from the parties while the pistols were loading, and Mr Peterkin having signified to Mr Macdonald that it was improper for any but the seconds and surgeons to be present, Mr Ritchie, on Mr Macdonald's suggestion, left the field.

The Scotsman certainly cannot be accused of sensationalising their account. It is interesting that Ritchie sought to give some support to his friend and colleague but apparently did nothing to suggest the shooting should not go ahead.

So *The Scotsman* continued on its highly-principled course, but sometimes it too was dominated by the reporting of events, not on its political or literary discourse, and one of the biggest stories in Scotland was about to hit the headlines, and the embryonic press were to play a vital part in ensuring that justice was done.

Chapter two

True crime

It was a tale of two cities, two Edinburghs. On one hand the city was a centre of learning, still basking in the intellectual afterglow of the Scottish Enlightenment, when the great philosophers of the day had created new ways of thinking.

As part of that intellectual surge Edinburgh had become a centre of medical excellence. The city was a leading international destination for those wishing to learn the most up to date techniques and procedures, for those wishing to learn from the men – and it was just men – literally at the cutting edge of medical development.

Edinburgh had some of the top teachers in the developing science of anatomy, including Alexander Monro and his son also called Alexander, John Bell, John Goodsir and of course Robert Knox.

But the teaching of anatomy, for which there was great demand (Knox reported he could get up to 400 people in his class) meant there was a huge demand for corpses, without which the classes could not go ahead.

There were some legal restrictions around where the bodies for dissection could come from: those who died in prison, suicide victims, and the bodies of children whose families could not be found.

But despite huge help from the conditions in the cramped and disease ridden Old Town, this supply could not keep up with demand. And in the struggle to make a living that many in the teeming tenements faced, the rewards from the anatomists were very appealing indeed, from £7 to £10 for each body.

With such an attractive prospect it probably did not take too long before other means of obtaining bodies were found, and the practice of robbing graves became commonplace. In fact it was so widespread that grieving families used to undertake a number of strategies to avoid their dearly departed disappearing, including posting

A sketch of Robert Knox, 1870.
Credit: Wellcome Library, London. Wellcome Images
Images@wellcome.ac.uk

Line engraving of Robert Knox.
Credit: Wellcome Library, London. Wellcome Images
images@wellcome.ac.uk

Portraits of serial killers William Hare and William Burke.

House of William Burke.

guards at cemeteries and even rolling a very large and heavy stone over the grave until the body had decomposed enough as to be worthless to the anatomists. The city had seen public protests at the increase in grave robbing. This had some effect on the supply of bodies and anatomists were said to have been becoming desperate to secure the necessary bodies. At the time Knox was undertaking dissections twice a day, and his advertising promised "a full demonstration on fresh anatomical subjects" as part of every course of lectures he delivered.

Some historians view the actions of Burke and Hare in murdering the victims before selling the bodies was simply a logical extension of what had gone before. In fact the first body they sold was that of a lodger who owed Hare rent and who had died before paying it. They saw the sale of the body simply as covering a debt owed.

When the murders became known Knox's role came in for much criticism, with members of the public questioning why he was not in the dock with Burke and his wife Helen McDougal, after Hare turned king's evidence. In the end he was not even called to give evidence.

The most damning evidence that Knox at least suspected foul play was in the case of the murder of James Wilson, an 18-year-old man with a limp caused by deformed feet. He also had obvious learning difficulties. A familiar figure who begged on the streets, he was known as Daft Jamie.

When his body turned up on the dissection slab some of Knox's students recognised him, but Knox said they were wrong in their identification. However Knox dissected the body ahead of others that were being held in storage and the head and feet were removed before the main dissection

In a move that we would consider bizarre today the trial of William Burke and Helen McDougal started in Parliament House off the Royal Mile on Christmas Eve, and would sit almost continuously until Boxing Day.

The Scotsman published its account of the trial on December 27 and the editors knew that the public could not get enough of this shocking story, the story ran to a length of 12,000 words. In the modern tabloid *Scotsman* that would be the equivalent of having the story on pages 1-16, something only done for the biggest of stories.

They also ran what today would have been called backgrounders, a long article on what was a very hot topic of the day, phrenology. This was a popular science where people's characters and personalities could be divined by reading the bumps on their heads. *The*

William Hare and Mrs Hare at the trial of Burke and McDougal for the West Port Murders, 1828.

Hare's lodging-house, Tanner's Close at the time of its demolition in 1902.

BURKE MURDERING MARGERY CAMPBELL.

William Burke murdering Margery Campbell – the last of the Burke and Hare murders.

Scotsman ran a story headlined: "Phrenological Observations on the head of William Burke". They also ran a big profile of Burke, and in a leading article called for a change where no teacher of anatomy could dissect a body without knowing whose it was and where the body had come from.

Of the press coverage of the Burke and Hare story, the historian Owen Dudley Edwards, who may well have been bitten by a reporter as a child as he is obviously no fan of journalists, writes: "In an age when we have taken note of the vilest libels and corrupt practices by newspaper employees serving billionaire magnates to answer their every whim and fill their papers with every profitable lie they can imagine, how agreeable to contemplate the press in the days of Burke and Hare when the reporters were as ruthless in their inventions to fill space and win attention.

"The Scottish media in 1828-1829 got what they could and invented what they couldn't, plagiarised and contradicted one another, wheedled gossip about the accused and the evidence from policemen, legal clerks, clergy, medical students or anyone else with the feeblest grasp of new information, dreamed up informants and evidence as deadlines approached, editors demanded, publishers snarled and public after public yearned, with those who could not read badgering those who could."

I think that by any reasonable interpretation that is a very jaundiced view and takes no account of the very great service the press reporting of the case did for justice.

Nowadays the press are very strictly limited by law as to what they can write and when in regards to court proceedings so as not to prejudice trials, but back in the day of Burke and Hare when newspapers and press reporting were in their infancy there were no such restrictions.

But that lack of restriction on the press, and the enthusiasm so derided by Dudley Edwards, actually proved a turning point in the treatment of Burke.

In the course of their murderous spree Burke and Hare had murdered 16 people,

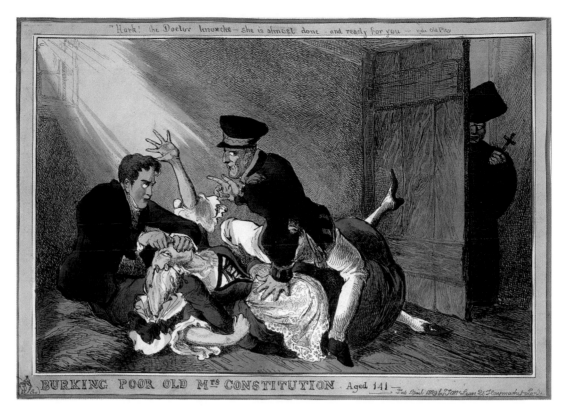

The Burke and Hare murders became so famous that they were used for satirical purposes in political cartoons, as in this one where Wellington and Peel are seen doing away with the constitution for Catholic emancipation.
Wellcome Trust

"Hark! the Doctor knocks – she is almost done – and ready for you – you old Prig."

BURKING POOR OLD Mrs CONSTITUTION. Aged 141

but there was only evidence in the case of their last victim, after blood-stained clothing had been found and the body had been discovered on Knox's dissection table. But the police were convinced there must have been more murders, but were severely hampered by the lack of bodies.

It was the stories run by the papers that meant other people whose loved ones were missing thought that they may have been victims of Burke and Hare and came forward to the police.

A local baker came forward and told police that Burke's nephew had been seen wearing trousers belonging to Daft Jamie, and the four were also charged with that murder. Then the Lord Advocate took a tried and tested tactic and offered Hare immunity from prosecution if he confessed and testified against the others. Because a person cannot testify in court against their spouse, Hare's wife also escaped prosecution, leaving Burke and McDougal the only ones in the dock.

On 4 December formal charges were lain against Burke and McDougal for the murders of Mary Paterson, James Wilson and Mrs Docherty.

The Scotsman reported the closing remarks of the Lord Justice Clerk at length. He was a man who believed that wherever possible sentencing should precisely fit the crime.

"The only doubt I have in my mind is, whether to satisfy the violated laws of your country, and voice of public indignation, your body ought not to be exhibited in chains to bleach in the winds, in order to deter others from the commission of similar offences. But taking into account that the public eye would be offended by so dismal a spectacle, I am willing to accede to a more lenient execution of your sentence, and that your body should be publicly dissected. I trust therefore that if it is ever customary to preserve skeletons, your skeleton will be preserved, in order that posterity may keep remembrance of your atrocious crimes."

The public dissection of Burke's corpse

EXECUTION of the notorious WILLIAM BURKE the murderer, who supplied DR KNOX with subjects.

Execution of Burke in the Lawnmarket, Edinburgh, 28 January 1829.
Credit: Wellcome Library, London. Wellcome Images Images@wellcome.ac.uk

was a very popular event. *The Scotsman* reported: "A prodigious crowd collected at an early hour in the forenoon and besieged the classroom door, eager to gain admission, and it was with great difficulty the regular students could gain access. The lecture was very long, and about one o'clock the crowd outside manifested signs of impatience at the delay and proceeded to evince their disapprobation by throwing stones and snowballs at the police.

"The officers in their endeavours to preserve order were obliged to have recourse to their batons, but were promptly opposed by walking sticks and umbrellas. A dreadful scuffle ensued which lasted a considerable time. In the meantime Dr Monro had concluded his lecture, the hall was cleared and large parties were admitted in rapid succession to see the corpse."

On the following day the corpse was still on show in the college, and the report ran: "The corpse lay exposed for seven and a half hours. The progress of the "stream of people" was slow but constant and yesterday the body was seen by upwards of 24,000 individuals. Incredible as it may appear, it is nevertheless true, that seven females pressed in amongst the crowd. They were treated as their want of decency and right feeling deserved and not one of them will ever again go to a gadding in the dress they had on at the time. Burke's body will be seen no more by the public."

But, as is laid out in the Lord Justice Clerk's ruling, to this day Burke's skeleton is on display at the Anatomical Museum at Edinburgh University to which the public have limited access.

Chapter three

The Scotsman's biggest scoop

For newspapers of course, then as now, it is all about stories. There is always a need to break the big exclusive stories to your readership, and everyone is always on the hunt for the big scoop. In 1840 *The Scotsman* had been credited for "a scoop on gigantic scale" and what has been called "*The Scotsman's* biggest scoop" - the Ice Age.

Looking back now it might be perceived that the presentation of the story was very different then than it would have been today, but they were different times and newspapers were still really in their infancy. There were no big banner headlines or multiple spreads.

But in scientific terms it was a great breakthrough, and it relied on the basic but sound journalistic practice of the paper's then editor, John Hill Burton.

It was a time of great scientific endeavour in many fields, and particularly in the field of geology to establish the origins of the earth. Now the subject of climate change regularly hits headlines and dominates political agendas, but back in 1840 was the very beginning of our understanding of the forces that shaped our planet and continue to do so.

John Hill Burton was born in Aberdeen in 1809 and studied to become a lawyer. He moved to Edinburgh but pursued a career in writing rather than a full-out legal career. He was a historian and a follower of philosophy. He wrote an eight-volume *History of Scotland: from Agricola's invasion to the extinction of the last Jacobite insurrection*. He contributed pieces to *Blackwood's Magazine* and *The Scotsman*, and became editor of *The Scotsman*.

He was aware that eminent geologists William Buckland and Louis Agassiz were visiting the Scottish Highlands, Agassiz had earlier published his theory that the world had been subjected to an Ice Age and that the evidence of that was reflected in mountain structures and geological

Louis Agassiz.

A bust of John Hill Burton as portrayed on his wife's grave in Dean Cemetery in Edinburgh (carved by William Brodie in 1881). Stephen C Dickson

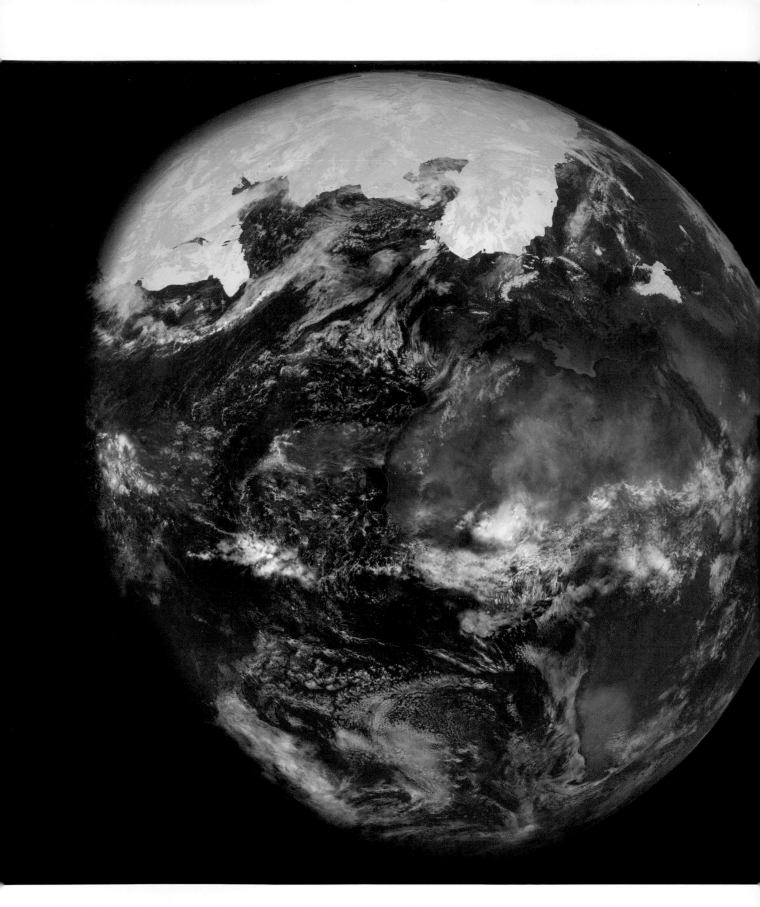

Earth during the last glacial maximum - the last glacial period when ice sheets were at their greatest extension - of the current ice age.
Based on: "Ice age terrestrial carbon changes revisited" by Thomas J. Crowley (Global Biogeochemical Cycles, Vol. 9, 1995, pp. 377-389)

Ben Nevis.

Scandinavia from space in winter.
Jacques Descloitres, MODIS Land Rapid Response Team at NASA GSFC

scarring of the landscape.

He travelled to Scotland with Buckland to find evidence to back up his theory. John Hill Burton sent a reporter from *The Scotsman* to accompany the scientists as they sought to find evidence to back up their theory in the Scottish mountains. The result was an exclusive story published in *The Scotsman* on 7 October that year. Before Charles Darwin came forward with evidence to back up his theory of evolution, here was proof that the earth was much older than thought and controversially that it had not been created in seven days, which at the time was a bombshell discovery.

As to the logic of the Note, we think there be but one opinion—that it convicts the ch Government of gross inconsistency and aith, and in showing that the pretended in- offered to it have no existence, demonstrates its blustering tone is without a shadow of se.

hoever looks at the map will see, that while emet Ali possesses Syria, and can station an of 100,000 men at Marasch or Samosat, he in the most literal sense the *key* of Asiatic ey. He is not placed on the borders of the try, but occupies a position precisely in its e, from which he can with equal ease, and early the same time, march to Bagdad, na, or the Bosphorus, to Trebisond or Mo- and he is equally in a condition to prevent Turkish officers in one of these districts from uring those in the others. If we suppose vading enemy to occupy Berwickshire, the Lothians, with Fife and Perthshire, and to a powerful army encamped in the last of counties, his position in Scotland would be r to that of Mehemet Ali in Asiatic Tur- France agreed with England that Turkey to be upheld as an independent state. The n assigned was "the maintenance of the ba- of power," which in this case means, that issolution of the Ottoman Empire would be ggrandizement of Russia, a power already trong for the security of Western Europe. greed also, that the integrity of that empire in peril by the encroachments of the Pasha. then was the danger to be averted?

he original opinion entertained by her Majesty's nment, and which was made known in June, to the other Four Powers, France included, was, he only arrangement between the Sultan and net Ali which could ensure permanent peace in evant, would be that which should confine Mehe- Ali's delegated authority to Egypt alone, and re-establish the direct authority of the Sultan whole of Syria, as well as in Candia and the ities; *thus interposing the Desert between the Sultan's authority and the province to be administered by the* ; and her Majesty's Government propo-ed that, compensation for the evacuation of Syria, Mehe- Ali should receive the assurance that his male ndants should succeed him as governors of Egypt the Sultan."

e soundness of this proposition is obvious. sert 150 miles in breadth, impassable for ry, and where an army cannot find either r water, is an excellent barrier, better far the Rhine or the Danube. The compensa- offered, too, is not without value. Mehemet , and assumes to be, nothing more than the of the Sultan, who would be entitled to re- possession of Egypt at the Pasha's death, strong enough, would unquestionably make ttempt. Mark the opinion of the French nment upon the subject :—

this proposal the French Government objected, that *such an arrangement would undoubtedly be , if there were means to carry it into effect*; but Mehemet Ali would resist it, and that any mea- of force which the allies might employ to compel yield would produce consequences which would re dangerous to the peace of Europe, and to the endence of the Porte, than the present state of between the Sultan and Mehemet Ali could be."

re we have the French Government admit- that the object sought by the Four Powers only reasonable and legitimate, but the eligible of any, and merely objecting to the sed danger attending its execution. Now, he execution been confined to Russia alone, bjection would have had some force; but Britain, Austria, Prussia, and France too chooses, are associated with her in the prise, where is the danger? Even a Russian in the Mediterranean, which some dread, really lessen the risk, because it would uivalent to a pledge put into the hands of n, which would be forfeited if Russia should her power to the injury of the Porte.

nce, though professedly satisfied with the disapproved of the mode of action proposed e other Powers, and for a while objected to nployment of force against the Pasha under rcumstances. Even this point, the only es- l point on which she differed from her co- tors, was at length conceded.

September 1839, Count Sebastiani, the French sador at the Court of London, proposed that *a uld be drawn east and west, from the sea somewhere Beyrout, to the Desert near Damascus*, and that all south of that line should be administered by net Ali, and all to the north of that line, by the

The concluding paragraph of the Note is equally just in sentiment, and dignified—

"Her Majesty's Government feels confident that Europe will acknowledge the integrity of purpose which has actuated the Four Powers on this occasion; for their object is disinterested and just. They look to reap no selfish advantage from the engagements which they have contracted; they seek to establish no exclusive influence, and to make no territorial acquisition; and the ends they aim at must be as beneficial to France as to themselves, because France, like themselves, is interested in the maintenance of the balance of power, and in the preservation of general peace."

DISCOVERY OF THE FORMER EXISTENCE OF GLACIERS IN SCOTLAND, ESPECIALLY IN THE HIGHLANDS, BY PROFESSOR AGASSIZ.

Professor Agassiz of Neufchatel has recently been studying the glaciers of the Alps with great care, and has been led by his investigations to certain bold, novel, and highly interesting conclusions respecting the part which these singular bodies have acted in the physical history of the globe. We were present when he explained his views in the Geological Section of the British Association at Glasgow, and subjoin a short outline of them, drawn up, we believe, under his own eye. To this we are enabled to add a most interesting communication, addressed by him to Professor Jameson, bringing out the important fact, that *he has discovered distinct indications of the ancient existence of glaciers at Ben Nevis, and elsewhere in the Highlands*. There are other geological phenomena which lead us to conclude that the climate of this country at a former, but, geologically speaking, a recent epoch, was much colder than it now is; and that such a state of things is consistent with the course of nature, is shown by the fact that Mr Darwin found glaciers reaching down to the level of the sea on the west coast of Chili, in latitude 46 degrees, that is, 11 degrees nearer the equator than Ben Nevis. The evidence on which M. Agassiz's experience in the Alps has taught him to rely, consists, first, of the striated and smoothed surfaces of the rocks, the direction of the striæ being along the valley; secondly, of *morains*, or long narrow ridges of gravel, which are deposited on the flanks of the glaciers; and, thirdly, of large transported fragments of rock, which are borne along by the glaciers in their course, or floated off by icebergs when the glaciers reach the sea. In a work just published, he has adduced powerful arguments to show that the great valley of Switzerland, between the Alps and Jura, fifty miles in breadth, was formerly covered by one great sheet of ice. The following is a brief notice of the communication made by Professor Agassiz *viva voce* to the Association, "On the Glaciers and Boulders of Switzerland:"—

"Professor Agassiz of Neufchatel gave a most valuable communication upon the glaciers of Switzerland, in which he particularly drew their attention to *facts* relative to the manner of their movements, which he attributes to the continual introduction of water into all their minutest fissures, which, in freezing, continually expands the mass. The effects of the movement produced by this expansion upon the rocks beneath the ice, are very remarkable. The basis of the glaciers, and the sides of the valleys which contain them, are always polished and scratched. The fragments of the rocks that fall upon the glaciers are accumulated in longitudinal ridges on the sides of the ice by the effects of the unequal movement of its middle and lateral masses. The result is longitudinal deposits of stony detritus, which are called *morains*; but as the glaciers are continually pressed forwards, and often in hot summers melted back at their lower extremity, it results that the polished surfaces, occasioned by friction on the bottom and sides, are left uncovered, and that the *morains*, or curvilinear ridges of gravel, remain upon the rocks formerly covered by the ice, so that we can discover, by the polished surfaces and the *morains*, the extent to which the glaciers have heretofore existed, much beyond the limits they now occupy in the Alpine valleys. It even appears to result from the *facts* mentioned by Professor Agassiz, that enormous masses of ice have, at a former period, covered the great valley of Switzerland, together with the whole chain of the

TOWN COUNCIL PROCEEDINGS.

TUESDAY, Oct. 6.

The LORD PROVOST in the Chair.

The Lord Provost, before proceeding to the ordinary business of the day, begged to be allowed to correct a misrepresentation which had gone abroad respecting a matter in which he was concerned. Statements or misrepresentations affecting himself, whether proceeding from newspapers or otherwise, he was usually in the habit of treating with that silent contempt which they merited; but when statements affecting one's feelings of honour, or the honourable feelings of others, were put into circulation, it became necessary to notice them. He understood that, in a newspaper of that morning, which dealt very much in these sort of floating rumours, it was stated that there was a sort of understanding between his honourable friend opposite (Mr Drysdale) and himself, or at least between their respective friends, on a certain event which might take place—that, in short, there was to be a kind of coalition between them. He (the Lord Provost) must say that there was no intention of any coalition, so far as he was aware; he did not know what support, in any circumstances, he was to receive from either one side of the table or the other; but he believed he would receive no support but what would be honourably given, and which he could honourably receive—without any abandonment of principle on either side—without the slightest compromise or understanding between any one (hear, hear).

Mr Drysdale also denied the knowledge of any coalition of the kind alluded to.

SELF-DENYING ORDINANCE.—On the reading of a report by the Trinity Hospital Committee, on contracts for bread, butcher meat, and coals, Mr Gray rose to move the abolition of the self-denying ordinance, which prevented members of Council from competing with their neighbours; but was informed that his motion could not be received without a week's previous notice, which he then agreed to give.

CHARITY WORKHOUSE.

There was next read a letter from the Treasurer of the Charity Workhouse, enclosing minutes of meetings of the ordinary and general managers, on the subject of the present embarrassments of the institution.

Mr Drysdale said, he was exceedingly sorry to observe that the managers were giving the Council unnecessary trouble in this matter. It was stated that the Council had virtually left the managers without the means of carrying on the institution. This was a perfect mistake. Before coming to the Council, he (Mr D.) had called at the office of the Collector of Poor-rates, and was informed by that gentleman, that notwithstanding the arrestments, he had already collected out of the new assessment the sum of £537 (hear, hear), and that he would guarantee the production of ways and means from the same source to keep up the institution at least for a month. In these circumstances, then, it was perfectly idle to come and tell the Council that they would all at once give up their important and valuable trust into their hands, because, forsooth, they had not enough of funds to carry it on. *There was another fact which he was sorry to notice*—he meant the arrestments—because the Banks knew perfectly well that they had a memorial before counsel, which they themselves had revised; and they were not entitled, in the midst of these arrangements, to go and take steps at law. What the Council should do, was to remit the matter to the Law Committee to take immediate steps for loosening any arrestments that have been laid on, or which might hereafter be laid on. He would stake any professional reputation that he had ever had at the bar upon the opinion, that the Banks had no power to arrest the poor-house assessment, which was in the nature of an alimentary debt, and which could never be arrested.

Mr Macaulay seconded the motion.

Treasurer Stodart said they had come now to a crisis in the history of the Workhouse; and he was sorry to see, from the discussions of the Managers, that there was something like bad feeling between them, the Banks and the Town Council; some misunderstanding, which he thought a few words of explanation would at least soften down. It appeared to him from the interview he had had with the Banks the other day, that they seemed to think the Council were wanting to shut out their claim altogether—that they did not intend to meet it fairly. He appealed to the Council if this was true? (hear, hear.) Had they not that day passed accounts from between £1000 to £1200 incurred in seeking to obtain a bill, one great object of which was to provide for the payment of this very debt? Had *they not also at that moment a case in the hands of* counsel to ascertain what power they had to pay that debt? And did not that imply that if they had the power, they would follow it up by laying on an assessment for that purpose? In this state of things, to assume that the Council did not wish to pay this debt, seemed to him most extraordinary; and the sooner the Banks were disabused of this the better. He appealed to these facts as the strongest contradiction to their assertion. With regard to the Managers, *it appeared to him that they had shown a degree of impatience* which the circumstances did not warrant. The Town Council, he admitted, were the proper constituted authorities for providing funds for the Workhouse by laying on assessment; and, after considering a vidimus of what was necessary for the year, they had provided this and more by authorizing an assessment

ceived from the West Kirk of the minute of Session emb that, being still of the same propriety of their resolution but to abide by it; but, in c modation of the public, the mittee to consider and rep employing hearses more fre rendering unnecessary the us mourners.

Bailie Thomson, in movin that enough had been stated vious meeting to warrant the clusion that it was now ind additional accommodation sh purpose of burying the dead There was no individual re that the West Kirk Session in this condition. He did ex of last meeting would have h them to rescind their resoluti and far from his wish, to th Kirk Session. He was disp gentlemen that they were ac done by the purest motives. he would take the liberty of had placed themselves in a f zeal in preventing the dese had carried them too far. outstripped their prudence (h altogether of the obstacles wl way of Sunday funerals, h had sufficient reason to encou the measure now contemplate fied, if they found a suitabl placed it under proper man not only afford great accon lic at a much cheaper rat give a sufficient return of capital (loud cheers). Scotland had had, till within an entire monopoly of the mar grounds; and he believed n more to bring the Sessions in gulations which they had so u posed to the feelings, privile of the public (applause). H was safe in stating, that in ev accommodation had been pr very great benefit to the local placed, and also remunerated perfect satisfaction. Upon th move, "That the West Kirk S acquiesce in the late express ference to Sabbath Funerals, a dated 'West Church, 22d S agreed to adhere to their resol on Sabbaths,' this meeting resolution referred to is opp convenience of the inhabitants it is necessary to take steps to

Councillor Ritchie said, he seconding the resolution; an in which it had now been in unnecessary to say anything word, however, he would say, marvelled exceedingly at the ing ever passed such a foolish was it all about? It was nei putting forward the pretend nience of a few gravedigge trampling on the high and ho inhabitants (loud cheers), whi rated. He agreed most cord Thomson had said, and had n ing his motion.

Mr Andrew Wilkie, jewe another resolution, which h means of remedying the evi meeting had agreed to the rese son, that something must be d as possible; and he had there is now rendered necessary, fr provide other burying-ground approve of a company being f which, under proper manageme the evil complained of, but a the public at much lower rates t

Mr Rodgers, tailor, seconde

Councillor Stewart moved committee to carry these resol was seconded by Mr A. D. C

Mr M'Aulay moved the names of labouring men to th agreed to.

Mr Campbell, journeyman name was one of those prop made a few rambling remarks ing a scheme like the present j lar basis, and not allowing monopolized by the middling gested that no shareholder, he held, should have more tha lisses).

Mr Balleny then read the p pany which had been prepared which was now submitted to posed that the capital should scribed for in shares of £1 eac

Mr Adie, journeyman mason of committee), in reference Campbell, bore testimony to which had been rendered to t

Discovery of the former existence of glaciers in Scotland, especially in the Highlands, by Professor Agassiz

Professor Agassiz of Neufchatel has recently been studying the glaciers of the Alps with great care, and has been led by his investigations to certain bold, novel and highly interesting conclusions respecting the part which these singular bodies have acted in the physical history of the globe.

We were present when he explained his views in the Geological Section of the British Association at Glasgow, and submitted a short outline of them, drawn up, we believe, under his own eye. To this we are enabled to add a most interesting communication, addressed by him to Professor Jameson, bringing out the important fact, that he has discovered distinct indications of the ancient existence of glaciers at Ben Nevis, and elsewhere in the Highlands.

There are other geological phenomena which lead us to conclude that the climate of this country at a former, but, geologically speaking, a recent epoch, was much colder than it now is; and that such a state of things is consistent with the course of nature, is shown by the fact that Mr Darwin found glaciers reaching down to the level of the sea on the west coast of Chile, in latitude 46 degrees, that is, 11 degrees nearer to the equator than Ben Nevis. The evidence on which M. Agassiz's experience in the Alps has taught him to rely, consists, first, of the striated and smoothed surfaces of the rocks, the direction of the strim being along the valley; secondly, of morains, or long narrow ridges of gravel, which deposited on the flanks of the glaciers in their course, or floated off by icebergs when the glaciers reach the sea. In a work just published, he shows that the great valley of Switzerland, was formerly covered by one great sheet of ice. The following is a brief notice of the communication made by Professor Agassiz viva voce to the Association, "On the Glaciers and Boulders of Switzerland:" –

"Professor Agassiz of Neufchatel gave a most valuable communication upon the glaciers of Switzerland, in which he particularly drew their attention to facts relative to the manner of their movements, which he attributes to the continual introduction of water into all their minutest fissures, which, in freezing, continually expands the mass. The effects of the movement produced by this expansion upon the rocks beneath the ice, are very remarkable. The basis of the glaciers, and the sides of the valleys which contain them, are always polished and scratched. The fragments of the rocks that fall upon the glaciers are accumulated in longitudinal ridges on the sides of the ice by the effects of the unequal movement of its middle and lateral masses. The result is longitudinal deposits of stony detritus, which are called morains; but as the glaciers are continually pressed forwards, and often in hot summers melted back at their lower extremity, it results that the polished surfaces, occasioned by friction on the bottom and sides, are left uncovered, and that the morains, or curvilinear ridges of gravel, remain upon the rocks formerly covered by the ice, so that we can discover, by the polished surfaces and the morains, the extent to which the glaciers have heretofore existed, much beyond the limits they now occupy in the Alpine valleys.

It even appears to result from the facts mentioned by Professor Agassiz, that enormous masses of ice have, at a former period, covered the great valley of Switzerland, together with the whole chain of the Jura, the sides of which, facing the Alps, are also polished, and interspersed with angular, erratic rocks, resembling the boulders in the morains, but so far different, that the masses of ice not being there confined between two sides of a valley, their movements were in some respects different – the boulders not being connected in continuous ridges, but dispersed singly over the Jura at different levels.

Professor Agassiz conceives that at a certain epoch all the north of Europe, and also the north of Asia and America, were covered with a mass of ice, in which the elephants and other mammalia found in the frozen mud and gravel of the Arctic regions, were embedded at the time of their destruction. The author thinks that when this immense mass of ice began quickly to melt, the currents of water that resulted have transported and deposited the masses of irregularly-rounded boulders and gravel that fill the bottoms of the valleys; innumerable boulders having at the same time been transported, together with mud and gravel, upon the masses of the glaciers then set afloat. Professor Agassiz announced that these facts are explained at length in the work which he has just published, "Etudes sur les Glaciers de la Suisse," illustrated by many beautiful plates, which were laid before the Geological Section.

Professor Agassiz is also inclined to suppose that glaciers have been spread over Scotland, and have everywhere produced similar results. If we understood him rightly, he means to follow up his valuable researches in the Highlands of Scotland during his stay in this country, where he confidently expects to find evidence of such glaciers having existed, particularly around Ben Nevis."

Today the Ice Age is common knowledge, but at that time it was revolutionary.

Chapter four

Boldly going

The mid-19th century had a world that was still to be filled in. There were large sections of the world uncharted, but one Scot was going to make a massive impact on that, and *The Scotsman* was there to ensure his discoveries and the importance of them did not go unnoticed by the nation of his birth, and he became one of the biggest national heroes of the age.

David Livingstone was a passionate believer in taking the message of Christianity to the peoples in the African interior, and an ardent opponent of the slave trade, in fact he believed his incredibly arduous and risky exploration of interior routes would hasten the end of the trade in human misery.

This was a time of empire building. In Britain almost every effort was in some way directed at the expansion of the empire and this was even more so in Scotland. The people at the forefront of carving out this new world and getting rich and famous in the process, the generals, the industrialists and of course the explorers were the celebrities of the day.

The values they represented, of innovation, courage, selflessness and enterprise were the aspirational values of the age, and they became entwined with how the nation saw itself. Scotland believed it was by far the purest reflection of the values of empire, and believed it played a disproportionate part in the success of the UK, to such an extent that Scottish politicians were demanding increased representation at Westminster to reflect the greater part it was playing in the UK's fortunes.

Livingstone was born at Blantyre on 19 March 1813. He studied medicine and theology in Glasgow and decided to become a missionary doctor.

In May 1856, four years after leaving the Atlantic coast of Angola, the Scot reached the mouth of the

David Livingstone.

Birthplace of David Livingstone in Blantyre, Scotland.

Zambezi on the Indian Ocean, becoming the first European to cross southern Africa. He was everything the public wanted in an Empire hero.

There are some wonderful insights from *The Scotsman* coverage at the time, not least in the eyewitness account of his return to Southampton, and the physical description of him.

WEDNESDAY, 17 DECEMBER, 1856

Dr Livingstone, the African Traveller

Dr Livingstone reached Southampton from London at seven o'clock on Thursday night. Mr Randall, with whom Mr Livingstone has been staying, and other gentlemen, met him at the railway station.

On Friday, a number of gentlemen paid their respects to him, although his arrival in the town was not generally known.

He is nearly forty years of age, his face is furrowed through hardships and is almost black with exposure to a burning sun.

He hesitates in speaking, has a peculiar accent, is at a loss sometimes for a word, and the words of his sentences are occasionally inverted.

His language is, however, good, and he has an immense fund of the most valuable and interesting information, which he communicates most freely.

He is in good health and spirits. He has scarcely spoken the English language for the last sixteen years. He lived with a tribe of Bechuanas, far in the interior, for eight years, guiding them in the paths of virtue, knowledge and religion.

He, in conjunction with Mr Oswald, discovered the magnificent Lake Ngami, in the interior of Africa. He traced by himself the course of the great river Zambesi, in Eastern Africa, and explored one of the extensive and arid deserts of the African continent.

Dr Livingstone explored the country of the true negro race. He saw a multitude of tribes of Africans and several races, many of whom had never seen a white man until he visited them. They all had a religion, believed in an existence after death, worshipped idols and performed religious ceremonies in groves and woods. They considered themselves superior to white men, who could not speak their language.

An engraving of a Zulu dance from Livingstone's *Narrative of an Expedition to the Zambesi and its Tributaries*. The Zulus were inhabitants of lands along the Zambezi.

The Scotsman's more traditional account of the hero being feted by the London establishment plays in to recognising the importance of the Scots in Britain's greatness. Although *The Scotsman* does appear to refer to him as English, a mistake that would not be easily forgiven by *Scotsman* readers today. Perhaps because he was in London Dr Livingstone also credits "the English people" for their commitment to the ending of the slave trade.

WEDNESDAY, 17 DECEMBER, 1856

Dr Livingstone's African Discoveries

The members of the Royal Geographical Society of London held a special meeting on Monday night to present the Society's gold medal to the Rev. Dr Livingstone for his discoveries in Central Africa.

The Society's room was crowded to excess. The chair was taken by Sir Roderick Murchison, President of the Society. The President, in opening the proceedings, said they were met to welcome Dr Livingstone on his return from South Africa to his native country after an absence of sixteen years, during which, while endeavouring to spread the blessings of Christianity through lands never before trodden by the foot of a British subject, he had made geographical discoveries of incalculable importance, which had justly won for him the Victoria or Patron's gold medal of that Society. (Cheers.)

When that honour was conferred in May 1855 for traversing South Africa from the Cape of Good Hope by the Lake Ngami to Linyanti, and thence to the west coast, Lord Ellesmere, their then President, spoke of the scientific precision with which the unarmed and unassisted English missionary had left his mark on so many important stations of regions hitherto blank. (Hear, hear.)

If for that wonderful journey Dr Livingstone was justly recompensed with the highest distinction their Society could bestow, what must now be their estimate of his prowess when they knew that he had retraversed the vast regions which he first opened out to their knowledge; nay, more, that after reaching his old starting point at Linyanti, in the interior, he had followed the Zambesi, or continuation of the Leamhye river, to its mouths on the shore of the Indian Ocean, passing through the Eastern Portuguese settlement of Tête, and thus completing the entire journey across South Africa?

In short, it had been calculated that, putting together all his various journeys, Dr Livingstone had not travelled over less than 11,000 miles of African territory; and he had come back as the pioneer of sound knowledge, who, by his astronomical observations, had determined the site of numerous places, hills, rivers, and lakes, nearly all hitherto unknown, while he had seized upon every opportunity of describing the physical features, climatology, and even the geological structure of the countries he had explored and pointed out many new sources of commerce as yet unknown to the scope and enterprise of the British merchant. (Cheers.)

Dr Livingstone was received with much cheering. After expressing thanks he said: "The English people and Government have done more for Central Africa than any other in the way of suppressing that traffic which proves a blight to both commerce and friendly intercourse. (Cheers.)

"May I hope that the path which I have lately opened into the interior will never be shut, and that in addition to repression of the slave trade, there will be fresh efforts made for the development of the internal resources of the country. (Hear, hear.)

"Success in this, and the spread of Christianity alone, will render the present success of our cruisers in repression permanent. (Hear, hear.) I cannot pretend to a single note of triumph. A man may boast when he is putting off his armour, but I am just putting mine on; and, while feeling deeply grateful for the high opinion you have formed of me, I feel also that you have rated me above my deserts, and that my future may not come up to the expectations of the present."

And as you would expect he remained true to his word, he turned his back on the celebrity circuit and returned once more to Africa, but his success was not to be repeated.

Six years after departing on an expedition that had seen the death of his explorer wife Mary, in 1864 he was ordered home by a dissatisfied government.

But still he would not give up, yet again he rallied opposition to the slave trade and departed again after receiving funding for a mission to discover the source of the Nile.

He set off in 1866 but was soon missing, not being heard of for many months. He was of course by this time a global superstar, so the New York Herald sent its reporter Henry Stanley to the heart of Africa to find him. And he did, immortalising the greeting he gave on their meeting: 'Dr Livingstone I presume?'

Livingstone died on 1 May 1873 while still on his mission. To sum up how he was regarded in his time, his self-effacing modesty and yet selfless ambition, his intellect and scientific prowess, and the global impact his journey had, it is worth looking at the gushing leading article in the usually sober *Scotsman*.

Henry Morton Stanley meets David Livingstone.

WEDNESDAY, 24 DECEMBER, 1856

Dr Livingstone's great achievement may be described in a few words: he has explored the whole of the immense region of Southern Africa, from the Atlantic to the Eastern Ocean. He has discovered rivers, lakes, cities, nations, even a new climate. First, he penetrated from the Cape of Good Hope upwards to Lake Ngami, and thence, by a direct route, to Linyanti, a point more than twenty-four degrees from the southern extremity of the continent. Being now within ten degrees of the equator, he struck off to the west, and succeeded in reaching the Portuguese settlements on the coast. Following these indications on the map, the reader will immediately perceive what vast blanks of geography were removed in the course of this single journey.

From the western coast, Dr Livingstone returned to Linyanti, and followed the course of the Zambesi river to its junction with the eastern waters in the channel of Mozambique. Mark these routes upon the map with a red line, and it will intersect Africa from the south hundreds of miles beyond the limits of all former research; and from ocean to ocean, west to east, through regions hitherto as unknown as America before the voyages of Columbus.

Moreover, Dr Livingstone carried with him a proficient knowledge of at least five sciences, so that as he journeyed he made incessant observations, astronomical, geological, and geometrical, marked the varieties of climate, and took botanical and zoological notes innumerable. Still further, he collected a large store of information connected with the commercial products of the various territories he travelled, the industrial habits of the natives, their disposition to trade.

For seventeen years, smitten by more than thirty attacks of fever, endangered by seven attempts on his life, continually exposed to fatigue, hunger, and the chance of perishing miserably in a wilderness shut out from the knowledge of civilised men, the missionary pursued his way, an apostle and a pioneer, without fear, without egotism, without desire of reward. Such work, accomplished by such a man, deserves all the eulogy that can be bestowed upon it,

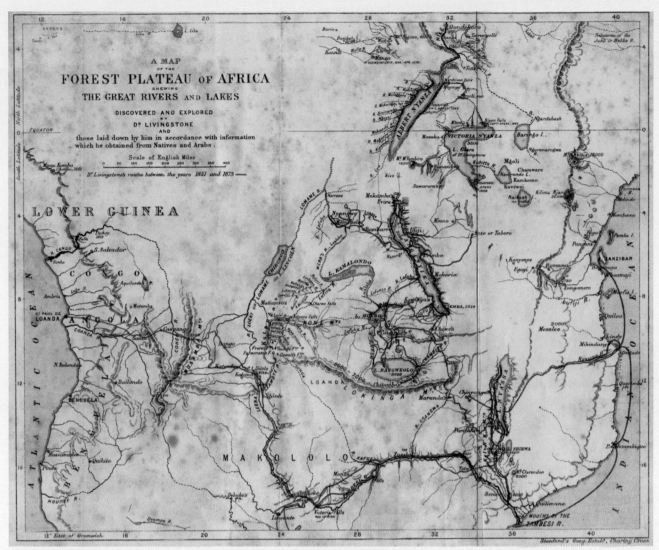

The journeys of Livingstone in Africa between 1851 and 1873.

The Last Journals of David Livingstone, in Central Africa, from 1865 to His Death, Volume II (of 2), 1869-1873, by David Livingstone.

for nothing is more rare than brilliant and unsullied success.

More interesting, however, than the geographical delineation of interior Africa is effected by Dr Livingstone in his account of its varieties of climate and population.

Turn to any Gazeteer, and we find the mysterious expanse of the south described as blazing in the rays of an insufferable sun, and only tolerable to the tropic constitution of the Ethiopian race. Many circumstances combined to perpetuate this illusion. As the Portuguese in the East, during

the sixteenth century, were accustomed to describe the Spice Islands as inaccessible desolations, encompassed by rocks, shoals, and all the dangers of the sea, so the Boer settlers along the outskirts of African civilisation were eager to build up a barrier of invisible terrors between the coast and the central kingdoms of the south.

Their object was monopoly, of course. Had Dr Livingstone been persuaded by their representations, he would never have ventured into a region. But he refused to take

alarm and pushed on. Sixteen degrees of latitude were found as hot and arid as they had been pictured; the western coast was indeed a serpent-breeding mass of swamps and forests; the eastern coast was often uninhabitable by Europeans; but beyond the twentieth degree of south latitude, not only a different race, but a different country was found. It was elevated, it was cooled by pleasant breezes, it abounded in fruit and grain, it was watered by a perfect maze of rivers and streams of all sizes. Some of them were broad and deep and never dry during the hottest season.

This was the true home of the Nigritina family, not of the rusty Bechuann, but of the curly-headed, jet-black Negro, who was once transported from these remote kingdoms to the British West Indian settlements, and who is even now brought down, at times, to the coast, and shipped for Cuba or Brazil. These nations have never carried on, however, any direct communication with the sea, the maritime tribes and colonists having cut them off - a policy which it will be difficult to carry out after the researches of Dr Livingstone have been made known to the commercial communities of Europe and America. It will no longer be possible to delude the natives by accounts of English cannibalism.

The great river discovered by Dr Livingstone, which intersects the southern region of the continent from one seaboard to another, traversing in the interior territories abounding in natural riches, and inhabited by an intelligent though simple race of people, is a pledge to Africa of future intercourse with Europe, and of comparative civilisation. The most extraordinary circumstance announced by Dr Livingstone is the salubrity of these vast countries. "In some of the districts of the interior and among the pure negro family many of the diseases that affected the people of Europe are unknown.

"Small-pox and consumption have not been known for twenty years, and consumption, scrofula, cancer, and hydrophobia are

seldom heard of." So healthy are the natives, and so free from weakening taints, that pure-blooded negroes from beyond the twentieth degree of south latitude are treasures in the Cuban or Brazilian market. They are brought down to the coast, men and women, in chains, and so far from being willing to quit their homes, are in most cases captured after a fierce and sanguinary battle with the tribe to which they belong.

This great traveller deserves a monument, and will, probably, build one for himself. He will publish the record of his wanderings, and that book will be a more enduring and appropriate memorial to his unostentatious genius and simple heroism than any tablet, or statue, or emblem whatever.

Engraving entitled *Gang of captives met at Mbame's on their way to Tette* from Livingstone's *Missionary travels and researches in South Africa*, published in 1857.

And of course no chronicling of the exploits of adventurers would be complete without the report that told of one of the great mysteries of the age – the disappearance of the expedition seeking the elusive Northwest passage commanded by arctic explorer Sir John Franklin. He had set sail in May 1845 with his two ships, HMS Erebus and HMS Terror, which were equipped with some of the most advanced inventions of the time, notably steam engines giving a top speed of four knots and a steam-based heating and distillation system that served the dual purpose of keeping the ship warm and providing fresh water for the engine's boilers. The crew were also well provisioned, with three years' worth of tinned supplies.

But the intrepid adventurers were last seen moored to an iceberg just outside Lancaster Sound, between Devon Island and Baffin Island, on 26 July, 1845 and never seen again.

There had been such high hopes for the expedition, and there were always stories of people surviving after shipwreck for years afterwards, that the loss and the potential finding of the Franklin expedition became one of the great quests, probably helped by the Admiralty putting up a £20,000 reward for anyone who found them. Even *The Scotsman* could not believe such a well-equipped expedition had met its end.

Sir John Franklin.
Credit: Wellcome Library, London.
Wellcome Images images@wellcome.ac.uk

Jane Griffin (later Lady Franklin), 24, in 1815. She married John Franklin in 1828, a year before he was knighted.

SATURDAY, 28 AUGUST, 1852

Arctic expedition - Sir J Franklin

What news of Sir John Franklin? Have any traces of his whereabouts been discovered? Has any light been thrown upon the fortunes of himself and his crews? We hasten to say; on the authority of those best qualified to form an opinion upon the subject, that hope of Sir John Franklin's safety is by no means to be abandoned, for the probabilities of his existence in some Polar region not yet explored are far greater and more numerous than the probability of his total loss. We say total loss - because in any other case than that of foundering in deep waters some vestige of wreck would, ere this, have been detected by the many keen-sighted and experienced investigators engaged in the search. We will remind the impatient or ill-informed that the total extinction of two British men-of-war, commanded by such officers as Sir John Franklin and Captain [James] Fitzjames, and manned and equipped as the vessels of his expedition were, is an event so contradictory to all experience of the causalities of the Polar regions, as to amount to the strongest improbability. The arguments of those who maintain the improbability of maintaining life in higher latitudes than those already explored are refuted by well-established facts, to which we will presently advert more in detail.

Sir John Franklin sailed from Kent, with the Erebus and Terror in May 1845, and arrived at the Whalefish Islands on 4 July. His last despatches were from this point, bearing the date July 12. The Erebus was spoken for on the 22nd of the same month by Captain Martin, of the whaler Enterprise, in latitude 75 deg. 10 min., longitude 60 deg. west. The Prince of Wales whaler reported that on the

A chart of the American Arctic expedition in search of Sir John Franklin in 1850/51.

26th of July, 1845, she saw Franklin's vessels in latitude 74 deg. 48 min., longitude 66 deg. 13 min. They were then moored to an iceberg awaiting an opening in the middle ice to enable them to cross over to Lancaster Sound. Between this period and 23 August, 1850, five years and a month, when the first traces were discovered by Captain [Erasmus] Ommanney, of her Majesty's ship Assistance, at Cape Riley, no intelligence, direct or indirect, was received of the missing ships. The evidences afforded by these first traces were added to largely four days after (27 August, 1850), by Captain [William] Penny's alighting at Beechy Island upon the spot where Franklin spent his winter of 1845-6. Early in 1850 the admiralty placed four ships in commission under the command of Captain Horatio T. Austin, C.B., who had served in an exploring voyage under Sir Edward Parry, for the purpose of examining Barrow's Straits, under a notion that Sir John Franklin might be retracing his course eastward in boats, or even in the ships themselves, having relinquished the hope of making a north-west passage. The squadron under Captain Austin consisted of his own ship the Resolute, the Assistance, Captain E. Ommanney, and the steam-tenders Pioneer, Lieut. Osborn commanding, and Intrepid, Lieut. Cator commanding. The Lords of the Admiralty ventured to associate William Penny, an experienced whaling captain of Dundee, with their own commissioned officers. Mr Penny, after receiving instruction from the Admiralty, proceeded to Aberdeen and Dundee, where he purchased two new clipper-built vessels, which were named respectively the Lady Franklin and Sophia, the latter in compliment to Miss Sophia Cracroft, a niece of Sir John Franklin, and most devoted companion of his noble-hearted wife. These vessels were placed under Mr Penny's command.

[At Beechy Island] Mr Penny discovered unquestionable traces of Sir John Franklin on the 27th August, and here the ships were moored to examine it as carefully as possible. The landing party was under the orders of Mr Stuart, commander of the Sophia, to whose intelligence, perseverance, and zeal, Captains Austin, Penny and Dr Sutherland combine in bearing testimony.

"Traces," observes the latter, "were found to a great extent of the missing ships: tin canisters in hundreds, pieces of cloth, rope, wood in large fragments and in chips: iron in numerous fragments, where the anvil had stood, and the block which supported it; paper, both written and printed, with the dates 1844 and 1845; sledge marks in abundance; depressions in the gravel resembling wells which they had been digging; and the graves of three men who had died on board the missing ships in January and April 1846."

Here, then, was unquestionably a station of Sir John Franklin's party, and occupied until the 3rd of April, 1846, at least. In the opinion of Captain Penny and others it was occupied for a look out up the Wellington Channel, to watch the first opening of that icy barrier which so frequently seems to block it up. Sir John Franklin's instructions, in 1845, were to proceed to the Wellington Channel, and if possible, through it, and the marks of a hasty departure thence may be more reasonably accounted for by a sudden opening in the ice, of which the ardent spirit of Franklin would prompt him instantly to avail himself, than the wild supposition which has been broached of his retreat from an onslaught of savages - a feat quite inconsistent with the habits and disposition of the harmless and inoffensive Esquimaux.

There is a narrative of four Russian sailors who subsisted in Spitzbergen on the product of the country for six years and three months reprinted in Captain Mangle's volume from the Annual Register for 1774. If four Russian mariners, with a few ounces of tobacco, twelve musket charges of powder and shot, and a small bag of flour, as their only stores to start with, could subsist for six years and three months in Spitzbergen, how long can the crews of two English men-of-wars, commanded by officers of the Arctic experience, fertility of resource and unconquerable courage of Sir John Franklin and Captain Fitzjames, preserve their lives? We leave others to work out this sum, and for ourselves say, Nil Desperandum.

Probabilities of his existence are far greater than the probability of his total loss.

And that was the view of most people. Many tried to find the missing men, and many died trying, but it took a Scottish whaling captain John Rae to end the mystery in 1854, and reveal that the end had involved cannibalism. This honest revelation which was not in keeping with the adulation of explorers as heroes was not popular and for his honesty Rae was never accorded the proper credit for his discovery. Here is how *The Scotsman* reported the solving of the maritime mystery.

WEDNESDAY, 25 OCTOBER, 1854

The fate of Sir John Franklin

Intelligence which may be fairly considered decisive has at last reached this country of the sad fate of Sir John Franklin and his brave companions. Dr [John] Rae, whose previous exploits as an Arctic traveller have already so highly distinguished him, landed at Deal on Sunday, and immediately proceeded to the Admiralty, and laid before Sir James Graham the melancholy evidence on which his report is founded.

Dr Rae was not employed in searching for Sir John Franklin, but in completing his survey of the coast of Boothia. He justly thought, however, that the information he had obtained greatly outweighed the importance of his survey, and he has hurried home to satisfy the public's anxiety as to the fate of the long-lost expedition, and to prevent the risk of any more lives in a fruitless search. It would seem from his description of the place in which the bodies were found that both Sir James Ross and Captain [Joseph] Bellot must have been within a few miles of the spot to which our unfortunate countrymen had struggled on in their desperate search. A few of the unfortunate men must, he

thinks, have survived until the arrival of the wild-fowl about the end of May 1850, as shots were heard and fresh bones and feathers of geese were noticed near the scene of the sad event.

The following is Dr Rae's report to the Secretary of the Admiralty:- Repulse Bay, July 29, 1854 "Sir, - I have the honour to mention, for the information of my Lords Commissioners of the Admiralty, that, during my journey over the ice and snows this spring, with the view of completing the survey of the west shore of Boothia, I met with Esquimaux in Pelly Bay, from one of whom I learned that a party of 'white men' (Kabloonans) has perished from want of food some distance to the westward, and not far beyond a large river containing many falls and rapids.

"Subsequently, further particulars were received, and a number of articles purchased, which place the fate of a portion, if not all, of the then survivors of Sir John Franklin's long-lost party beyond a doubt - a fate as terrible as the imagination can conceive.

"The substance of the

information obtained at various times and from various sources was as follows: In the spring, four winters past (spring, 1850), a party of 'white men,' amounting to about forty, were seen travelling southward over the ice and dragging a boat with them by some Esquimaux, who were killing seals near the north shore of King William's land, which is a large island. None of the party could speak the Esquimaux language intelligibly, but by signs the natives were made to understand that their ship, or ships, had been crushed by ice, and that they were now going to where they expected to find deer to shoot. From the appearance of the men, all of whom except one officer looked thin, they were then supposed to be getting short of provisions, and they purchased a small seal from the natives.

"At a later date the same season, but previously to the breaking up of the ice, the bodies of some thirty persons were discovered on the continent, and five on an island near it, about a long day's journey to the NW of a large stream, which can be no other than Back's Great Fish

River (named by the Esquimaux Oot-ko-hi-ca-lik), as its description and that of the low shore in the neighbourhood of Point Ogle and Montreal Island agree exactly with that of Sir George Back. Some of the bodies had been buried (probably those of the first victims of famine); some were in a tent or tents; others under the boat, which had been turned over to form a shelter, and several lay scattered about in different directions. Of those found on the island one was supposed to have been an officer, as he had a telescope strapped over his shoulders and his double-barrelled gun lay underneath him.

"From the mutilated state of many of the corpses and the contents of the kettles, it is evident that our wretched countrymen had been driven to the last resource - cannibalism - as a means of prolonging existence.

"There appeared to have been an abundant stock of ammunition, as the powder was emptied in a heap on the ground by the natives out of the kegs or cases containing it; and a quantity of ball and shot was found below high water mark, having probably been left on the ice close to the beach before the spring commenced. There must have been a number of telescopes, guns (several of them double-barrelled), &c., all of which appear to have been broken up, as I saw pieces of these different articles with the Esquimaux, and together with some silver spoons and forks, purchased as many as I could get.

"None of the Esquimaux with whom I had communication saw the 'white' men, either when living or after death; nor had they ever been at the place where the corpses were found, but had their information from those who had been there, and who had seen the party when travelling.

"I offer no apology for taking the liberty of addressing you, as I do so from a belief that their Lordships would be desirous of being put in possession at as early a date as possible of any tidings, however meagre and unexpectedly obtained, regarding this painfully interesting subject."

John Rae acquired the first Franklin expedition relics from the Inuit and reported on starvation and cannibalism among the dying crewmen.

Relics of Franklin's lost expedition.

Chapter five

The death of Queen Victoria

Victoria was a monarch who was remarkable in many ways, not least her 63-year reign and the fact she proposed to her husband-to-be at a time when not many women were doing so. But one of the special aspects of Victoria was her relationship with Scotland. Historians have written that the Queen was obsessed with Scotland and that Scots considered themselves her favourite subjects. Certainly this all came at a time when the national image of Scotland was changing and Victoria helped foster a romanticised view of The Highlands, at a time when the industrialised central belt of Scotland was probably not a very attractive place.

Quite how big a part ghillie John Brown played in Victoria's love of Scotland is not clear, but theirs was certainly a very involved relationship, and he certainly embodied her view of the strong and dependable Highlander.

But her interest in Scotland was there long before she met John Brown. She was a fan of Walter Scott's novels and was keen to see the setting over which she reigned. She and Prince Albert honeymooned in Taymouth Castle in 1840 and she set out on her first royal visit to Scotland only five years after being crowned, and she appears to have been smitten. She wrote in her diaries: "The impression Edinburgh has made upon us is very great, it is quite beautiful, totally unlike anything else I have seen, and what is even more, Albert, who has seen so much, says it is unlike anything he ever saw it is so regular."

She went on: "The enthusiasm was very great, and the people friendly and kind."

The Queen and Prince Albert liked the country so much they bought their own castle and estate, Balmoral in 1852. The Deeside property was purchased privately by Prince Albert and it remains the Royal Family's private property today, not the property of the Crown. Prince Albert even had a hand in the design of the new castle they built there, as the original was deemed too small.

After Albert died in 1861 the Queen went in to deep mourning and it was said that the influence John Brown had on her was very great, he became one of her most trusted advisers.

There have been reports the couple married in secret, and that documentary evidence of the marriage had been destroyed by the Royal Family. That would to most people be reinforced by

Albert, Victoria and their nine children, 1857. Left to right: Alice, Arthur, Albert, Edward, Leopold, Louise, Victoria with Beatrice, Alfred, Victoria and Helena.

Victoria and John Brown at Balmoral, 1863.
Photograph by G.W. Wilson.

Queen Victoria photographed for her diamond jubilee, 1897.
W. and D. Downey

what Victoria had buried with her in her coffin, which included a plaster cast of Prince Albert's hand and one of his dressing gowns, but she also had with her a lock of John Brown's hair and a picture of him. But most telling of all perhaps was the wedding ring of John Brown's mother, which Victoria was given by Brown.

So Scotland genuinely had a place in Victoria's heart, and it can also be said that Victoria had a place in Scotland's heart if the reporting of her death in *The Scotsman* can be taken as a measure.

WEDNESDAY, 23 JANUARY, 1901

Death of the Queen

We deeply regret to announce that the Queen died at Osborne at half-past six last evening. The gravity of the bulletins of the last few days must, in some measure, have prepared Her Majesty's subjects for the sorrowful announcement made to-day. The sad news was conveyed to the nation in the following bulletin, timed Osborne, 6.45 p.m., and signed by Sir R. Douglas Powell, M.D.; Sir James Reid, M.D.; and Sir Thomas Barlow, M.D.: - "Her Majesty the Queen breathed her last at 6.30 p.m., surrounded by her children and grandchildren." It is a remarkable fact that the Queen has died within a few hours of the anniversary of her father's death, which occurred eighty-one years ago. The Duke of Kent died, after a brief illness, at Sidmouth, Devonshire, on January 23, 1820.

The Prince of Wales telegraphed to the Lord Mayor of London, at 6.45 last evening: - "My beloved mother, the Queen, has just passed away, surrounded by her children and grandchildren." The Lord Mayor immediately replied to the Prince of Wales: - "Your Royal Highness' telegram announcing the nation's great loss I have received with profound distress and grief, and have communicated its most sad intimation to my fellow-citizens. Her Majesty's name and memory will live for ever in the hearts of her people. May I respectfully convey to your Royal Highness and to all the members of the Royal Family the earnest

THE SCOTSMAN

EDINBURGH, WEDNESDAY, January 23, 1901.

WE deeply regret to announce that the Queen died at Osborne at half-past six o'clock last evening. The gravity of the bulletins of the last few days must, in some measure, have prepared Her Majesty's subjects for the sorrowful announcement made to-day. The sad news was conveyed to the nation in the following bulletin, timed Osborne, 6.45 P.M., and signed by Sir R. Douglas Powell, M.D.; Sir James Reid, M.D.; and Sir Thomas Barlow, M.D.:—"Her Majesty the Queen breathed her last at 6.30 P.M., surrounded by her children and grandchildren." It is a remarkable fact that the Queen has died within a few hours of the anniversary of her father's death, which occurred eighty-one years ago. The Duke of Kent died, after a brief illness, at Sidmouth, Devonshire, on January 23, 1820. The Prince of Wales telegraphed to the Lord Mayor of London, at 6.45 last evening:—"My beloved mother, the Queen, has just passed away, surrounded by her children and grandchildren." The Lord Mayor immediately replied to the Prince of Wales:—"Your Royal Highness' telegram announcing the nation's great loss I have received with profound distress and grief, and have communicated its most sad intimation to my fellow-citizens. Her Majesty's name and memory will live for ever in the hearts of her people. May I respectfully convey to your Royal Highness and to all the members of the Royal Family the earnest sympathy and condolence of the City of London in your great sorrow?" A detailed sketch of the Queen's long and illustrious reign will be found in another part of the paper.

PARLIAMENT meets to-day. The official announcement was issued this morning. The object of the meeting of Parliament is to enable Peers and members of the House of Commons to take the oath of allegiance to the King.

AN immense sensation was created in London by the announcement that the Queen had passed away. The theatres and the other places of amusements, many of which were already well filled, were instantly closed. A gloom seemed to fall over the entire City. A similar feeling prevails throughout the country, as indicated by numerous telegrams.

AT an early hour this morning telegrams were beginning to come to hand describing the intense grief which the death of the Queen has occasioned throughout the British Empire and in foreign countries. The President of the United States at once dispatched by cable an affectionate message to His Majesty the King at Osborne House. The Senate of the United States adopted a resolution declaring that the

a popular mistake to suppose that the task of a constitutional Monarch is an easy one. The functions that have to be discharged are, perhaps, more difficult and delicate because of the restrictions on personal initiative and personal inclination and the necessity of exerting personal influence within the strict lines of the Constitution. During the Queen's reign there has been a complete disappearance of jealousy of the Royal prerogative, because nobody has been more watchful against infringement of the rights and liberties of Parliament than the Queen herself. Yet her personal influence has been as constant as the attention she has bestowed on public affairs, and the Statesmen who have been her most intimate and responsible advisers know best how real and valuable and wisely directed it has been. If she has been careful not to exceed her prerogative, she has been equally judicious in her aloofness from the contentions of political parties. Being not only a Queen, but a woman of an active mind and independent judgment, and not wanting in will or in keen interest in the questions of the day, her sympathies must at times have set strongly in favour of one party and one cause. But the country never felt that the Queen was a partisan, and in act and word she was never a partisan. On how many important occasions she has played the part of mediator in the strife of parties and has helped to tide the country over perilous waters the public are still unaware. But they know of one such occasion in 1869, when the indirect but potent intervention of the Queen averted a crisis threatened by the powerful forces arrayed against each other over the Irish Church Bill. This was an example of the power of personal influence which only the Sovereign could have exercised effectively, and which, nevertheless, involved no exercise of Royal prerogative. In so far as the Queen's government was personal, it has been a moral government, working through moral and social channels by the persuasive influence of example and of words spoken and acts performed in the right way and at the right season. As Queen and woman she has done much to elevate the morals and purify the manners of the nation. The chief reason for thankfulness that her reign has been so long is that she has not only set precedents of priceless value, but her wise precedents have had time to grow into what may be fairly regarded as habits and characteristics of the British Monarchy. Even if the country were less assured than it is of the wisdom and apt qualifications of the King, it might rest assured that for a long lapse of time no British Sovereign could forget to walk in the ways of Queen Victoria.

The power of her personality and the loyalty and devotion of her people have grown

the Waverley Station by the 10.50 East Coast last night for London.

Among the visitors at the Foreign Office yesterday afternoon were the French and American Ambassadors, and the Portuguese, Netherland, Chinese Ministers.

In consequence of the death of the Queen, Andrews University have resolved to postpone installation of Lord Balfour of Burleigh to Chancellorship of the University.

Mr Scott Dickson, M.P., Solicitor-General; Hon. Thomas Cochrane, M.P., Mr Thomas Q.C., M.P., and Captain Sinclair, M.P., travelled by the East Coast route from the Waverley Station last night for London.

The "Hong-Kong Government Gazette" of December 1900 contains the following notification:—"Reginald Fleming Johnston to be private secretary to his Excellency the Governor, in the absence of the Earl of Donoughmore, or until further notice."

Lady Russell, wife of Sir Edward Russell, of "Liverpool Daily Post," died at her residence, Abercromby Square, Liverpool, yesterday morning. The deceased lady was the daughter of Mr Bradley Bringe, Canterbury, and married Sir Edward in ... Lady Russell was taken ill about a week ago, ... no serious consequences were anticipated, ... pneumonia developed.

The Berlin correspondent of the "Times," telegraphing on Monday, says:—The "Kreuz Zeitung" learns that the Empress Frederick was prostrated on hearing the grave news regarding condition of the Queen, and that the grief of Imperial Majesty was rendered more poignant by inability to leave her sick room. Her Imperial Majesty is overwhelmed by the bitter consciousness which prevents her from being with the Queen.

A marriage has been arranged, and will take place in April, between the Rev. H. M. Lamont, minister of Coldingham, late of Edinburgh, and Edith, younger daughter of the late Sir Samuel and Lady Home-Stirling of Renton and Glorat.

BURNS CLUBS AND THE SHILLING FUND.—The death of the Queen has led to the abandonment of the Burns anniversary celebrations on January at which it was proposed to make a collection for "The Scotsman" Shilling Fund on behalf of the widows and orphans of our soldiers. The Executive Committee of the Burns Clubs who undertook the organisation of the collection, and who had received most gratifying promises of support, have issued a circular expressing a hope that the object of the collection will not be lost sight of. The Committee are confident that the Burns fraternity, by adopting such a method as may commend itself to the respective clubs, will support them in carrying out the purpose of relieving the widowed and fatherless, a purpose that was always so dear to the heart of Her Majesty.

THE GENERAL MANAGERSHIP OF THE CALEDONIAN RAILWAY.—Mr Robert Millar was yesterday appointed general manager, ad interim, of the Caledonian Railway in succession to the late Mr W. Patrick. It is only a fortnight ago that Mr Millar was promoted to be superintendent of the western district of the company's lines, and he had assumed his new duties when the further appointment was conferred on him yesterday. Mr Millar, it may be recalled, belongs to Stirling, and entered the service of the Caledonian Railway twenty-seven years ago as a clerk in Buchanan Street goods station, Glasgow. He was soon promoted to be a canvasser, and for ten years he was the representative of the company in Ireland. Eventually he was drafted to the head offices in Glasgow to take charge of the canvassing in Scotland. Four years ago he was transferred to the general manager's office, and for the last twelve months he has been an unattached district superintendent. In the various positions he has occupied, Mr Millar has acquired an experience which eminently qualifies him for the duties he will now be called upon to discharge. His appointment will be very popular throughout the service as well as with the traders of the country, among whom he is widely known.

ROYAL SCOTTISH GEOGRAPHICAL SOCIETY.—In consequence of the death of Her Majesty the Queen, the meeting of the Royal Scottish Geographical Society, which was to have been addressed yesterday by Sir Thomas Holdich, with General Chapman in the chair, did not take place. The meeting arranged for Sir Thomas at Glasgow and Dundee have also been cancelled.

EDINBURGH PLUMBERS AND REGISTRATION

sympathy and condolence of the City of London in your great sorrow?"

FEELING IN SCOTLAND

EDINBURGH Flags flew half-mast high in the sunshine yesterday, at the Castle, the City Chambers, public institutions, hotels, and other buildings. They were the outward expressions of the profound sorrow which the citizens, one and all, felt at the loss of the loved and venerated Sovereign of these realms. In other ways this feeling of grief was manifested.

There was a general opinion that with the nation in mourning it would be unseemly if the more ordinary affairs of life should not be suspended for the moment, and all engagements of a pleasurable nature indefinitely postponed.

Many meetings were in this way put off; the Court of Session and the Stock Exchange met and adjourned, and the University and the public schools of all grades also closed their doors for the day.

Naturally the decease of the Queen was the chief topic of conversation, though the tendency of human nature to look ahead even under such circumstances was also shown in the speculations that were indulged in as to the proceedings of the Privy Council, the title which the new King was likely to adopt, and as to the day when he would be proclaimed at the Cross of Edinburgh.

Without waiting for a Lord Chamberlain's order, many of the citizens of Edinburgh yesterday appeared in mourning. Princes Street was crowded in the afternoon both with ladies and gentlemen, and the number of the former wearing black was quite remarkable. The gentlemen for the most part had put on black neckties. Many of the shop windows along Princes Street and other thoroughfares displayed mourning goods, and the demand which was made for them is said to have been very great.

In the afternoon, on instructions from the War Office, a minute-gun salute of eighty one rounds - one gun for every year of the Queen's age - was fired from Edinburgh Castle. Many people thought it would have been more appropriate if the Queen's death had been made known to the community by the firing of the guns, and that the "salute" yesterday afternoon was rather belated. The booming of the guns was heard all over the town.

GLASGOW "We are not in a frame of mind to conduct business to-day," said a prominent Glasgow shipowner at a meeting yesterday afternoon, and his remark fittingly described the situation. The Royal Exchange remained open, but there was an entire absence of the usual bustle which on ordinary occasions distinguishes the place where merchants congregate. The "iron ring" did not meet, and few members of the Exchange were present in the room at any part of the day.

The Stock Exchange was open in the morning, but it was at once decided to adjourn, and a similar course was adopted at the Corn Exchange. Indeed, in commercial circles generally there was an almost complete suspension of activity.

At the Sheriff Courts suitable references to the nation's loss were made by Bench and Bar, and thereafter the Courts were adjourned for the day.

The City Chambers were also closed, and under the superintendence of Councillor Shearer, the buildings, both inside and outside, were elaborately draped with black cloth. Flags at half-mast were displayed by shipping in the harbour, and on many public buildings similar emblems of the city's sorrow were to be seen.

ABERDEEN Though the shops were not closed, and in the public works labour did not cease, many signs of mourning met the eye, and the chief topic of conversation was the national loss.

At the harbour the ships flew their flags at half-mast, and in the city the Corporation banner floated from the Town House tower; while the Royal tradesmen draped the coat-of-arms over their doorways.

The ordinary business of the Sheriff Court was adjourned. No classes were held at the University; and the University Court is to meet to-day to give formal expression to the sense of the loss entertained by this ancient seat of learning, in whose welfare the Queen took a special interest. At the United Free Church College, also, the classes did not assemble. The theatre was closed for the evening.

Chapter six

Scott of the Antarctic

Robert Falcon Scott.

But the Empire went on even in the event of the death of the Empress, and British explorers were still competing with others from other nations for the global bragging rights of feats of endurance, and the expeditions that most captured the public's imagination and interest were those of the Antarctic explorers, and of course that included the most dramatic story of all – that of Robert Falcon Scott - or "Scott of the Antarctic", as he became known, who was beaten in the race to the South Pole by Norwegian Roald Amundsen.

What was remarkable in *The Scotsman's* coverage of the tragedy was the publication of only the bare announcement that Scott's body had been found before a paragraph in italics that read: "The above message was still in the course of transmission when we went to press". And that publication came almost a year after the men had actually perished. News still moved very slowly from some corners of the globe.

From left to right at the Pole: Oates (standing), Bowers (sitting), Scott (standing in front of Union Jack flag on pole), Wilson (sitting), Evans (standing). Bowers took this photograph, using a piece of string to operate the camera shutter.

Antarctic disaster

Captain Scott and four companions perish.

Overwhelmed by blizzard returning from the pole

CHRISTCHURCH, NZ, Tuesday 8AM The Terra Nova, which went South to bring back, as it was hoped, Captain Scott and the other members of the British Antarctic Expedition, arrived at the base at Cape Evans on January 18 of this year, and obtained the following information there from the shore party:-Captain Scott reached the South Pole on January 18, 1912, and there found Amundsen's tent and records.

On the return journey the whole of the Southern party perished.

Captain Scott, Dr Wilson, and Lieutenant Bowers died from exposure during a blizzard about March 29, 1912, and their last camp, 11 miles to the south of the "One Ton" depot, or 155 miles from the hut at Cape Evans.

Captain Oates died from exposure on March 17, and Seaman Evans died from concussion of the brain on February 17.

The health of the remainder of the expedition, including Lieutenant Campbell's Northern party, who wintered in Terra Nova bay, is excellent.

STORY OF THE STRUGGLE.

The history of the expedition is as follows:-Before the Terra Nova left for New Zealand in March last, Surgeon Atkinson, who had been left in charge of the Western party until the return of Captain Scott, dispatched Mr Cherry Garrard and the dog driver Demetrie with two dog teams to assist the Southern party, whose return to Hut Point was expected about March 10, 1912.

Surgeon Atkinson would have accompanied this party, but was kept back in medical charge of Lieutenant Evans, the second in command, who, it will be remembered, nearly died of scurvy.

This relief party reached "One Ton" depot on March 3, but was compelled to return on March 10 owing primarily to the food for the dogs running short, and also to the persistent bad weather and the poor condition of the dogs after the strain of a hard season's work.

The dog teams returned to Hut Point on March 16, the poor animals mostly frostbitten and incapable of further work.

Mr Cherry Garrard collapsed as the result of having overstrained his heart, and his companion was also sick.

UNUSUALLY SEVERE WEATHER.

As it was impossible to communicate with Cape Evans, the ship having left and the open sea intervening, Surgeon Atkinson and Petty Officer Keohane, the only two men left, sledged out to Corner Camp to render any help that might be wanted by the Southern party.

They fought their way out to Corner Camp against the unusually severe weather, and realising that they could be of no assistance were forced to return to Hut Point after depoting one week's supply of provisions.

In April, when communication with Cape Evans was established, a gallant attempt to relieve Lieutenant Campbell was made by Surgeon Atkinson, Mr Wright, Petty Officer Williamson, and Petty Officer Keohane. This party reached Butter Point, but they were there stopped by open water. Their return was exciting, and nearly ended in disaster owing to the sea ice breaking up.

THE SEARCH PARTY

A search party left Cape Evans after the winter on October 30 last. It was organised by Surgeon Atkinson, and consisted of two divisions, Surgeon Atkinson taking the dog teams with Mr Cherry Garrard and Demetrie, while Mr Wright was in charge of a party which included Mr Nelson, Mr Gran, Mr Lashley, Petty Officer Williamson, Petty Officer Keohane, and Steward Hooper. Seven Indian mules were taken with the second party. Provisions were taken for three months, it being anticipated that an extended search would be necessary.

"One Ton" Camp was found to be in order and all provisioned. Then proceeding along the old southern route Mr Wright's party on November 12 sighted Captain Scott's tent.

FINDING OF THE BODIES.

Within it were found the bodies of Captain RF Scott, Royal Navy; Dr EA Wilson, chief of the scientific staff; and Lieutenant HR Bowers, of the Royal Indian Marine. From their records the following information was gleaned:- The first death was that of Seaman Edgar Evans, Petty Officer, RN, official number 160;225.

The above message was still in course of transmission when we went to press.

Chapter seven

The Great War

The black cloud over Europe bringing the events that were to completely dominate the 20th century was making its entrance.

The Great War was to begin just a year after the reporting of Scott's death, and was to touch every family in Scotland and reach in to almost every aspect of daily life, including that of *The Scotsman* and the journalists and others that worked there.

The tension leading up to the war brought seismic changes to the paper. In July 1914 the paper ran the headline SHADOW OF EUROPEAN WAR and it re-wrote all the rules for newspapers up until then, when it introduced something that is absolutely commonplace today: it carried the headline across three columns. Up until then no headline – regardless of the importance of the news it heralded – went over more than one column.

At the advent of war *The Scotsman* was enthusiastic and confident, mirroring the views of the land in general, and it joined in calls for men to enlist. And its workers joined the throngs eager to do their patriotic duty, and it was easy for them to get caught up in this because there was a recruiting office in its new state-of-the-art office buildings at North Bridge in Edinburgh.

It revealed the onset of war to the nation in very non-sensational prose.

WEDNESDAY, 5 AUGUST, 1914

Britain and Germany at war

Great Britain declared war against Germany at 11 o'clock last night. A declaration of war was also made by Germany.

Earlier in the day a British Ultimatum was addressed to Germany protesting against the German violation of Belgium's neutrality, and demanding a reply before midnight.

The British request was summarily rejected, and the British Government have declared to the German Government that a state of war exists between the two countries as from 11pm on August 4. The British Note conveying an Ultimatum to Germany was sent direct to Sir E. Goschen our Ambassador at Berlin, a copy being at the same time forwarded to the German Embassy.

Sir Edward Grey asked Prince Lichnowsky, the German Ambassador, to see him at the Foreign Office this morning.

It has been arranged that the United States will take over the affairs of the German Embassy.

The King, in a message to Admiral Sir John Jellicoe, sends an assurance of his confidence that the officers and men of the Fleets will revive and renew the old glories of the Royal Navy, and prove once again the sure shield of Britain and her Empire in the hour of trial.

Two Turkish battleships built and building in this country, and two destroyer leaders ordered by the Government of Chile, have been taken over by the British Government.

Admiral Sir J.R. Jellicoe has been appointed to the supreme command of the British Home Fleets, and Rear-Admiral Charles E. Madden has been appointed his Chief of the Staff.

The King, in a message to the people of the Overseas Dominions, expresses his appreciation of the messages received from them "at this time of trial."

The momentous announcement of the British Ultimatum to Germany was made by Mr Asquith in the House of Commons yesterday afternoon.

Mr Asquith told how the King of Belgium had asked for "diplomatic intervention" by

this country to prevent the threatened German infringement of Belgian neutrality.

This was however too late, for the German Ambassador had already officially intimated that, in the view of the threat of a French attack across Belgium, open quote "which was the plan, according to an impeachable information," Germany had "consequently to disregard Belgian neutrality as a matter of life and death."

The Prime Minister said this was not "in any sense satisfactory communication, and the British Government had again asked for and assurance with regard to Belgium's neutrality, and expected an answer before midnight."

Mr Asquith read a message from the King, saying he was calling out the Army Reserve and embodying the Territorials.

German forces have entered Belgium near Verviers and are marching on France.

The Germans are also advancing on France through Luxembourg, another independent state, whose integrity has been ruthlessly violated. Three German columns are pressing forward in the direction of Longwy, Villerupt, and Thionville.

After firing on the town of Bona, Algeria, the German producer Breslau steamed towards the west, where she is said to have been engaged with the British Fleet.

The diplomatic rupture between Germany and France is now complete. The German Ambassador, who has left Paris, informed the French Government that Germany considers herself at war with France.

The German Emperor addressed the Reichstag Deputies, and called upon the party leaders to come forward and give him their hands in witness that they were firmly resolved, without distinction of party or creed, to hold together with him "through thick and thin, through need and death."

Germany is to raise a credit of £250,000,000, to meet non-recurring extraordinary expenditure.

Germany has made representations to Italy for help, but Italy holds to her attitude of neutrality.

The German liner Kronprinzessin Cecilie, with two millions of specie [coins] on board, has succeeded in returning to American waters, having arrived at Bar Harbour, Maine, yesterday morning.

In some parts of this country the demand for provisions and food-stuffs was excessive yesterday, and many shops were closed. Retail prices were advanced by as much as 50 per cent.

Twenty weeks' supply of wheat or flour, or 12,610,000 quarters, is estimated by Dornbusch, to be in sight for the United Kingdom, independent of stocks held at present through the country.

An order in Council has been issued declaring it expedient that the Government should have control over the railways in Great Britain.

In consequence of the government assuming control of the railways, military commands and requisitions will take precedence over all passenger and freight traffic, and all special and excursion trains in Scotland has been cancelled.

American tourists stranded in Europe will, it is expected, be relieved by 2,500,000 dollars in gold, to be sent in an armoured cruiser by the Government, while vessels will be sent to convey the tourists home.

NOTICE TO CORRESPONDENTS.

We cannot undertake to return rejected communications.

In all cases in which matters of fact are involved Correspondents must furnish us with their names and addresses—not for publication, but as a guarantee of good faith.

Notices of Presentations, Dinners, or Entertainments given to Private Persons, Charitable Donations, or of Examinations of Schools or other Educational Institutions can be inserted only as advertisements.

The charge for Society and Fashionable Notices, except those relating to official incidents, is at the rate of One Guinea when not exceeding five lines, and at the rate of 2s. 6d. for each additional line.

THE SCOTSMAN

EDINBURGH, TUESDAY, August 4, 1914.

	SUN.	MOON (Full, 6th.)
Rises	4.22 A.M.	Rises ... 8.10 P.M.
Sets	8.14 P.M.	Sets (5th) .. 2.57 A.M.

IN the House of Commons Sir Edward Grey made a long and important statement about the European situation. He said that, though we had no engagement to send forces abroad, we could not permit the Channel ports of France to be attacked, nor could we sanction Germany's proposal to pass troops through Belgium in order to attack France. In the later hours of the sitting a number of Radical and Labour members urged that the Government should still preserve neutrality. Mr Redmond made a speech in which he suggested that Ulster and the other three Provinces would be found united behind the Government if war arose.

(pp. 4-5.)

THE Belgian Government received an ultimatum from the German Government asking it to facilitate the passing of German troops through Belgium. The Belgian Government refused, on the ground of respect for the principle of neutrality. No important military movements on the Franco-German frontier are reported to-day. There was an encounter on Germany's eastern frontier, where German troops drove back a Russian force, and occupied several points in Russian Poland. An engagement is reported to have taken place

to Hunter's Quay, but keen competition was witnessed. The principal winners were Ithona, Runag, Sarina, Ethne, Gonda, Tringa, and Elsinore. (p. 3.)

AT Sandown Park race meeting the winners were Margreen, Militant, Volta, Agnate, Fancy Nurse, Nenuphar, and Woodwild. (p. 2.)

IN English cricket, Hobbs, playing for Surrey against Notts, made 226 in four hours and twenty minutes. (p. 3.)

WEATHER FORECAST.—Scotland.—North and East—Southerly winds, moderate or fresh; cool; changeable, some showers. (p. 5.)

AT any moment Great Britain may be at war with the German Powers. Her people will accept this destiny with quiet and enduring courage. "Up to the last moment, and beyond the last moment," Britain has striven, first to preserve the peace of Europe, and then to prevent the Empire from being drawn, without sacrifice of British honour and interests, into the vortex of the great struggle of the Continental Powers. In neither of these endeavours, although earnestly and incessantly pursued night and day, have the efforts of the Government been crowned with success. Wherever the blame of failure can be laid, it cannot be placed at the door of Sir Edward Grey and of the country he represents. His statement of last night was, perhaps, the gravest that has been made by a British Minister for a century past. It was in every way worthy of a solemn occasion. It was convincing in its sincerity of tone, in its calm and dispassionate marshalling of facts, in its noble appeal to the national sense of duty, as well as of self-preservation. There can be no doubt that it will meet with full and warm approval from the British people, including, as Mr Bonar Law reminded the House of Commons last night, our fellow-citizens in the Overseas Dominions and other lands under our flag. It will be felt that the British temper and the British attitude could not have found a better exponent than the Foreign Secretary, and that as he took the right steps at the right time, he spoke the right words in the right way. Yet the prospect which Sir Edward Grey's words have opened before these Kingdoms, and before the whole Empire under the rule of the King, is more deplorable than anything that has been known in our time.

and before them, the defection of It the smaller States are arming then tualities. The en has become so unh calamity to her if certainly will—an destiny if it were succeed. For a G Dictator of Europ right of the swor hatred and jealous and races, could r come to a good en Teutonic régime Napoleonic genius it could hardly be power or a di among the pe trenched behind asked to confront a She faces her lute spirit which century ago to g other Colossus wh Europe and crush Happily the natic the Army—one co other now in co never more efficien we have, what wa last great Eurc moral and mater who own Britain whole-hearted and her cause is one country's pride of trial. Even reckoned as a sou fort and encoura gency. Mr Red good purpose, ne his country and tion, as when in Parliament he Nationalist Volu shoulder with the the shores of Ire British flag. A presented by the the Labour party Radicals. Mr R were those of a speech, felt hims the case on whic been destroyed

THE EUROPEAN WAR.

BRITISH ATTITUDE TO GERMANY.

IMPORTANT DECLARATIONS BY SIR EDWARD GREY.

The whole of Central Europe, from the Franco-German border on the west to the Russo-German and Russo-Austrian frontiers on the east, and from Copenhagen in the north to Belgrade in the south, is embraced within the map given above. It therefore brings into view the three seats of warlike operations on land—in Poland and other parts of the common boundaries of Prussia and Russia; in the parts of France adjoining Alsace - Lorraine and Luxemburg; and in Servia. It exhibits the position of Belgium, Holland, Switzerland, and Luxemburg in relation to the belligerent Powers in the western theatre of war; and it shows part of the Baltic basin (including Libau, reported as having been attacked by a German war-ship) and the southern coasts of the North Sea, together with the connecting channel of the Kiel Canal. Several of the places mentioned as scenes of invasion and in the dispatches are marked on it, Kalisz, the Polish frontier town and which is said to have been captured, short fight, by the Germans.

THE WAR.

GREAT BRITAIN'S ATTITUDE.

BELGIUM'S REPLY TO

only twelve miles to the north-east of Liège.

According to a Berlin telegram, there was a fight between German and Russian troops near Lublinitz. The Russians were repulsed, and the Germans occupied Czenstochowa. Benoyin and Kalisz, in Poland, have also been occupied by German troops.

to indemnify or give national insurance against war risks on all foodstuffs for discharge in the United Kingdom.

GERMAN ULTIMATUM TO BELGIUM.

the number of men available in war, including depots, will eventually come to about 350,000.

The field Army consists of 5 divisions and 2 cavalry divisions. The former are composed of three or four mixed brigades (two infantry regiments, making eight battalions, one troop gendarmerie, a machine gun company), nine batteries, one cavalry regiment, one cyclist company, and one battalion of pioneers.

An "aeronautical company" has been formed. It consists of the aeronautical school and

To give some indication of just how all-consuming the coming conflagration would be, two days later the following short story appeared.

FRIDAY, 7 AUGUST, 1914

Scottish banks: appeal to public

The offices of the Scottish banks will be reopened this morning for business as usual.

Arrangements have been made from meeting the reasonable requirements of the public, as shown by the following notice which will be posted in the various officers: - Notice.

1. *Customers of the bank are reminded that only small sums of cash are actually required for ordinary purposes. Checks should, therefore, be used for making payments to the utmost extent possible.*

2. *This is a great national emergency. The banks are not in any way responsible for the financial situation which has arisen, but they have made arrangements which will be amply sufficient for meeting all reasonable needs.*

3. *Depositors are assured that their interests are absolutely protected. Under the moratorium the obligation of the banks to pay deposits ceases for the time, but they are anxious that their customers should be put in a position to meet payments from this for necessary requirements.*

4. *The notes of the Scottish banks are now legal tender throughout their branches in Scotland, and the wish of the government as expressed by the Chancellor of the Exchequer being that gold should not be parted with merely to be hoarded.*

Patriotism therefore, demands that all should join in strengthening the hands of the banks at this time of national trial.

For *The Scotsman* and other newspapers the war brought editorial challenges, both physically in how to actually cover the stories and report them, and also intellectually, in as much as how would the reporting of brutal truths and supply shortages affect national morale. The government's view, as it always is in these cases, was clear. It was in favour of bolstering morale at the expense of the truth and it, again as usual, has a large degree of control over where journalists could go and how they could get their reports back to their offices.

A colonel from the Black Watch Regiment in conversation with another officer.
Reproduced by permission of the National Library of Scotland

The Scotsman's account of the first day of the Somme was published two months after the battle. It is a very moving account given what we know now of the cost in lives of the battle. It talks of the soldiers' bravery and coolness, even to the point where as they were preparing to go over the top "you would have thought we were going to a picnic."

MONDAY, 4 SEPTEMBER, 1916

The Royal Scots' splendid part in the Great Advance

So gigantic is the scale of the war, and so rapidly moving are its chances and changes, that events are fated to become old very soon. To say that they become old is not to imply that they are forgotten. Many of them are stamped indelibly on the nation's memory and on the pages of the world's history, but so prolific of stirring action and gallant episode is the war that comparatively recent events already seem far away.

But the opening of the great British and French offensive on the Somme red-lettered the First of July among even the greatest days, and information which has just come to hand indicates the splendid manner in which the Royal Scots bore themselves on that occasion. The glory that was by the regiment on that fateful morning will be shared too by the community of Manchester, for many of the sons of that city were also prominent in the assault. Where the standard is so high as it is in the British Army, outstanding reputations are far from easily earned, but the fame of the regiment has spread along the front, and it is known as among the foremost of Kitchener's Army.

Like many others they had, of course, spent dour and trying times in the trenches, and so far as the ordinary run of things goes "out there" they had been through it. But they had never been "over the bags", which is Tommy's descriptive phrase for mounting the trench and going into action. How they cocked their ears when the word at long last came that they were to go forward! The prospect of "going over the top" had opened up to them at last.

The morning of the 1st July was a glorious one in a weather sense too, and the drama of the battlefield was enacted in the limelight of resplendent sunshine. While the men of the Royal Scots waited to mount the parapet they were a jovial company. They sang and they laughed. They had the honour of going out first. Here, truly, was an incentive. The men felt they had a great duty imposed upon them, and they rose nobly to the occasion. Led by their pipers and their most inspiring music, the men set across the open for the enemy trenches. The distance to be traversed, I am told, was roughly about 700 yards. So the men started steadily to march. "They were as cool as could possibly be," said one of them who is now a convalescent at home. "You would have thought we were going to a picnic - the sun was shining and the lads were so cheery." But the ground was

somewhat difficult underfoot, and comrades began to fall here and there as the enemy bullets pierced the lines. The men never wavered. On they went in most amazing fashion considering that the deadly experience was new to them. Each of them was resolved to die gamely.

On they trampled across that stretch of ground, which was pitted with shell holes and broken by the engines of war. When they neared the German lines they doubled their determination, if that were possible, and went for the enemy tooth and nail. Our bombardment had reaped a plentiful harvest. The enemy barbed wire was pulverised, and after passing over it the Royal Scots went steadily through to the fourth line of German trenches. There were many enemy dead in the area. Others who lived through the bombardment appealed for "Mercy, Camerade." But there was plenty of fight in some of them. The resolve and steadiness of the Royal Scots was irresistible. Here is what an officer, writing proudly from France, says of the day's achievement: "Everyone did wonderfully well, none better. The men were just splendid, and the regiment won undying fame."

Pipe majors at a horse show behind the lines during World War I. Soldiers at the Front were not on constant trench duty. There were periods allowed for recuperation and relaxation.

Reproduced by permission of the National Library of Scotland

Highlanders working on a road in France. They are all in kilts and most of them are wearing Balmorals. Some of the men appear to be wearing a cover or 'apron' to protect their kilt.

Reproduced by permission of the National Library of Scotland

Soldiers and two women hard at work, as Seaforths help the French in potato fields. The soldiers' kilts can just be seen under their long coats.

Reproduced by permission of the National Library of Scotland

A Highland regiment marching.
Reproduced by permission of the National Library of Scotland

As the British army became increasingly desperate for men, the various Highland regiments that constituted the Gordon Highlanders were ordered to expand rapidly during World War I.
Reproduced by permission of the National Library of Scotland

Two soldiers and their German helmet collection, during World War I. Both men look a little worse for wear, but seem relaxed and quite cheerful. They are, however, sitting in quite a confusing and alien landscape, which gives the image a surreal atmosphere.
Reproduced by permission of the National Library of Scotland

PEACE.

TERMS OF THE ARMISTICE.

GERMAN ARMY DISARMED.

Evacuation of Occupied Lands and Alsace-Lorraine.

THE RHINELAND AS PLEDGE.

Great Surrenders of Ships and Guns.

The Great War is ended. The armistice was signed at five o'clock yesterday morning, and hostilities ceased on all fronts at 11 A.M.

The historic announcement of the signing of the armistice was made by the Prime Minister in a statement issued shortly after ten o'clock yesterday morning. Everywhere the news evoked rejoicings over the Allies' magnificent victory and profound feelings of thankfulness that the long struggle was at last over. In all the cities and towns of the Empire and of the Allied countries memorable scenes were witnessed.

Mr. Lloyd George had an enthusiastic reception when he rose to read the terms of the armistice in the House of Commons. After the Prime Minister's speech the House immediately adjourned, on his motion, to proceed to St Margaret's Church in order to give reverent thanks for the deliverance of the world from a great peril.

The armistice terms will be found in full below. They include:—

Immediate evacuation of Belgium, Alsace-Lorraine, and Luxemburg.

Evacuation by the enemy of the Rhineland to be completed within 31 days.

The occupation of evacuated territory by Allied and United States troops will keep pace with the evacuation.

Allied garrisons to hold main crossings of the Rhine at Mainz, Coblenz, and Cologne, together with bridgeheads and a 30-kilometre radius on the right bank.

A neutral zone is also to be set up on the right bank of the Rhine.

Military food stores and munitions not to be removed from evacuated territory.

Means of communication not to be impaired.

The surrender of 5000 locomotives and 5000 guns (2500 heavy and 2500 field), 30,000 machine guns, 2000 aeroplanes, bombers, and night bombing machines.

Railways of Alsace-Lorraine to be handed over.

Immediate repatriation (without repatriation of Germans) of all Allied and United States prisoners.

All German troops in Russia, Rumania, and elsewhere to be withdrawn.

Complete abandonment of the Treaties of Bukharest and Brest-Litovsk.

Immediate stoppage of all hostilities at sea.

The handing over to the Allies and the United States of all submarines.

The following are to be disarmed:—Six battle cruisers, 10 battleships, 8 light cruisers, and 50 destroyers of the most modern type.

All other surface-water ships to be concentrated in German naval bases to be designated by the Allies, and to be paid off and disarmed under the surveillance of the Allies.

The Allies reserve the right to occupy Heligoland in order to enforce the terms of the armistice.

Freedom of access to and from the Baltic to be given to the naval forces of the Allied Powers.

The existing blockade of Germany to remain unchanged.

All Black Sea ports to be evacuated by the Germans. All Russian warships seized by Germany in the Black Sea are to be handed over.

The immediate restitution of cash deposits of the National Bank of Belgium.

The restitution of Russian and Rumanian gold.

The duration of the armistice is to be 36 days.

Canadian troops of the First Army captured Mons early yesterday morning. Belgian troops entered Ghent.

It is reported that the Kaiser, who has taken refuge in Holland, will be interned by the Dutch Government.

ARMISTICE SIGNED AT 5 A.M. YESTERDAY.

HOSTILITIES STOPPED AT 11 A.M.

PRIME MINISTER'S ANNOUNCEMENT.

THE CESSATION OF FIGHTING.

HEADQUARTERS' BULLETINS.

The following bulletins were received from the various General Headquarters last night:—

BRITISH (Monday, 8.32 P.M.)—Hostilities were suspended at 11 o'clock A.M. to-day. At that hour our troops had reached the following general line:—Franco-Belgian frontier east of Avesnes, Jeumont, Givry, 4 miles east of

---

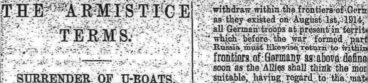

THE ARMISTICE TERMS.

SURRENDER OF U-BOATS.

FLEET TO BE DISARMED.

ALLIED CONTROL OF HELIGOLAND.

GUNS AND EQUIPMENT TO BE HANDED OVER.

FREEDOM FOR ALLIED PRISONERS.

FROM the Press Bureau the conditions of the armistice with Germany were issued yesterday afternoon in the following terms:—

SCHEDULE OF CLAUSES.

(A) CLAUSES RELATING TO THE WESTERN FRONT—1 to 11.
(B) CLAUSES RELATING TO THE EASTERN FRONTIERS OF GERMANY—12 to 16.
(C) CLAUSE RELATING TO EAST AFRICA—17.
(D) GENERAL CLAUSES—18 AND 19.
(E) NAVAL CONDITIONS—20 TO 33.
(F) DURATION OF ARMISTICE—34.
(G) TIME LIMIT FOR REPLY—35.

(A) CONDITIONS OF AN ARMISTICE WITH GERMANY—CLAUSES RELATING TO WESTERN FRONT.

(1.) Cessation of operations by land and in the air six hours after the signature of the armistice.

(2.) Immediate evacuation of invaded countries, Belgium, France, Alsace-Lorraine, Luxembourg, so ordered as to be completed within 14 days from the signature of the armistice.

German troops which have not left the above-mentioned territories within the period fixed will become prisoners of war.

Occupation by the Allied and United States forces jointly will keep pace with evacuation in these areas.

All movements of evacuation and occupation will be regulated in accordance with a note (Annexure 1.)

(3.) Repatriation, beginning at once, to be completed within 14 days, of all inhabitants of the countries above enumerated including hostages, persons under trial or convicted.

(4.) Surrender in good condition by the German armies of the following equipment:—
5000 guns (2500 heavy, 2500 field),
30,000 machine guns,
3000 minenwerfer,
2000 aeroplanes (fighters, bombers—firstly D.7's—and night bombing machines.)

The above to be delivered in situ to the Allied and United States troops in accordance with the detailed conditions laid down in the note (Annexure I.)

(5.) Evacuation by the German armies of the countries on the left bank of the Rhine.

These countries on the left bank of the Rhine shall be administered by the Local Authorities under the control of the Allied and United States garrisons holding the principal crossings of the Rhine (Mayence, Coblenz, Cologne), together with bridgeheads at these points of a 30-kilometre radius on the right bank, and by garrisons similarly holding the strategic points of the regions.

A neutral zone shall be set up on the right bank of the Rhine between the river and a line drawn 10 kilometres distant, starting from the Dutch frontier to the

---

withdraw within the frontiers of Germany as they existed on August 1st, 1914.

All German troops at present in territory which before the war formed part of Russia, must likewise return to within the frontiers of Germany as above defined, as soon as the Allies shall think the moment suitable, having regard to the internal situation of these territories.

(13.) Evacuation by German troops to be at once, and all German instructors, prisoners, and civilian as well as military agents now on the territory of Russia (defined on August 1st, 1914) to be recalled.

(14.) German troops to cease at once all requisitions and seizures and any other undertaking with a view to obtaining supplies intended for Germany in Rumania and Russia, as defined on August 1st.

(15.) Abandonment of the treaties of Bucharest and Brest-Litovsk, and of supplementary treaties.

(16.) The Allies shall have free access to the territories evacuated by the Germans on their Eastern frontier, either through Danzig or by the Vistula, in order to convey supplies to the populations of the territories, or for the purpose of maintaining order.

(C) CLAUSE RELATING TO EAST AFRICA.

(17.) Unconditional evacuation of all German forces operating in East Africa within one month.

(D) GENERAL CLAUSES.

(18.) Reciprocity within a maximum period of one month, in accordance with detailed conditions hereafter to be fixed, all civilians interned or deported who may be citizens of other Allied or associated States than those mentioned in Clause —

(19.) With the reservation that any future claims and demands of the Allies and United States of America remain unaffected, the following financial conditions are required:—

Reparation for damage done.

While the armistice lasts, no public securities shall be removed by the enemy which can serve as a pledge to the Allies for the recovery or reparation for war losses.

Immediate restitution of the cash deposit in the National Bank of Belgium and, in general, immediate return of documents, specie, stock shares, paper money, together with money plant for the issue thereof touching public or private interests in the invaded countries.

Restitution of the Russian and Rumanian gold yielded to Germany or taken by that Power.

This gold to be delivered in trust to the Allies until the signature of peace.

(E) NAVAL CONDITIONS.

(20.) Immediate cessation of all hostilities at sea, and definite information to be given as to the location and movements of all German ships.

Notification to be given to neutrals that freedom of navigation in all territorial waters is given to the naval and mercantile marines of the Allied and Associated Powers, all questions of neutrality being waived.

(21.) All naval and mercantile marine prisoners of war of the Allied and Associated Powers in German hands to be returned without reciprocity.

(22.) Handing over to the Allies and United States of all submarines (including all submarine cruisers and mine layers) which are present at the moment with full complement in the ports specified by the Allies and the United States.

Those that cannot put to sea to be deprived of crews and supplies, and shall remain under the supervision of the Allies and the United States.

Submarines ready to put to sea shall be prepared to leave German ports immediately on receipt of wireless order to proceed to the port of surrender, the remainder to follow as early as possible.

The conditions of this article shall be carried out within 14 days after the signing of the armistice.

(23.) The following German surface war ships which shall be designated by the

But as the war drew on it took its toll across the nation, as any visit to almost any small Scottish village or community will testify with the names on the war memorials, with fathers and sons and brothers, land owners and land workers all represented there in awful numbers.

So when Armistice Day came, *The Scotsman* once again captured the national mood – rejoicing tinged with knowledge of great loss. As the bells rang out to mark the joyous occasion, those who lost their lives were certainly not forgotten. The mood of the country was taken with reports from around the land.

TUESDAY, 12 NOVEMBER, 1918

Peace is declared

TERMS OF THE ARMISTICE

The Great War is ended. The armistice was signed at five o'clock yesterday morning, and hostilities ceased on all fronts at 11 a.m. The historic announcement of the signing of the armistice was made by the Prime Minister in a statement issued shortly after ten o'clock yesterday morning. Everywhere the news evoked rejoicings over the Allies' magnificent victory and profound feelings of thankfulness that the long struggle was at last over. In all the cities and towns of the Empire and of the Allied countries memorable scenes were witnessed.

Mr Lloyd George had an enthusiastic reception when he rose to read the terms of the armistice in the House of Commons. After the Prime Minister's speech the House immediately adjourned, on his motion, to proceed to St Margaret's Church in order to give reverent thanks for the deliverance of the world from a great peril.

The terms of the armistice were then set out. The duration of the armistice is to be 36 days. Canadian troops of the First Army captured Mons early yesterday morning. Belgian troops entered Ghent.

It is reported that the Kaiser, who has taken refuge in Holland, will be interned by the Dutch Government.

EDINBURGH: STIRRING SCENES

News of the conclusion of the armistice was received in

Edinburgh a little before eleven o'clock. Special editions of the evening papers were immediately published, and by midday the glad tidings had spread generally over the city.

There was no outburst of unbridled demonstration. The public took the news joyously and thankfully, but in the main quietly. The first public celebration took place in the Waverley Market, where a gathering of several hundreds had assembled for the opening of the Edinburgh War Loan Campaign. The ceremony was appropriately converted into a peace celebration, in which the Lord Provost expressed the sentiments evoked by a great occasion.

The proceedings opened with the singing of "God Save the King." Gradually as the day advanced the streets assumed an air of festivity. Flags were displayed on the prominent buildings. Smaller flags, as by magic, seemed to blossom forth in every direction. They were fluttered by numerous promenaders, especially by the younger people. Large bands of girls, freed from their munition work, passed along the streets singing and displaying red, white and blue colours in a variety of forms. Flags flew from the windows of dwelling-houses in all directions. The prolonged sounding of horns conveyed the news to the outskirts of the city, and syrens from vessels in the Forth also served to disseminate the news.

Occasionally there was a hint of tragedy amidst the rejoicings. Amongst those, for instance, who stood at one of the street corners and waved a white handkerchief to a joyous company of soldiers who had commandeered the top of a car was a young widow attired in black.

Family parties during the early part of the afternoon were conspicuous everywhere, and their participation in the celebrations clearly indicated the removal of a shadow which had been hanging over the home.

An appropriate celebration in mid-air was furnished by a covey of aeroplanes, which circled over Waverley Market at noon. The planes performed spectacular evolutions and dropped smoke balls, while three of them at one stage flew along Princes Street low down over the heads of the crowd.

Bands of young munition girls paraded with flags, singing popular songs, the old familiar song "Till the Boys Come Home," being frequently heard. A company of naval men sealed the Wellington Monument at the Register House, and, by arranging flags on his person, forced the hero of Waterloo to participate in the celebrations.

All Edinburgh in the evening came out into the streets. The tramcar traffic was stopped at eight o'clock, and the thoroughfares were left to the promenaders. Princes Street became a channel along which, from one side to the other, flowed a broad stream of humanity.

Searchlights, no longer used as a defensive precaution, played on the clouds overhead. The outstanding feature of Princes Street was a searchlight on a motor waggon, whose brilliant shaft was directed on the crowd, to the Scott Monument, and up skywards by turns. Groups of young people sang popular choruses as they moved along, and the din was considerable. With the public-houses closed early in the evening, cases of intoxication were very rare. The early retiring habits acquired during the war period began to show their sedative influence by ten o'clock, after which the city quickly quietened down.

GLASGOW: ALL CLASSES CELEBRATE

Since the armistice negotiations commenced crowds of the public had gathered at the Post Office and the newspaper office nightly, anxious to learn the latest information, and on Saturday night and Sunday night - even till early on Monday morning - they had waited for the information that the Germans had accepted the terms which Marshal Foch had to communicate, and had gone home rather disappointed that the moment for celebration had been delayed. But that disappointment only reinforced the joy of actual accomplishment.

The news reached Glasgow shortly after ten o'clock, and spread throughout the city within a remarkably short time. Public places like the City Chambers and Exchanges received the tidings "across the wire"; newspaper offices were inundated with telephone inquiries; and from mouth to mouth the fact that the armistice had been signed passed, scepticism being abolished by the appearance of special editions of the newspapers. Gradually flags appeared, tardily at first, and then in ever-increasing number till the streets of the city were bedecked in colour. Business in shops and offices and warehouses became unsettled, and members of the staffs gave up the attempt to work calmly, and went outside.

There they found themselves joined by workers from the big industrial establishments, by students from the University, and children from the schools, by munition workers, and by staid citizens whose ordinary mode of life was influenced by immediate environment. Without organisation or pre-arrangement processions were formed in various parts of the city, and headed by isolated musicians - usually a piper - they marched to George Square, which was the point of convergence for most of the demonstrators.

There Lord Provost Stewart, mounting a lorry, announced the glorious news, but his speech was cut short by the full-throated cheering of the assembly, repeated again and again as the Union Jack was unfurled from the City Chambers and the Royal Standard displayed from the General Post Office.

It was frequently remarked by observers that there was no discordant note throughout the celebrations. The red flag effectively hid its diminished head, and the raucous Bolshevism which has disturbed public meetings so often of late was discreetly silent. Where public meetings took place reference was made to the event which had thrilled the nation, and the National Anthem was sung, while in many instances telegrams of congratulation were sent to the King, Admiral Beatty, and to Sir Douglas Haig. Bells were rung from the church steeples, guns were fired, and whistles resounded through the day and during the evening.

DUNDEE: CROWDS AT CITY CHAMBERS

In Dundee all classes of the community went on holiday, and from morning till night the streets were thronged with cheering crowds. In the forenoon sirens were sounded, and work was not resumed in the mills and factories, shipyards and engineering establishments after the breakfast hour. Great crowds gathered at the centre of the city.

At noon Lord Provost Sir William Don and the Magistrates assembled on an improvised platform in one of the arches at the City Chambers, and the Lord Provost addressed a huge crowd. He said they had received the announcement of the signing of the armistice with feelings of thankfulness to the Most High. On the call of the Lord Provost, the crowd sang the National Anthem with fervent goodwill, and amid a forest of flags, cheers were given for "Haig and the boys at the front."

Subsequently many peals of bells were rung, and bands paraded the streets with cheering crowds in their wake.

The temper of the people was in every way admirable. Everywhere there was the note of thankfulness that the war had terminated, but there was also a deeper and stronger note that the British cause had triumphed. A great feature was the decking with bunting of all the vessels in the harbour.

ABERDEEN: STREET PROCESSIONS

In Aberdeen the first intimation was the ringing of the great bell Victoria, for the first time since Hogmanay 1914, and the hooting of the syrens of the vessels in the harbour. Great crowds gathered in the streets.

At the Town House, where the flags of the Allies were hoisted, Provost Sir James Taggart appeared on the balcony, and called for three cheers for "our glorious boys" and for the King, which were warmly given. The Gordon Highlanders, with their pipe and brass bands, had an enthusiastic ovation.

The students from Marischal College paraded with flags and drums, and in the afternoon the Discharged Sailors and Soldiers' Association had a procession with their bands. Flags were everywhere - on the cars and at all public buildings. Rosettes of red, white and blue were prominent. All the schools were closed for the afternoon and most of the public works were also shut.

From the meeting of the Town Council telegrams of congratulation were sent to the King, the Prime Minister, Field-Marshal Haig, Admiral Beatty, and Marshal Foch. In several churches services were held at noon. The students had a torchlight procession in the evening.

In the forenoon sirens were sounded, and work was not resumed in the mills and factories.

Chapter eight

The tragedies continue

For Scotland in particular, and therefore *The Scotsman*, the stories from the First World War were far from over. The country saw two huge stories in 1919 in the Western Isles and the Northern Isles, both shocking but one of them delivering devastating consequences on an island community that had already suffered heavily.

The Iolaire was carrying 280 servicemen who had survived the horrors of the war and were on their way home to Lewis. Just as it neared Stornoway it hit rocks, and 205 of those on board lost their lives. Joy at reunion was turned instantly to tragedy, a tragedy that touched almost every village on the island.

The Iolaire.

THURSDAY, 2 JANUARY, 1919

Wreck at Stornoway

REPORTED LOSS OF 270 LIVES

NAVAL RATINGS ON HOLIDAY LEAVE

A disaster which has cast a gloom over Stornoway and Lewis took place early yesterday morning, when the steam yacht Iolaire, with 300 sailors from Kyle of Lochalsh to Stornoway - these men were all on New Year holiday leave - struck the Beasts of Holm, dangerous, jagged rocks situated to the right of Stornoway harbour entrance.

Of the 300 on board only about 30 were reported saved. They scrambled ashore as best they could, some of them very seriously injured, some

making marvellous escapes. All the officers and most of the crew of the Iolaire were lost.

Between 1am and 2am she was approaching Stornoway Harbour, the lights on Arnish Point and the beacon off the harbour entrance being quite visible. The passengers were in high spirits, eagerly anticipating their New Year holiday, the first since hostilities ceased. For some reason quite inexplicable the vessel, instead of turning into Stornoway Harbour, proceeded right across the harbour mouth, and ran ashore at full speed near Holm Head. By this time the wind had increased and there was a

high sea running on the leeshore, where the Iolaire had struck.

Some narratives have been gleaned from survivors, who unfortunately are few. Accurate figures are not available but the number is put variously at 35 to 50, so that the loss is over 200 men.

A young Naval Reservist, interviewed by our correspondent, said: "It was very dark, there being no moon, but the atmosphere was clear, and lights were distinctly visible at a great distance. As we were approaching Arnish Lighthouse we commenced getting our kit together, expecting to be safely alongside Stornoway Pier in a few minutes.

"It was about ten minutes to two, and I was in the salon when there came a great crash, and the vessel heeled heavily to starboard. It was so dark that we could not see the land, which was only 30 yards distant from the point we struck. I didn't think it was rock we struck, but just that we ran ashore. When the ship listed the seas came breaking over, and I should say 40 or 50 men jumped overboard. I think every one of them was drowned. There was a great panic on board.

"Two lifeboats were launched, and both were swamped. From the first, one man scrambled back on board. With this exception I think all the men who went into the boats were drowned. When the Iolaire struck she was bow on to the land, but about ten minutes afterwards she lifted and drove a little to seawards, afterwards coming in stern first, and falling broadside on to the shore. Rockets were fired, and by their light I could see that her stern was now not more than seven yards from a ledge of rocks jutting out from the shore, and amidships she was within twenty yards of the only available place for landing. The seas were breaking over the stern, but many were tempted to try to reach the rocks there which were so near. I don't think any of them succeeded, for there was a very strong current running between the ship's stern and the ledge of the rocks, and I believe there were scores of men dashed to death against the rocks.

"When the second or third rocket went up I observed a line hanging into the sea from one of the davits amidships, and as the vessel, broadside on, was breaking the force of the sea on the shore at this part I let myself down by the line, got hold of a bit of wreckage, and tried to make the shore. As far as I know I was the first man to reach land.

"I was very exhausted and dazed, and wandered about for an hour or two before I found a farmhouse, where all of us who got ashore were hospitably received."

After the hull of the Iolaire disappeared one plucky lad, Donald Morrison of 7 Knockard, continued to hang on to the mast. It was impossible to render assistance from the sea owing to the position of the wreck. When the storm subsided Morrison was taken off in a very exhausted condition, after being eight hours clinging in his precarious perch.

A list of the men lost can only be compiled by degrees as their names become known through their relatives, who are scattered throughout the hundred villages of Lewis. A complete list of the saved is also at present unavailable. So far, only 24 bodies have been recovered, but it is expected that a large number will come ashore on the next tide.

And later that year the Germans caused outrage by scuttling its fleet holed up at Scapa Flow in the Orkney Islands to stop them falling into British hands.

MONDAY, 23 JUNE, 1919

End of the German Fleet

70 WARSHIPS SUNK AT SCAPA SCUTTLED BY THEIR GERMAN CREWS

By an act of German treachery, almost all the German warships interned at Scapa Flow were sunk on Saturday. The Interned Fleet included: Battleships – 10, Battle Cruisers – 6, Light Cruisers – 8, Destroyers – 50. Of these none now remains afloat except one or two of the destroyers. Most of the others have been sunk and the remainder are beached.

According to the latest information, the fate of the ships is as follows: Battleships and Battle Cruisers - All sunk (some in shallow water), except the Baden, which was run aground in Swanbister Bay.

Light Cruisers - Five sunk and three beached, partly submerged.

Destroyers - All sunk, except 18 beached and four still afloat.

Skeleton German crews were

on the ships as caretakers, and there were no British guards on board. This was in accordance with the naval terms of the Armistice. The ships were regarded as merely interned until their fate was decided by the Peace conference.

The German Rear-Admiral and most of the Germans from the ships are in custody on-board His Majesty's ships.

Some boats from the ships refused to stop when ordered, and were fired on, and a small number of Germans were killed and wounded.

In accordance with the terms of Armistice, the German ships were interned with skeleton German crews as caretakers, and without British guards on board.

SCUTTLED WHILE BRITISH BATTLESHIPS WERE AT SEA.

Kirkwall, Sunday morning.

The end of the German fleet in Scapa Flow has been even more dramatic than its surrender to Admiral Beatty. At midday on Saturday the red flag and German ensign were hoisted on all the German battleships, battle cruisers, light cruisers, and destroyers, the Kingston valves opened, and, seemingly before the British well knew what was taking place, so many ships were doomed that now but one battleship remains afloat. The British battle squadron which, rightly or wrongly, has been regarded as the guard of the enemy float, was at sea exercising, it is believed.

The hoisting of the red flag seems to have been regarded at first by the British authorities as a simple mutiny on the part of the German seamen. Those of the members of the crews of the German ships who had not taken to boats leaped overboard. All of them were a considerable time in the water before being rescued. Some of the boats from the German ships refused to stop when ordered to do so. These were fired upon. The number of casualties is not known.

The British battleships were recalled to port, and every effort was made, with the assistance of the tugs, trawlers, and drifters already on the scene, to save the ships which still remained afloat. Many of the German vessels had disappeared before the arrival of the last of the British Battle Fleet.

EFFORTS AT SALVAGE

At 3p.m. practically all the enemy destroyers had been sunk or beached.

Three battleships and battle cruisers remained afloat, two of them lying deep and sinking fast, and of the five light cruisers remaining two seemed near their end.

Of the three heavy ships the Hindenburg, which had cast adrift in an attempt to beach her on the island of Cava, settled down a short distance from the shore with decks submerged and only masts and funnels showing.

Another, after ineffectual attempts to move her by a destroyer, a trawler, and a drifter, turned turtle, and in less than a minute nothing but the bubbling water where her anchorage had been. The third ship around 4.30pm was apparently regarded as safe, for at that hour a large white ensign, with the German flag below it, was hoisted at the main of the five light cruisers, one was cast adrift and came safely ashore Cava island. Two others were taken by tugs and destroyers to Swanbister bay, where they now lie on the sandy bottom. The fourth, while in charge of the tug, listed heavily to port and went down in deep water. The fifth sank by the stern while at anchor.

Of the great fleet of seventy vessels all that remain are thus one battleship; a few dull, reddish-coloured hulls peeping through the shallow waters; three small cruisers, partly submerged; and, on the western side of Fara Island, destroyers, perhaps numbering less than a dozen, no more than a stone's throw, so it seemed, from across the water, from the beach.

A PREMEDITATED ACT

Thurso, Sunday.

The sinking of the German ships by their crews recalls the behaviour of the crews on board the interned ships, who landed on the surrounding islands shortly after internment, and engaged in marauding among the defenceless homesteads of the islanders, carrying away such booty as they could, principally that which was service in replenishing their supplies. As the result of that occurrence, their facilities for a repetition were curtailed.

THE SURRENDER AND ITS SEQUEL A DRAMATIC FINALE

The sudden eclipse of the German Fleet at Scapa Flow makes a dramatic finale of one of the strangest stories of the sea to be found in history. Many extraordinary and

Scuppered German ships in Scapa Flow.

memorable events have occurred during the war, but for dramatic effect and appeal to the imagination there is nothing comparable to the surrender of the German fleet on the High Season on the morning of 21st November 1918. That spectacle the public have been enabled to visualise in a manner impossible with the more extended operations of the fighting on land. No one who was present on that historic occasion could have predicted that the end of the magnificent surrendered fleet would be. That they should have gone down simultaneously in the place of their internment possibly solves a difficult problem for the Allies, and at the same time it affords a companion picture of equally strange and unprecedented character to that episode of last winter in the Firth of Forth, when in the rich glow of sunset the flower of the German Navy came to anchor within the enclosing circle of British ships of war.

STORY ABOUT GERMAN ADMIRAL

None of the German sailors who succeeded in reaching the shore was allowed to land, but all were taken prisoners and sent to the British ships.

Eye-witnesses have various accounts of what occurred. People living in the vicinity of Houton Pier declare that the German Admiral succeeded in reaching Houton early, and that he asked the men at the Aviation Station to go out and rescue some of the German sailors who were in difficulties.

Several men were seen to jump into the water while the Emden was being towed shorewards. One of these Germans made for a buoy, and, reaching it, sat astride it for some hours before he was taken off by one of our small craft.

Mr Archibald Hurd says it is stated that the German Rear-Admiral von Reuter has affirmed that he understood the armistice came to an end on Saturday, and he accepts full responsibility for sinking the vessels, in accordance with an order given in the early stages of the war, rather than surrender them.

Many of the German vessels had disappeared before the arrival of the British fleet.

ALL-NIGHT RAID ON CLYDESIDE

Dwelling-Houses, Schools and Churches Damaged

FATAL CASUALTIES

German Bombers Return to Scotland Last Night

SCOTLAND experienced its longest and most severe air raid of the war on Thursday night. The main attack was delivered on Clydeside, where casualties and damage resulted, but some high-explosives and incendiaries were also dropped in scattered areas elsewhere in Scotland. Several districts in England were also attacked, Merseyside experiencing a heavy raid.

Thirteen German bombers were brought down during the night, eleven of them by R.A.F. fighters.

Enemy 'planes returned to the West and Central districts of Scotland last night. Their presence overhead was noted half an hour earlier than on the occasion of Thursday night's visit. Distant gunfire was heard.

As the evening advanced the gunfire became more and more intense, and at some stages it exceeded the volume of sound heard on the previous evening. The night was darker and the piercing searchlights were more visible against the sky. Exploding shells made brilliant splashes of colour, and sometimes, for seconds at a time, the area was as clearly lit as at midday. Once again the aeroplanes were flying at a terrific height and were invisible from the ground.

Up to a late hour in the evening no serious damage was reported. Nearly two hours after the raid commenced, it was still possible to report that no serious casualties had occurred.

OFFICIAL COMMUNIQUÉ

A *communiqué* on Thursday night's raids issued by the Air Ministry and Ministry of Home Security yesterday morning stated:—

"Last night's enemy activity over this country was on a large scale, and was widely spread over England and Scotland.

"A heavy and prolonged attack was made on Clydeside. Some industrial buildings and many houses were damaged. Several fires were started, but these were fought with determination, and all were extinguished or brought under control by the

not been fully removed by the time commercial traffic had begun for the day, and bus and tram services had to be diverted.

The terror tactics of the enemy completely failed to break the morale of the people. In one district where incendiaries rained down by the hundred, men and women, and even children, helped to put them out by means of sand and with stirrup pumps. In one large tenement an incendiary became lodged in an inaccessible corner of the roof. The top flat of the building was soon ablaze, and before the fire was quelled a number of families had been rendered homeless.

A number of people lost their lives when a high-explosive bomb struck a working-class tenement near an industrial establishment. The latter premises escaped with a few broken windows, but many homes around were rendered uninhabitable by blast. Tenants who took cover in the back-court brick shelters were unhurt, though some of them found their way out temporarily blocked by a high pile of debris.

The ingenuity of cinema and theatre managements was equal to the occasion. When it was realised that patrons must spend the best part of the night under their care, impromptu concerts were staged after the normal programme had been given, and in some "houses" the audience was entertained to tea, biscuits and cake. A cheerful atmosphere was maintained, but as the morning wore on many patrons were to be seen sleeping soundly in their seats.

Transport services were practically normal throughout the Alert, and workers during the morning found there was little or no interruption in their routine.

A representative of *The Scotsman* who toured the bombed area at the height of the raid found everywhere the defence services fully mobilised to cope with any call that might be made upon them. In areas where damage had been caused, the rescue squads and firemen were quickly rushed to the scene, and within minutes they had commenced their task of bringing succour to the victims.

TRIBUTES TO CIVIL DEFENCE PERSONNEL

ETHIOPIAN TROO

Within 100 Miles Addis Ababa

IMPERIAL ADVANC

EMPEROR HAILE SELASSIE'S Patrio has now reached the vicinity of Marcos, strategic key town 100 north of Addis Ababa, the cap Abyssinia.

Operations in Abyssinia "are according to plan," said a military man at G.H.Q., Cairo, last night, co ing (says Press Association) on the advance by the Imperial and Emper Selassie's Patriot forces.

"It is impossible to say what sh enemy will put up at Debra Mar it is estimated that an enemy force 20,000 men is concentrated in this he added. "After Debra Marcos t Nile runs in a wide sweep through gorge which provides an obstacle."

Led by British officers, the operating in this region, have been ha the retreat of the Italian garriso Burye, the fortress captured rece

The capture (already reported) o 300 miles west of Addis Ababa, by a operating from Kurmuk, on the Suda tier, is officially confirmed.

SERIOUS CASUALTIES OF EN

The latest Army *communiqué* from Cairo, stated:—

Abyssinia.—Our troops have c Asosa, and are now advancing al Mendi road.

After their successful advance from during which they have continued to serious casualties on the retreating Patriot forces have now reached the of Debra Marcos.

Reporting the operations from the Somaliland, the *communiqué* sa "Yavello (South-West Abyssinia) h occupied by Patriots, who are follo the Italian withdrawal towards Neg conjunction with Imperial forces o from the Dolo area."

"MOPPING UP" IN SOMALIL

The following *communiqué* was is military headquarters in Nairobi day:—

"Operations in Abyssinia continue ing to plan.

"Mopping-up operations in Italian land are rapidly ending with the ca surrender of the last remnants of t

"Since the advent of the topees an hats of our Imperial troops, now as a feature of Italian Somaliland recently were in Kenya, fresh confid been installed in many of the na habitants, and conditions through occupied territory are rapidly b normal."

HEAVY RAIDS ON TRIPOL

A *communiqué* issued at R.A.F. Mid headquarters yesterday states:—

"TRIPOLITANIA.—The naval basin main quay at Tripoli were heavily h Wednesday night. Bombs fell an entire length of the quayside caus

Chapter nine

World War II

It was not long before the shadow of war would again stretch over the world, only this time it would be truly a global conflict, a conflict that would cost tens of millions of lives and have a direct impact on almost every inhabitant on the planet.

With a war of this magnitude it obviously produced many, many great stories, in the politics leading up and in all the way to the eventual peace, a long and agonising six years down the road.

For the staff at *The Scotsman* it meant some of the same experiences of World War One, in that also staff went off to fight. However those that did not also played a part in the military plans – *The Scotsman* formed its own Home Guard unit.

At this time there were great fears of German invasion or raids from German parachutists, so the Home Guard was formed. It consisted largely of those too old or too young to serve on the front line or those unable to do so for medical reasons. Its reputation these days has not been done any favours by the sitcom Dad's Army.

The Scotsman's Home Guard company, was formed by drama critic Charles Graves, who had been an officer in the Royal Warwicks in World War One. The company used to hold regular training exercises, that occasionally got a little too heated. On one such time the "attacking force" had managed to take control of the advertising office in *The Scotsman's*

A defused German 1000kg Luftmine (parachute mine). Glasgow, 18 March 1941.
From the collections of the Imperial War Museums

very palatial offices on North Bridge, but the defenders were seeing some success in repelling them by throwing bags of sand.

Suddenly fearing damage to the ornate wooden carvings and majestic marble pillars of the offices, company secretary John Noble called a halt to proceedings, much to the chagrin of Lt Graves, who believed in the necessity of life-like exercises.

"I seriously thought of putting Noble under arrest," Graves is reported to have said.

This was a war that was to plumb the depths of man's inhumanity to man, and technological advances meant many new strategies were devised. The development of aircraft in to heavy bombers with a range able to strike at the enemy's industrial resources meant a huge threat to the civilian populations that were inevitably densely clustered around these new targets. It was not just London's civilians that suffered from the nightmare of the blitz, but the blitz spirit of a stoic response is reflected in *The Scotsman's* coverage.

All-night raid on Clydeside

DWELLING HOUSES, SCHOOLS AND CHURCHES DAMAGED, FATAL CASUALTIES

Scotland experienced its longest and most severe air raid of the war on Thursday night. The main attack was delivered on Clydeside, where casualties and damage resulted, but some high explosives and incendiaries were also dropped in scattered areas elsewhere in Scotland.

Several districts in England were also attacked, Merseyside experiencing a heavy raid. Thirteen German bombers were brought down during the night, eleven of them by RAF fighters. Enemy planes returned to the West and Central districts of Scotland last night.

As the evening advanced the gunfire became more and more intense. Exploding shells made brilliant splashes of colour, and sometimes, for seconds at a time, the area was clearly lit as at mid-day. Once again the aeroplanes were flying at a terrific height and were invisible from the ground. Several tenement houses, schools, churches and other buildings suffered on Thursday in Clydeside's first all-night air raid, which left a trail of casualties, many of them fatal.

Caught out of doors when the raid started, many people sought safety in the nearest shelter, and like the thousands who were patronising the cinema and theatre, had to remain there for hours. Waves of bombers loaded with high explosives and incendiaries swept over the area, which was bathed in moonlight, and were immediately met by a terrific antiaircraft barrage. The flash of tracer bullets indicated that our fighters were also in action.

Many flares were dropped by the enemy machines, some of the chandelier type. A number of these were shot out before they reached the ground. Following one heavy burst of gunfire, a bomber flew low with its engine running irregularly, and unconfirmed reports state that this machine and another ultimately crashed. Some of the crew managed to bale out before the bomber burst into flames.

The civil defence services emerged triumphant from their testing ordeal. Acts of heroism in the face of indiscriminate bombing have won them the admiration of the population. Two policemen and two auxiliary firemen lost their lives in carrying out their duties.

Clydeside went calmly about its ordinary duties after the all-night attack. From all the working class districts throughout the area, some of which suffered considerable damage, the workers left home at their usual hour grimly determined to carry on their jobs without interruption. The women folk were as quietly heroic. Despite the harassing experiences of the night, they pluckily went to it to put their homes right and clear away any accumulation of debris.

Two families were wiped out by a direct hit on two houses in a scheme in the Glasgow area. Three men and a woman were killed at one town in the district which suffered severely. They were in a building damaged or struck by a high explosive. This town bore the brunt of the attack. Incendiary bombs were showered down and a church was struck. The minister had an alarming experience when a heavy bomb fell near his house, but fortunately without causing any great damage. A tenement occupied by many families in another working class area was demolished by a bomb. Men, women and children were trapped. The lot of the rescue workers, as well as that of those trapped in debris, was rendered worse by further bombing during rescue operations.

Paying tribute to the high courage of the victims, an Air Raid Precautions warden said he saw one little girl about three years old in the wreckage. When he tried to get to her, all she said was: "Let me sleep, let me sleep." The child was brought out soon afterwards, and seemed little the worse for her ordeal. One ARP worker who took a leading part in the rescue operations lost his wife and two children when the tenement collapsed. In spite of this, he continued the task of extricating neighbours trapped in the debris. Among those rescued were two babies a few months old. One of them had been partially buried for more than an hour.

One tenant, trapped to the neck in rubble, joined the rescue squad immediately after he had been released. A number of the casualties were caused when the victims were walking in the street. One man was found dead in a telephone box.

A number of people lost their lives when a bomb struck a working class tenement near an industrial establishment. The latter premises escaped with a few broken windows. Tenants who took cover in back court brick shelters were unhurt, though some of them found their way out blocked by a high pile of debris.

The ingenuity of cinema and theatre managements was equal to the occasion. When it was realised that patrons must spend the best part of the night under their care, impromptu concerts were staged after the normal programme had been given, and in some "houses" the audience was entertained to tea, biscuits and cake. A cheerful atmosphere was maintained, but as the morning wore on many patrons were seen sleeping soundly in their seats.

Searching the rubble of bombed buildings along Dunbarton Road.

The tone of these reports shows that *The Scotsman*, like other newspapers, was keen to play its part in the greater good and keep with the positive, morale-boosting tone of the time. But as always for newspapers this desire to do the right thing had to be tempered yet again with their duty to report accurately and make sure the public were not being dangerously misled by the government. So inevitably there were conflicts, and this led *The Scotsman* to strike out on its own and in a principled decision it defied the government and broke bad news to the people of Scotland which the Government had expressly demanded be covered up.

RMS Lancastria was a Cunard Liner, built on the Clyde, that was requisitioned by the government at the outbreak of war and became a troop ship. In June 1940 she was part of a naval force evacuating British troops and nationals from France two weeks after the Dunkirk evacuation. Because of the need and circumstances her captain was ordered to take as many people on board as was humanly possible, and told to disregard normal safety procedures. She was struck by three bombs from a German aircraft. No-one knows for sure how many were on board but it is estimated 4,000 were killed, making it the worst single loss of life in British maritime history.

Fearing the effect the news would have on morale, at this desperate stage of the war, Winston Churchill ordered a D Notice to prevent the news being published for 100 years.

But *The Scotsman* refused to accept the disaster should be hidden from the public and took the decision to print the story after the facts had been put in to the public domain by a U.S. report. Showing just how torn it was over the decision to publish and any impact on morale, it headlined on the number who had been saved – 2,500 – instead of the far bigger number of losses. It also published an editorial comment stating why it thought it had done the right thing by revealing the news.

FRIDAY, 26 JULY, 1940

Sinking of the Lancastria

2500 KNOWN TO BE SAVED

Nearly 2500 are known to have been saved – and more may be in enemy hands – from a total of 5300 aboard the transport Lancastria, which, it was admitted in London yesterday, was sunk on June 17 by the enemy during the evacuation of the B.E.F. from France.

The Lancastria, a Cunard-White Star liner, was lying at St Nazaire and was about to weigh anchor when the Nazi bombers launched their attack. After half an hour's ineffectual bombing she was hit by a salvo, took on a heavy list, capsized and sank.

As the ship went down Tommies sang "Roll out the barrel" and "There'll always be an England." Women and child evacuees, of which there were a number in the ship, jumped overboard – the heavy list hampering the launching of the lifeboats – only to be machine-gunned by the raiders.

The majority of survivors were picked up by small craft which were engaged in ferrying other personnel from the docks to troop-ships. Some, however, managed to swim and wade ashore in the shallow water.

Two thousand four hundred and seventy-seven survivors are known to have been picked up, but it is possible that the actual number may have been larger, and that others may have made their way ashore and have fallen into enemy hands.

There is great difficulty in estimating what are the exact figures in view of the difficult circumstances under which evacuation was taking place. Survivors all paid tribute to the magnificent courage displayed by the ship's crew and all ranks at the time the ship was struck.

RMS Lancastria sinking after being hit by German bombers.

EDITORIAL COMMENT

The loss of the Lancastria has been revealed after some delay. A former liner, the Lancastria was being used as a troopship to evacuate British forces from France. After embarking over 5000 passengers, including a number of women and children refugees, the vessel, while still at anchor, was attacked and sunk by German aircraft. Almost 2500 were picked up, and others may have succeeded in reaching the shore, but the number of casualties must have been deplorably high. Such losses unfortunately cannot be avoided in withdrawal operations, and it may be wondered why the fate of the Lancastria was not disclosed, until a report, not altogether accurate, had appeared in the American Press. The Government have given repeated assurances that it is not their policy to conceal news of losses and reverses, since they know that the people of this country are not easily depressed by misfortunes. There is no reason to suppose that in general the Government are not fulfilling their undertaking of dealing honestly with the people in the publication of information, and there may have been special reasons for delaying the announcement of the loss of the Lancastria.

Yet it is obvious that the belated release of news gives an opportunity for rumour to get busy, and to embellish facts in a sensational form. It also spreads suspicions that the Government's policy is to tell the public what they think is good for them to know, and no more. People with an itch for news are always prone to imagine that they are being kept in the dark, and that much is happening behind the scenes. Frank and timely publication of information, good or bad, is the best antidote for gossip and distrust.

Of course there were other dramas in the war, but there was one that was outstanding in its singularity and its direct involvement of Scotland.

Rudolph Hess was the Deputy Fuhrer in Nazi Germany, the third most powerful man in the country's hierarchy. In 1941 he flew secretly to Scotland with the intention of speaking to the Duke of Hamilton in a bid to start negotiations to bring the British Government in to peace talks. He lost his bearings trying to find the Duke's estate and his aircraft ran out of fuel, forcing him to parachute out.

He landed at Floors Farm at Eaglesham, south of Glasgow, and was discovered by David McLean, a local ploughman. He alerted the Home Guard, and Hess was taken in to custody. *The Scotsman* plays the story with a very straight bat.

THURSDAY, 15 MAY, 1941

Hess lands to help Britain overthrow Nazi tyranny

It is now permitted to be stated that Rudolf Hess flew to Scotland in an attempt to visit the Duke of Hamilton, whom he is said to have met on several occasions before the war in connection with matters of sport, in which they were both interested.

According to a semi-official statement issued in Berlin last night, Hess was desirous of bringing the war to a close and "thought that Hamilton and his colleagues in Britain had the necessary influence." It can also be disclosed now that Hess had made an attempt to communicate with the Duke of Hamilton by letter some months ago. The Duke immediately placed the letter in the hands of the security authorities and no reply was made to Hess.

It has, of course, already been stated in authoritative circles in London that Hess did not arrive with any peace overtures, that he was not on a mission or carrying any message, that his flight was an escape, and that he came in defiance of authority.

PENCIL RING AROUND DUNGAVEL

Hess's destination was Dungavel, the Duke's home, which is about six miles south of Strathaven, in Lanarkshire, near the border of Ayrshire. He landed near the Renfrewshire village of Eaglesham, about 12 or 14 miles north-west of Dungavel.

Hess had a map on which his route from Augsburg, South Germany, was marked in blue pencil. The line ended at Dungavel, which was ringed in blue pencil. When, on Saturday night, he baled out in Renfrewshire, some eight miles from Glasgow, the first thing he asked Mr David McLean, the ploughman who assisted him out of his parachute harness, was the way to Dungavel.

He had mistaken a large house he had sighted as the mansion he was seeking, and, failing to find a suitable landing ground, decided to descend by parachute. Despite the injury to his ankle, he wanted to be taken to the Duke's house, which he thought was nearby. According

to Mr McLean he did not say why he wanted to see the Duke, but he was obviously very anxious to do so. The Duke, who is on active service with the Royal Air Force, was not in Dungavel.

WHAT HESS SAID

Hess is reported to have told the farm people of the hardships now being experienced in Germany, and of the great distress that prevails among the people there over the bombing by the RAF of the towns and the sufferings of the civilian population. He said he had a message of great importance to deliver to the Duke of Hamilton, with whom he had been previously associated, and who shared his interests in skiing and flying, and in whose exploits in flying over Mount Everest he was particularly interested.

He said that when the Duke was Marquess of Douglas and Clydesdale he knew him well, and that he had flown to Scotland and made his estate his objective, as he had valuable information to give the Duke. He said that this

information would be of great use to the British in overthrowing the tyranny that now prevailed in the Reich.

BERLIN'S EXPLANATION

A semi-official statement issued in Berlin runs:- "Rudolf Hess left a considerable number of notes behind him before starting off for Britain. From these it may be deduced that he thought himself in a position to reach a peaceful understanding between Germany and Britain, if he could succeed in 'bringing the truth to Britain.'

"The motive of his action, which was in complete misunderstanding of the actual possibilities – and in the manner in which it was carried out can only be explained by the existence of mental derangement – appears, in the first instance, to have been prompted by reasons of humanity, for which he was very receptive by reason of his physical ailment.

"Rudolf Hess was naturally not initiated in the plans of the High Military Command of the Reich, which are known only to a very small circle, but he knew enough to be convinced that the prosecution of the war by the Germans and the British to the bitter end, irrespective of what support Britain might receive, would end not only in defeat but in the destruction of Britain. He knew Britain had made false statements, not only about the military but also about the economic conditions in Germany.

"He believed that it would be possible to convince Britain of the insane attitude of her leaders, if he could succeed in enlightening other British personalities as to the true position."

HESS IN GOOD SPIRITS IN HOSPITAL

Rudolf Hess is making good progress towards recovery. His injured ankle is yielding to treatment, and the slight abrasions to his arm are healing rapidly. He is stated to be in excellent spirits, and enjoys the light diet of chicken, fish and eggs. He may be sufficiently rested in a few days to leave the hospital where, of course his room is unostentatiously under military guard. He is reading a lot, generally light English literature, and short stories. He hears the BBC bulletins, and converses with the officer on guard and the nurses.

PLANE TO BE EXHIBITED

He has already talked at length to Mr Ivone Kirkpatrick, who, on Foreign Office instructions, flew from London to his bedside. It is understood that Hess has talked freely, and has given the British authorities a considerable amount of data that can be catalogued as "highly useful information." Detectives checked all arrivals yesterday at the hospital where Hess is detained. A military guard has also been posted at the gates. Authorised persons alone are allowed to pass. The remains of his plane are to be exhibited during London's coming War Weapons Week.

After Hitler's suicide on 30 April, 1945 Germany surrendered unconditionally on 7 May. The following day had been officially marked as the day of celebrations, but the British people were very understandably unwilling to wait. Natural joy at the end of a horrific six-year ordeal was not going to be put aside, despite the stoicism and willingness to obey all kinds of orders that has thus far been demonstrated. But as *The Scotsman* reports make clear, although celebrations were heartfelt, there were many who still mourned the loss of husbands, wives, sweethearts, parents, children and friends.

WEDNESDAY, MAY 9, 1945

Peace in Europe

One minute after midnight hostilities in Europe officially ended. Any German troops who continued to resist thereafter would, Mr Churchill intimated in his broadcast to the nation announcing the termination of the war, be treated as brigands and be hunted down by the forces of the United Nations.

Germany's defeat is total. There can be no doubt about that this time. Count von Krosigk, the German Foreign Minister, has himself referred to the "collapse of all physical and material forces." Once more Britain has saved herself by her exertions, and Europe by her example. While giving thanks to God for a great deliverance, we should, in the words of His Majesty the King in his broadcast to his peoples last night, remember first those who will never come back, and then the living who have brought victory. To the dead we owe it to strive for the better world and lasting peace for which they died. With the living we must go forward to that restoration throughout the world of freedom and respect for law and human personality without which this tremendous struggle will have been in vain. It was, as His Majesty said, the knowledge that in defending ourselves we were defending the world's liberties, as well as the realisation that our freedom, independence, and national existence were at stake, that upheld us, and it is in the conviction that a stricken world looks to us to lead it back to peace and sanity that we must now shoulder other, though less heavy, burdens. That the task before us will be easy, no one imagines.

Mr Churchill yesterday declared that it would require all our strength and resources, and President Truman put the matter in a nutshell when he said that the watchword for the coming months was "work, work, work." Both statesmen were thinking chiefly of the war against Japan, which in the hour of victory in Europe we must not forget will call for great exertions by this country, as well as by the United States, before it is brought to a successful conclusion. Japan still holds large portions of Eastern Asia, and there can be no worldwide peace and security until she, too, surrenders unconditionally and pays the just penalty for the injuries and detestable cruelties of which she is guilty. How long she will continue to resist now that, as Generalissimo Chiang Kai Shek said yesterday, the whole stupendous weight of humanity is about to come down on her, remains to be seen. Her Foreign Minister's references to the desertion of Japan by Italy and Germany betray an uneasy state of mind. Nevertheless, we must reckon on her fighting to the bitter end. Field-Marshal Smuts, speaking at San Francisco yesterday, appealed to the Allied nations assembled there not to destroy the present victory by lapsing into isolationism or selfish living. Here in Britain, rejoicing, as we do, in the liberation of the last remaining countries held captive by Nazi Germany, and not least in the deliverance of our own fair Channel Islands, we pause for relaxation after our long period of toil but to renew our strength for the immense task of restoring Europe as well as of defeating Japan. At San Francisco yesterday Mr Mackenzie King, the Canadian Prime Minister, spoke of the suffering to be relieved and the devastation to be repaired in the liberated countries. With defeated Germany as well to be saved from chaos, our burden is not such as to admit of the slightest slackening. We must strive on if the return of peace to Europe is to be anything but a name.

HOW EDINBURGH SPENT VE DAY

Edinburgh's official recognition of the ending of the war in Europe took the form of a short meeting of the Town Council in the City Chambers, at which Lord Provost J.S. Falconer paid a tribute to the endurance of the British people and to the part played by Scottish men and women in the war. The meeting was followed by a brief ceremony at the Mercat Cross, at which the Dean of the Thistle read the 76th Psalm, which formed part of a service held in the same place in 1588, as a thanksgiving for the defeat of the Armada. Unofficially, the end of the European War was celebrated in a very different way. Wet weather had not appreciably affected the spirits of the thousands of Servicemen and women, factory workers, shop girls and others who paraded the streets. In the afternoon crowds began to gather outside the American Red Cross Service Club and the Register House, and additional police had to be called to regulate the crowd outside the Club and to prevent accidents in the street. Thousands of young people had gathered outside, and, from the balcony and windows, chewing gum and chocolate were showered upon them. Hats were tossed into the street and a marine on the balcony, constituting himself conductor, led community singing. "Roll Out the Barrel," "The Yanks are Coming," "Tipperary," and "Land of Hope and Glory" were among the choices. A Red Flag waved from the balcony was cheered. In American fashion, torn-up paper fluttered from the windows down to the street.

WELLINGTON'S STATUE

The focal point at the Register House was Wellington's statue, which was climbed by several soldiers and sailors. For a time a British soldier stood perilously balanced on the mane of the horse and from this height tried to catch caps which were thrown to him. He succeeded in trying on several. The climbers drew a large crowd, which gathered on the steps of the Register House and on the pavement below. Flags were flown from a large number of buildings, public and private. The Union Jack predominated, but from a number of windows hung the Scottish Standard, the Stars and Stripes, the Red Flag of the Russians with its golden sickle, the French, Belgian, and other national flags. Strings of pennants floated on the air, and window sills and balconies were decked with bunting. It is hoped that these decorations will be kept in place for the visit of the King and Queen next week.

CROWDED GLASGOW STREETS

Despite the liveliness of the evening hours, Glasgow commenced its VE celebrations quietly. Commercial and business establishments were closed, most shops and… firms continued "business as usual." Among industrial concerns, some managements recognised the day as a holiday, but many workers had not heard the B.B.C. late announcements, and, with their morning papers arriving after they had left for work, they turned up, complete with dinner "pieces," to find closed gates. Saturday's scenes of bread queues were repeated. There was uncertainty with regard to the closing of bakers' butchers', and other food shops with the result that housewives were determined to lay in whatever foodstuffs they could procure. Many bakers were sold out by noon. There was similar confusion in relation to restaurants and tearooms. Many remained open, and while the lunch hour was busier than usual, the crowds in the city had increased to such an extent by the late afternoon that the demand for teas was similar to that of International Day at Hampden. Victory Night in flag-draped Glasgow should long be remembered by the many who visited the heart of the city late in the evening for the spontaneous display of gaiety by the vast crowds in the street. For a brief spell the populace were out to cheer and make merry by way of expressing thanks for a great military victory and the relief

GEORGE SQUARE A FOCAL POINT

of a heavy burden of anxiety.

George Square was the focal point of the evening's demonstration of jubilation, and from eight o'clock onwards the spacious area became a seething mass of humanity. There was a constant hum of noise and singing, and the corps of mounted policemen had an exacting job in keeping the thoroughfares free from tram traffic. The mild, bright weather was ideal for the occasion. Throughout the evening, bonfires were lit in all districts – in streets and in open spaces. Many Church services were held in the city. At the service in the Cathedral… a glowing tribute to the valour of British youth was paid by the Rev. Dr .A. Neville Davidson, in his address.

EVENING ILLUMINATIONS

The carnival spirit was heightened in the evening when the illuminations were switched on at 10.35 at George Square. Over 1000 green, red, yellow, white and blue fairy lights weaved a colourful pattern among the trees and on some of the monuments, while the façade of the City Chambers had an imposing appearance under the brilliant glare of six batteries of flood-lamps arranged on either side of the Cenotaph. Simultaneously, the University buildings on Gilmorehill were floodlit. The street standard lights, which for economy reasons had not operated since the beginning of this month, were turned on at 10.30.

GREAT CROWDS CELEBRATE IN LONDON

Royal Family and Premier on Balcony of Palace

FROM OUR LONDON STAFF

Buckingham Palace was the magnet for perhaps the greatest crowds in London yesterday. They began to collect from an early hour— a constant stream of people passing down the Mall and Birdcage Walk, overflowing into St James's Park and the Green Park, and coming to rest before the Palace, where they squatted on the grass between the tulip beds, which were gorgeous masses of bloom.

The sun had come out after a violent thunderstorm in the early hours, and the trees in the Mall and St James's Park were showing the freshest green of spring. Prepared for a long wait the people sat down where they could, even on the kerb stones of the roadway. They were massed on the Victoria Memorial, which promised the best viewpoint. In front was a battery of ciné-cameras with protruding long focus lenses.

There was plenty of incident by and by. Before noon the new Palace guard marched along the Mall with fifes and drums. There were cheers for them and for the Irish Guards band playing the old guard back to Wellington Barracks.

There was another chance to cheer when Mr Churchill arrived to lunch with the King and Queen. He wore morning dress and came in an open car. The cheering crowds closed round it, and the police had difficulty in keeping open passage for the car. Mr Churchill was smiling broadly and repeatedly gave the crowd the "V" sign as he drove into the Palace. He left a little before three o'clock by a garden entrance. The front gates of the Palace had had to be closed because of the pressure of the crowds.

The King and Queen and the two Princesses had heard the Prime Minister's historic announcement in their private apartments, and the words of it had come to the crowds from loud-speakers hung in the forecourt.

CALL FOR THE KING

There had been calls, "We want the King," and after Mr Churchill had broadcast, the King appeared on the centre balcony which was draped with a crimson and gold hanging. The King was bareheaded and in naval uniform. For a few seconds he stood alone, smiling. The packed crowds pressed close against the forecourt railings and extending far back up the Mall were at that moment eloquent of an Empire's rejoicing. This was the central scene of it all.

The King was joined by the Queen and the Princesses. Her Majesty was in soft powder blue. Princess Elizabeth in her uniform of second subaltern of the A.T.S., and Princess Margaret in blue. They stood for several minutes while the people cheered.

With a Guards band leading them the crowd sang the National Anthem. Repeatedly the King, the Queen and the Princesses waved to the crowd. The Palace façade, with its bomb-spattered stonework, windows as yet unglazed and makeshift railings, was a fitting background to this happy ending of years of stress and havoc. Above it had flown all day the Royal Standard.

There was more cheering and waving of flags when an hour later the King and Queen with the Princesses appeared a second time. Their Majesties again came to the balcony with Mr Churchill, who had arrived at the Palace with the other members of the War Cabinet. So the day wore on, with enthusiasm unabated, until the evening when the King broadcast, and the Palace was floodlit against the night sky.

---

the day, and at all times the congregation was large—one of civilians, young and old, and of Service men and women of all nationalities. The protective scaffolding behind the altar of St Paul's still stands as reminder, if that were necessary, of the dire attacks that threatened the life of the City and of much else besides. There still, too, waits to be removed the vast brick wall enclosing the monument to the Duke of Wellington, with its bronze group depicting "Truth plucking out the tongue of calumny."

By mid-day a great crowd had gathered on the steps of the Cathedral, that place which more than any other had come to be the brave, familiar symbol of an indomitable City. It was a memorable scene. The crowd must have numbered thousands. In Service uniform and civilian dress, brightened by buttonholes of red, white and blue, they stood packed together listening to the music of a military band which played in the forecourt. Then, suddenly, there in the shadow of St Paul's the people burst out singing when the familiar airs sounded not of the songs of recent years, but of those of 1914-1918. They joined, quietly at first and then heartily, in the choruses of "Pack Up Your Troubles," "Keep the Home Fires Burning," and "Tipperary." The poignant emotions of some of the singers were plainly evident.

CARNIVAL SCENES

As the hour of the Prime Minister's announcement drew near signs of excitement heightened in the City streets. In Fleet Street, windows were cascaded with newspaper office "tape," and it was thrown and scattered, in the American manner of carnival, from one side of the roadway to the other. It hung on buses and cars which drove along, white streamers fluttering in the breeze, to be caught and pulled by laughing people. One observer who remembered the Armistice Day scenes of 1918 said: "This is altogether different. The crowds have not gone mad. They are happy, but they are aware." This observer might, indeed, later in the day at some points in London, have seen fit to revise his opinion, but on the whole irresponsible and thoughtless "mafficking" seems to have been confined to the minority element. The City crowds, however, were gay. Groups of young people wore paper hats and wielded rattles, shouting and singing. Numbers of sightseers had somehow procured pony carts and the spectators on bicycles were numerous.

As 3 o'clock approached people were still streaming to and from St Paul's. A few 'planes roared low overhead. The moment had come for which not only London had waited through the amazing years.

THE VOICE

Those who heard the voice of the Prime Minister, calm, clear, incisive, and devoid of emotion save for the ringing lift of his tone at the close of the most tremendous pronouncement of all history, were unashamed this time to show themselves stirred. Mr Churchill had once again, in characteristically adequate words, touched profundities of feeling which up till now neither received nor needed superficial expression. But on this occasion London's imperturbability could be relaxed. And it was. The cheers resounded in City streets and so did the singing and the laughter.

Hours later the crowds were still moving about. Vast numbers of Londoners had evidently determined to spend no part of the day at home, and had kept to their plan in spite of the discomfort and uncertainties of travel to and from the suburbs. London Transport had decided at the last moment to run only a Sunday service. Buses were

---

IN PARLIAMENT SQUARE

LATION CEREMONY AT REIMS

SURF

Allied

For

AGUE

**General Jodl,
victors would**

hill in Britain,
ulle in France.
been published

; midnight.
capture yester-
nd of Dresden

agreement for
rounding area,
gned yesterday
d the German

ratitude of every
1 Nations."
nch cathedral city
so much at the
rism in the First
of the war against
d of Hitler's Third

TALKS

1 arranged for the
to be brought to
for preliminary
isted of Admiral
k, a supply expert.
whole trip by
Brussels continued

nched at an R.A.F.
and "kiltie Scotch
Admiral Friede-
rectly out of the
loy it. The party
up car driven by
der, of Inverness.
preliminary meet-
as required to show
ority to represent
lear, however, that
surrender.
xplained to Friede-
e German military
xpressed the fear
rs would be killed
y were allowed to
Allied armies in

owed no sympathy
declared that the
to talk about any-
rrender to all the

howed no signs of
l of defeated Ger-

NTED

dmiral Friedeberg
Commander which
ap, calling for un-
l forces to remain
and for an under-
eacraft should not

the terms back to
n, where he and
sandwiches and
d for a time by
ther clarified the

d London were in
ral Eisenhower of
being explained
as authorised only
of the remaining
ern Front.
that discussion of
refused and that
ire the necessary
re to seek.

CAPITULATION AT PRAGUE

Surrender of Germans to Czech Patriots

HOSPITALS SHELLED

AN agreement for German capitulation in Prague and the surrounding area, scheduled to start at eight o'clock last night, was signed yesterday, according to Prague radio, all stations of which are now in the hands of Czech patriots. The agreement, said the radio, was signed by representatives of the Czecho-slovak National Army and the German general commanding the forces in Prague.

According to the agreement, all Wehrmacht units, S.S. troops, German police, and all German State organisations in Prague and surroundings had to start leaving by 8 p.m.

"German women and children, as far as they are not following the withdrawing troops, are being put under the protection of the representatives in Prague of the International Red Cross, who will care for their transport," said the announcement. "All heavy weapons are to be left at the outskirts of the town at the disposal of the units of the Czechoslovak National Army. All other weapons will be handed over to representatives of the Czech National Army at the demarcation line outside Prague.

"The Czechoslovak authorities are taking care that the Czech population does not impede the withdrawal of the German forces."

Prague radio followed the announcement by appeals to the Czech population not to attack withdrawing men and S.S. formations, or to impede their retreat. All barricades, however, must be strongly guarded by the Czechoslovak National Army, it added.

GERMAN "CEASE FIRE" ORDER

At 6.15 yesterday morning the radio had broadcast the following announcement:—

"At 1.30 a.m. to-day the German Command issued orders through all communications to German units to cease fighting.

"There are, of course, technical difficulties in the communication of this order in the shortest possible time. Therefore, inform the German units where necessary. The German military plenipotentiary is negotiating with the Czech National Council on details of unconditional surrender."

Despite the German Command's "Cease fire" order, fighting continued in Prague for the greater part of the day.

At 4.54 p.m. the following appeal was broadcast in English: "Prague calling. We request dive-bombers. Help us, we beseech you. The Germans are shelling Prague. Do not hesitate. Do not lose a moment. We need the aircraft urgently in the southern part of Prague, on the right bank of the Moldau River."

An hour earlier all the Prague stations issued the following:—"German artillery fire continues. Fight back, but don't waste ammunition."

A few minutes later the radio called upon the German artillery to stop shelling the general hospitals in Prague and the suburbs of Strahov and Bulovka, and not to shell rescue squads. There were individual as well as general appeals to respect work for the wounded, such as: "Cease firing at the Hospital of the Merciful Sisters, by order of the International Red Cross."

GERMANS MURDER CIVILIANS

A message from Prague reaching Czechoslovak quarters in London at 6 p.m. said:—

"During to-day, five German divisions have been preparing for an assault on Prague from the west. On Monday, Czech partisans and military units from all parts of Bohemia also moved towards Prague.

"We have been in telephone communication with Pilsen, and have asked for a speedy advance of the U.S. forces towards Prague. Help has not arrived.

"German troops continue to commit crimes against international conventions. The town of Konetopy near Brandys ??

The King and Queen with Mr Churchill on the balcony of Buckingham Palace. Their Majesties are acknowledging the cheers of the huge crowd gathered in front of the Palace.

EISENHOWER TO HIS TROOPS

"Every Man of Every Nation Has Contributed to the Outcome"

GENERAL EISENHOWER'S victory Order of the Day issued from S.H.A.E.F. yesterday stated:—

Men and women of the Allied Expeditionary Force—The crusade on which we embarked in the early summer of 1944 has reached its glorious conclusion. It is my especial privilege, in the name of all nations represented in this theatre of war, to commend each of you for valiant performance of duty.

Though these words are feeble, they come from the bottom of a heart overflowing with pride in your loyal service, and admiration for you as warriors. Your accomplishments at sea, in the air, on the ground, and in the field of supply, have astonished the world. Even before the final week of the conflict you had put 5,000,000 of the enemy permanently out of the war.

You have taken in your stride military tasks so difficult as to be classed by many doubters as impossible. You have confused, defeated, and destroyed your savagely-fighting foe. On the road to victory you have endured every discomfort and privation, and have surmounted every obstacle that ingenuity and desperation could throw in your path. You did not pause until our front was firmly joined up with the great Red Army coming from the East and other Allied forces coming from the South.

"FULL VICTORY ATTAINED"

Full victory in Europe has been attained. Working and fighting together, in a single and indestructible partnership, you have achieved a perfection in unification of air, ground, and naval power that will stand as a model in our time.

Blood of many nations—American, British, Canadian, French, Polish, and others—has helped to gain the victory.

Each of the fallen died as a member of the team to which you belong, bound together by a common love of liberty and a refusal to submit to enslavement. No monument of stone, no memorial of whatever magnitude could so well express our respect and

revering each honoured grave and be sending comfort to the loved ones of comrades who could not live to see this day.

MONTGOMERY'S SALUTES

"Let Us Now Win the Peace"

Field-Marshal Montgomery, in a message to all ranks under his command in the 21st Army Group, said:—

"I would ask you all to remember those of our comrades who fell in the struggle. They gave their lives that others might have freedom, and no man can do more than that. I believe that He would say to each one of them, 'Well done thou good and faithful servant.' We who remain and have seen the thing through to the end must remember to give the praise and thankfulness where it is due. This is the Lord's doing, and it is marvellous in our eyes.

"Let us never forget what we owe to our Russian and American Allies. This great Allied team has achieved much in war, may it achieve even more in peace.

"Without doubt, great problems lie ahead. There is much work for each one of us.

"We must face up to that work with the same fortitude that we faced up to the worst days of this war. It may be that some difficult times lie ahead for our country and for each one of us personally. If it happens thus, then our discipline will pull us through, but we must remember that the best discipline implies the subordination of self for the benefit of the community.

"It has been a privilege and an honour to command this great British Empire team in Western Europe. Few commanders can have had such loyal service as you have given me. I thank each one of you from the bottom of my heart.

"We have won the German war. Let us now win the peace. Good luck to you all, wherever you may be."

DEBT TO ROYAL NAVY

The following message was received yesterday by the First Sea Lord from Field-Marshal Montgomery to the Royal Navy:—

"Throughout our long journey from Egypt to the Baltic any success achieved by the British armies has been made possible only

BRI

ALLIED re
capitulation,
Earlier y
message from
addressed to

EXIT

Party H
Say

DIFFICUL

GRAND ADMIRA
in a speech to t
over Flensburg

"German me
addressed you c
announce the de
appointment as
my first task we
German men an

"In conformi
High Command c
the night of Ma
conditional surr
troops in all th

"From 23.00
European time)

"German sol
battles, are now
captivity, and th
fice for the life
and for the futu

"We bow in
which they have
We remember th

"I have prom
and children to
living conditions
to do so, in the

"I do not kno
to do to help yo
have to face fa

"The foundat
Reich was built
unity of State
The party has
of its former ac

OFFER TO

"With the occ
has passed into
forces. It depe
the Reich Gove
be able to conti

"If I can be
land by continu
My love for Ger
keep me at my
to personal cons

"I shall not r
is compatible wi
to the Reich.

"There is a di
one of us. We m
gallantry, and d
of our dead den

"We must be
our best in wor
which there car
life. We want
unity and justic
survive the hard

"We may trea
the time will co
live a free and
peace.

"I do not war
thorny path. If
in office, I shall
If, however, du
this step will he
and Reich."

"CEASE

New orders to
broadcast from t
man High Comm

Chapter ten

The birth of the world's greatest arts festival

In the immediate aftermath of the war everyone was looking for distraction and an antidote to death and destruction, for a benefit of peace and demonstration of the higher, more civilised characteristics of mankind, to repudiate the horrors of the conflict.

Edinburgh was no exception and in 1945 a committee was formed to create a new identity for the capital as "the cultural resort of Europe" with a Festival of Music, Art and Drama the centrepiece. This was the beginning of the Edinburgh Festival, which is still the biggest arts Festival in the world. It can be said with confidence that the aim of the original committee has been achieved. Edinburgh is without doubt now recognised as the Festival City, probably above anything else in many parts of the world.

The first festival took place in August and September 1947. Right from the very beginning there was a Fringe – companies who turned up uninvited and put on their shows regardless of official status, and 1947 also saw the birth of the Edinburgh International Film Festival, and it is now the longest continuously-running film festival in the world.

And the number of festivals has continued to grow with the shows and audiences. They now include the Edinburgh International Book Festival, the Edinburgh Art Festival, the Royal Edinburgh Military Tattoo, the Edinburgh Jazz & Blues Festival, the Scottish International Storytelling Festival, the Edinburgh International Science Festival, Edinburgh's Hogmanay, and the Edinburgh International Children's Festival. And there is also a Festival of Politics.

The Festivals continue to be important to *The Scotsman*, it publishes a daily guide with reviews and venues throughout the main festival period, and *The Scotsman* and its authoritative coverage continues to be important to the Festivals, with its Fringe First Awards and its reviews being coveted by the many acts that flock to Edinburgh.

So it is interesting to see how *The Scotsman* reported the birth of this phenomenon. The headline from January 1947 must surely rate as one of the most boring ever written.

Edinburgh International Festival

TWO BIG EXHIBITIONS TO BE HELD CONCURRENTLY IN CITY

Two notable exhibitions are to fit into Edinburgh's big-scale programme for the International Festival of Music, Art, and Drama which is to make the city "a magnet that will attract people from all over the world."

The quoted phrase was used by Professor Charles Sarolea when, heading a visit of members of the Consular Corps in the city to the City Chambers yesterday, he conveyed to Lord Provost Sir John Falconer their New Year greetings. The Lord Provost, outlining the extension of the Festival arrangements, stated that the Chamber of Commerce will present a very large Exhibition of Industries, Arts, and Crafts, for which it is hoped to use the windows of the shops along the whole length of Princes Street, and the Council of Design and Industry hope to hold an exhibition in the Royal Scottish Museum which will present Scotland in all its aspects.

The Lord Provost, in thanking the Consular Corps for offering the goodwill of the countries they represent, said that it was only on the basis of greater friendship that lasting peace could be expected. They must find a starting-place for the new era and translate into action their desire that their people should inter-mingle and pursue in unison the road to prosperity.

With that in view, they proposed to hold in Edinburgh an International Festival of Music, Art and Drama. "That is also very much our concern, for the future of our countries is inextricably interwoven and the prosperity of one affects the prosperity of all. We have fixed the last week of August 1947 as the date upon which we will definitely direct our steps towards this new future, a future in which we will, together, develop those things which will invigorate our trade.

"We will use this great event, when the finest music and drama will be presented, as a focus at which not only will those accomplishments be encouraged and enjoyed, but a great opportunity will be presented for showing the arts and crafts and industries of our country, and when businessmen and traders of all countries meet in a happy and fresh atmosphere to discuss questions of sale and exchange."

The Lord Provost mentioned that members of the Consular Corps would shortly receive the brochure showing that part of the event which belonged to the musical festival proper and which would last for three weeks, from 24th August to 12th September. It was under the patronage of the King and Queen. The programme would commence with a great service of praise in St Giles' Cathedral. Every day for those three weeks there would be performances of opera and drama and of chamber music.

There would be recitals and orchestral concerts, given by, among others, the Vienna Orchestra, conducted by Bruno Waller; L'Orchestre Colonne, conducted by Paul Parri; the Hallé, the Liverpool, the Scottish, and the B.B.C. Scottish Orchestra. These together would present a festival of a quality beyond any that had ever been held in the British Isles. "It will be held," added the Lord Provost, "with the advantage of the background of this old city, with its ancient castle, its palace, its courtyard and its gardens, all of which we hope will beat the disposal of the visitor and will form an incomparable relief of history and beauty and romance."

And let's not forget the importance of Royal patronage.

FRIDAY, 8 AUGUST, 1947

Queen's visit to Festival

HER MAJESTY TO ATTEND THREE PERFORMANCES

It was announced last night that the Queen will visit the International Festival of Music and Drama in Edinburgh on September 6, 8 and 9 and, among the three performances which she will attend will be that of Verdi's "Macbeth" by the Glyndebourne Opera Company at the King's Theatre on September 8. On September 6, Her Majesty will hear the Glasgow Orpheus Choir in the Usher Hall, and on September 9, the Vienna Philharmonic Orchestra, also in the Usher Hall. It was intimated during the recent visit of the Royal Family to Edinburgh that the Queen would come to the city for the Festival, and last night, Lord Provost Sir John Falconer told *The Scotsman* that Her Majesty had made particular inquiries as to the prospects of its success and had expressed enthusiasm and delight at the decision to hold it in Edinburgh. "Her Majesty," he stated, "took the latest brochure away with her so that she might study it most carefully, and I know she was looking forward with very great pleasure to attending as many performances as she could manage. Every arrangement will be made for her comfort and convenience, and Edinburgh is delighted and honoured that she should come."

But from these humble beginnings it became the massive event it is today, an event that over the decades has attracted some of the biggest stars in the world to the capital of Scotland. The fantastic breadth of the artistic offering, from opera and ballet, music and film to stand-up comedy meant that those at the top of their chosen calling attended and that those aspiring to become stars also attend. The list of attendees is such a stellar one it is hard to single out any, often stars like to come because they can use the time to see other shows and artists they admire or are curious about. In fact celebrity-spotting has become a recognised part of the Edinburgh summer and there are now lists of pubs and restaurants that should be patronised if getting up close and personal with the rich and famous is what you want to do.

Claire Bloom, Richard Burton and Fay Compton reading the Edinburgh Festival programme in August 1953. They were starring in the Old Vic production of *Hamlet*

Actor and director Orson Welles arrives at the Cameo Cinema during 1953 Edinburgh Film Festival to give a lecture where he declared that "the film industry is dying."

The Edinburgh Festival 1954. Margot Fonteyn admiring the exhibits at the Homage To Diaghilev exhibit.

Maria Callas, with her dresser, prepares for her role as Amina in *La Sonnambula* with La Piccola Scala opera company at the Edinburgh Festival 1957. She sang in the four performances she had been contracted to do, but when asked to do a fifth she refused citing nervous exhaustion. A press furore followed after Callas left for Venice, but for her replacement, Renate Scotto it proved to be a breakthrough performance.

The English Stage Company presented *Exit the King* at the Lyceum Theatre during Edinburgh Festival 1963 - Alec Guinness & Googie Withers.

American actress Carroll Baker clambers into her seat at the International Drama Conference held in McEwan Hall during Edinburgh Festival 1963.

Oxford Theatre Group Late Night Revue during Edinburgh Festival 1963 - Monty Python member Terry Jones behind Jayne Braysham's head. The others are Doug Fisher (next to Jones), Robin Grove-White and Ian Davidson.

Watched by Victor Spinetti (left) and Festival Director Lord Harewood (right), director Joan Littlewood faces the press after her production of *Henry IV* had been heavily criticised.
"Critics," she said, "are like old ladies. They like what they have been used to."

A scene from *Hamp* at the Lyceum Theatre Edinburgh Festival 1964. L-r: Richard Briers as Hargreaves, Leonard Rossiter as Webb, Tom Watson as the Padre and (kneeling) John Hurt as Hamp.

Marlene Dietrich and Burt Bacharach arrive at Turnhouse airport for the Edinburgh Festival 1965.

French mime Marcel Marceau at the Gateway Theatre during Edinburgh Festival 1967.

Violinist Yehudi Menuhin at Haddington during the Edinburgh International Festival 1968.

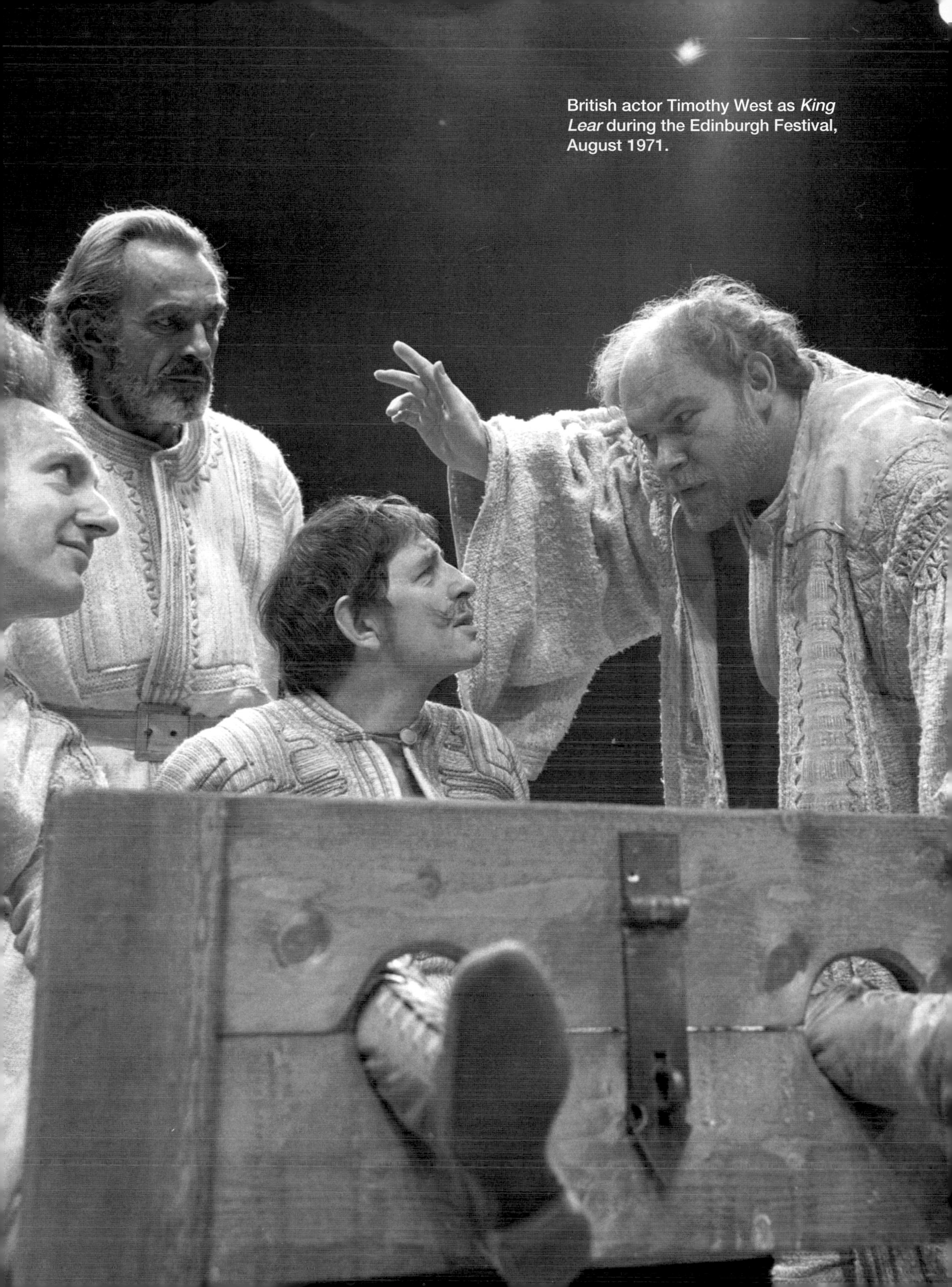

British actor Timothy West as *King Lear* during the Edinburgh Festival, August 1971.

The Offshore Theatre Company presented *The Great Northern Welly Boot Show* at the Waverley Market during the Edinburgh Festival Fringe 1972. In picture, Kenny Ireland (chorus, right) Bill Paterson (chorus, 2nd right) and Billy Connolly (in front).

Ian McKellen and Felicity Kendal in the Lyceum Theatre production of *Tis a Pity She's a Whore* during the Edinburgh Festival 1972.

Rudolf Nureyev and members of the Royal Ballet rehearse *Giselle* at the King's Theatre during the Edinburgh Festival 1975.

Alan Rickman and Anna Calder-Marshall in a Birmingham Repertory Company production of *The Devil is an Ass* at the Assembly Halls during the Edinburgh Festival 1976.

Fenella Fielding with two Edinburgh policemen during the Festival in 1976.

Burt Lancaster at the
Edinburgh Festival
Club in August 1976.

The Prospect Theatre Company present Chekhov's *Ivanov* at the Lyceum Theatre during Edinburgh Festival 1978 - Derek Jacobi as Nikolai Ivanov and Jane Wymark as Sasha.

David Suchet (right) in a scene from the Birmingham repertory production of *Measure for Measure* at the Edinburgh Festival 1976.

British actor Jude Law (aged 16) leads the cast of the National Youth Music Theatre (NYMT) production of *Joseph and the Amazing Technicolour Dreamcoat* at the Heriot Hall during Edinburgh Festival 1989.

Chapter eleven

The coronation of Queen Elizabeth II

Of course it was not just Edinburgh and Scotland that were keen to put behind the austerity and privations of World War Two. The prospect of the Queen's coronation held out an opportunity to demonstrate to the world the pomp and splendour of Britain at its best, and that opportunity was seized. Every chance to reinforce the escapism was taken.

In the run-up *The Scotsman* printed plans showing the route the royal procession would take, sketches of what Her Majesty's coronation gown might look like, timings for proceedings in London, and details of festivities in Scotland.

The Scotsman's coverage included a special six-page Coronation Supplement with a massive picture of the scene at Westminster Abbey on the front. Of course the coverage also reported the celebrations from all around Scotland.

Opposite
Queen Elizabeth II and Prince Philip, Duke of Edinburgh. Coronation portrait, June 1953, London, England.

Right
Queen Elizabeth II progresses past the Coronation Chair.

Unforgettable Reception by Her Subjects

SPLENDOUR OF PAGEANTRY UNDIMMED BY RAIN-LADEN SKIES

Scenes of tremendous splendour yesterday marked the Coronation of the Queen. Rain, at times heavy and continuous, failed to dim the brilliance of the pageantry or damp the spirits of those lining the procession route.

They watched Her Majesty borne along on a sea of cheers to her crowning in Westminster Abbey. After that solemn act and when the religious ceremony was over, the return to the Palace began in pouring rain, but as she "went forth to her people and her service," the rain stopped.

If the reception on the way to the Abbey had been memorable, that accorded the Royal pair on their homeward route was unforgettable.

Forty minutes after the triumphal return, the Queen, wearing the Imperial State Crown, stepped on to the balcony at Buckingham Palace with the Duke of Edinburgh and other members of the Royal Family.

They and the thousands below watched the fly-past of R.A.F. planes. Later the Queen and the Duke made a further brief appearance by themselves in response to the tumultuous waves of cheers.

Prince Charles saw the crowning and also all the other acts of investing his mother with the insignia of Royalty. Brought to the Abbey during the service, he sat between the Queen Mother and Princess Margaret.

Scotland's Day of Rejoicing

BONFIRES FROM SHETLAND TO THE BORDERS

Scotland marked the Coronation in full measure with a day of national rejoicing, and there was scarcely a hamlet but had its own special programme for the entertainment of its people, special attention being paid to the young and the old.

ORKNEY'S WINTRY WEATHER

It was mostly a "stay at home" Coronation in Orkney, where wintry conditions prevailed throughout the day. But if outside it was cold, miserable and grey, under every roof, from the smallest croft on the shores of Scapa Flow to the gaily bedecked ones in Orkney's two beflagged towns of Kirkwall and Stromness, the dignity of the Coronation service and the excitement and pageantry of the procession were conjured up by the radio.

In Shetland a bitterly cold northerly gale caused the cancellation of outdoor celebrations for children and, where possible, the children were taken to public halls.

Many bonfires were lit on the highest hills on the island last night. At Gallow Hill, near Scalloway, the ancient capital of Shetland, a bonfire was Shetland's link in the nation-wide chain of bonfires.

MORAY AND NAIRN

In spite of the weather the spirit of rejoicing in Moray and Nairn found enthusiastic expression in ceremonial parades, sports, picnics, dancers, fireworks displays and bonfires. They began with religious services in the morning in the larger centres of population and the festivities continued throughout the day and evening.

From the Califer Hill, which commands a view of seven counties stretching from Aberdeenshire to Caithness, a grandstand view was provided for a ring of bonfires that were lit in towns and villages right along the coast.

ABERDEEN - CROWDS DRAWN TO BIG PARADE

A procession which took an hour to pass the saluting base at the Music Hall was the highlight of Aberdeen's celebrations. Throughout the three-mile route crowds jammed the pavements and the 1600 Servicemen of the Navy, Army, and Air Force, who were accompanied by civilian and youth organisations, were loudly cheered as they marched along Union Street with pipes and drums and bands.

In the absence of Lord Provost J. M. Graham, who was attending the Coronation ceremony at Westminster, the salute was taken by Sheriff S. McDonald, senior Sheriff-Substitute. Pride of place in the trade and industry section, comprising 74 decorated vehicles was given to the "Craigievar Express" - a three-wheeled steam-driven car invented by Andrew Lawson, a Donside postman in 1897. It came through its test with great success.

Earlier in the day special church services throughout the city were well attended. Members of the Town Council, Magistrates, Sheriffs, officials and representatives of many organisations joined a congregation of 1500 at the city's official Coronation service in the West Church of St Nicholas.

As the Queen was being crowned, four guns drawn up on Castlehill Terrace fired a Royal Salute at the order of an officer listening in to the broadcast of the ceremony.

In the evening at Pittodrie Park, the first performance was given of the historical pageant "Bygone Aberdeen", which covered the city's history from the earliest times.

As darkness fell, bonfires were lit on high ground at Kincorth and Cairncry, and a fireworks display was given at the Links.

A party of estate workers from Balmoral were in London for the Coronation and the remainder took part in celebrations arranged by a Crathie committee which had Major Andrew W. Haig, the Queen's factor at Balmoral as chairman. After a dance in the new hall at Crathie in the evening, the festivities concluded with a bonfire on the top of Craighuie, a hill overlooking Balmoral.

Stonehaven put on the greatest show of its lifetime. A half-mile long procession was a pageant of colour, gaiety and history. Children and old people were specially entertained. There was a fancy dress parade, a swimming gala, a gymkhana, a display of motor car handling, old-time dancing and the day finished with the lighting of a giant bonfire on Cowie Cliffs and a display of fireworks.

THE CELEBRATIONS IN FIFE

Anstruther Town Hall, where the televised programme of the Coronation was on view to the old folks, was the focal point of celebrations in the united burghs in the morning. In the afternoon children's sports were held in Waid Park.

Open air dancing on the Folly was the attraction in the evening and finally came the fireworks display with a bonfire on a boat at the mouth of the harbour forming the climax.

At Crail the celebrations began with a service in Old St Mary's Church. Old folks were given an opportunity of watching the televised Coronation ceremony in Old St Mary's Church Hall.

In the afternoon there were spots in Beechwalk Park followed by teas for children and old folks. Then Coronation souvenirs were distributed. A football match was the attraction in the early evening and a film performance was provided for the children.

10,000 WATCH TV AT DUNDEE BIG SERVICES PARADE

Dundee had a full programme of Corporation-sponsored and privately organised events. A chilly east wind, however, made conditions poor for children's outdoor events and for crowds watching processions.

In the forenoon a large crowd watched a Royal salute being fired at Riverside Park by the Dundee battery of the 276 (Highland) Field Regiment R.A. T.A. The city's official service was held in Dundee Parish Church (St Mary's) where Baillie A. G. Hossick, acting Lord Provost, attended, accompanied by civic dignitaries. A queue formed at 6 a.m. for admission to the Caird Hall, where the Corporation sponsored a TV show. Twenty sets were in operation. Old age pensioners had been given tickets previously. About 2000 people packed the hall, and there was a steady flow of viewers, those going away being quickly replaced by others. During the day some 10,000 people passed through the hall.

Last night the celebrations included a massed pipe band display at Riverside Park, a Corporation fireworks display, and a huge bonfire by the Tay, flood-lighting of the Law War Memorial and a Coronation ball in the Caird Hall.

DUMFRIES HAS A FEU-DE-JOIE

Tree-planting ceremonies at the Dock Park, the Observatory, and at Burns Garden, which mark the opening of celebrations at Dumfries were delayed until early evening because of the televising of the Coronation. Afterwards crowds gathered in High Street at the Mid Steeple when Retreat was played by

the pipes and drums of the 5th Bn, King's Own Scottish Borderers.

The main celebrations started at 11 p.m. when there was an artillery salute at the Whitesands interspersed by a feu-de-joie by riflemen of the K.O.S.B. This display was the signal for illuminating the four bridges over the River Nith, a procession of illuminated boats on the river, a display of fireworks, and a bonfire. From a sports festival held in the afternoon by youth clubs in the town, a team of 12 boys relayed a message from the citizens of Dumfries to Carlisle.

BORDER BONFIRES

So unexpectedly large was the procession of children marching to the Coronation sports at Hawick that the organisers ran out of halfcrowns, one of which had been promised to each child. An emergency call had to be made at a local bank. There were over 2600 children and it cost £330 to give them each their half-crown. At night a huge bonfire was lit at the Miller's Knowes overlooking the town as one of the Boy Scout series which link-up with bonfires on the Cheviots, Minto Hills, Ruberslaw and throughout the country. A

fireworks display followed.

NIGHT SCENES IN EDINBURGH JOYOUS CELEBRATIONS

Coronation day was almost over before Edinburgh began her visible rejoicings. By day the city was still and silent, but as soon as darkness fell a brave attempt was made to bring back the light - or so it seemed - with bonfires, floodlighting and fireworks. And the people, having viewed and listened to the celebrating in London, came out in thousands, themselves, to celebrate.

Until well into the evening the town had almost a Sabbath stillness. By sunset, however, large, thickening crowds appeared on the streets.

Seldom had there been so rapid a convergence of people on the city centre, and traffic was slowed to a crawling pace. From all over Edinburgh they thronged into Princes Street. The stance chosen by most was opposite Waverley. From there, the view covered the fireworks display on Calton Hill, the bonfire on Arthur's Seat, the floodlit Castle, and the twinkling lights of flagbedecked Princes Street itself.

One of the best vantage points was the Castle esplanade but, surprisingly, not many people chose to

watch from there. About 10.15 the red glow of the bonfire appeared over the gaunt shoulder of Arthur's Seat, a few minutes later the Castle was illuminated, and at 10.30 the first rockets went up from the Calton Hill, the Braids, Corstorphine Hill and Leith Links.

A fire was burning brightly somewhere in the Pentlands, and spots of light began to appear along the coast of Fife, a reminder, perhaps, not only of other celebrations - those, for instance, that marked the crowning of Queen Victoria - but of the balefires that used to be started centuries ago to give alarm of inroads from England.

Managers of leading Edinburgh cinemas spent an anxious night waiting and hoping for the first newsreel shots of the Coronation.

These were being flown north from London, but the aircraft was held up by bad weather in the North of England, and although taxis were standing by at Turnhouse airport, it was impossible to collect the copies in time for the last evening performances.

A half-mile long procession was a pageant of colour, gaiety and history.

And although the fervour around exploring and discovery had died down somewhat from its peak in the 19th century, there were still some glittering prizes to be taken, not least getting to the top of the world – conquering Mount Everest. Of course in June 1953 there was only one prism through which the headline and the story could be written.

Edmund Hillary and Tenzing Norgay in 1953.

TUESDAY, 2 JUNE, 1953

Everest "gift" for Queen

NEW ZEALANDER REACHES SUMMIT

BRITISH CLIMBERS' SUCCESS

Mount Everest has been conquered. Late last night, a few hours before Coronation Day, came the news that E.P. Hillary, a New Zealand member of the British expedition, and the Sherpa Guide, Tensing, had planted the Union Jack on the summit last Friday.

Mr Holland, Prime Minister of New Zealand, said in London last night: "What a grand achievement on the eve of the Coronation. I would hope this terrific example of tenacity, the spirit of endurance and fortitude in this, our Coronation year, might be regarded as a symbol that there are no heights or difficulties which the British people cannot overcome."

Hillary, who is 34, is a New Zealand beekeeper who joined the expedition in India. He has had wide climbing experience in the New Zealand Alps, where heavy snowfalls and peculiar icefalls make conditions not unlike those in the Himalayas.

Tensing (39), leader of the Sherpa guides, is the stalwart veteran of more Everest attempts than any man on earth. He made an epic ascent last year with the Swiss climber, Raymond Lambert, reaching the previous record height of 28,215 feet.

The news of the conquest was given by New Delhi Radio, which broadcast a message from Colonel John Hunt, leader of the expedition. It is believed that improved oxygen equipment, combined with fair weather, were largely responsible for the British success.

The report was communicated to the Queen at Buckingham Palace and to Winston Churchill. In the United States radio and television programmes were interrupted to make the announcement.

Admiral Richard Byrd, the American Polar explorer, told Reuter's correspondent in Washington: "That is wonderful news." He said the conquest "was typical of the bulldog tenacity of the British, which always wins through. Reaching the top of Everest is an epochal event. I am so glad the British are the first to succeed."

He added: "This is a wonderful gift for the Queen."

The news was quickly passed to President Eisenhower at the White House. First reports from London of Colonel Hunt's dramatic message caught New Delhi sleeping, states Associated Press. Newspapers which had produced their last editions of the night prepared to bring out "specials."

Himalayan experts were jubilant Everest had been conquered in this, the eleventh attempt in 32 years. Enthusiasm was the greater in view of the fact that Colonel Hunt's team had twice failed, and unconfirmed reports from Katmandu had indicated that the supposedly dejected members of the team were proposing to return in the first week of June, before the monsoon struck.

Chapter twelve

The modern world

One of my earliest memories as a child is being in the back of the family car as it bumped down the steep cobbled ramps at South Queensferry and clanked on to the ferry to take us across to Fife. I must have been three years old. My mother and father hail from Fife so most Sunday afternoons were spent on duty visits to the grandparents, and in that solidly working class tradition we never went over for lunch or dinner, we left after lunch and got home for dinner, and for my parents it was tea and biscuits. In Burntisland my sister and I had a special treat, a small individual bottle of fizzy juice from the Kool 0 Pop factory just at the end of the road. For me it was the height of sophistication and luxury - none of your common diluting nonsense.

But those ferry journeys soon stopped and the Stewart family's Sundays were transformed by one of the engineering feats of the 20th century.

My mother says she took me to the opening of the bridge, but I have no memory of that. I had just turned four. The crowds turned out in their thousands.

It is hard to overestimate the impact the bridge had on Edinburgh, the East Coast of Scotland and beyond. A ferry service across the Firth here had been in continuous service for 800 years. By the 1950s, the ferries were making 40,000 crossings annually carrying 1.5 million passengers and 800,000 vehicles.

The bridge really was an engineering marvel, at the time it opened it was was the longest steel suspension bridge in Europe and 210,000 tons of concrete were involved in its construction, the total cost of the project including road connections and realignments was £19.5 million. Seven lives were lost during construction.

As the 21st century puts the Queensferry Crossing next to the Forth Road Bridge due to fears over the toll that time and traffic took on it, it is worth remembering how *The Scotsman* reported the opening at the time.

Men fearlessly walk ropes during construction of
the Forth Road Bridge, August 2, 1961.

The south side tower of the Forth Road Bridge at an advanced stage of construction.

People and cars turn out en masse in Edinburgh Road, South Queensferry, to see the opening of the Forth Road Bridge in September 1964.

Forth spanned again

GIANT STEP FORWARD INTO THE MOTORWAY AGE

Today sees the realisation of a scheme that was born some 40 years ago in the mind of a man of vision, and carried through to its magnificent conclusion by dint of pressure and enthusiasm in the face of caution and faint-heartedness.

The Forth Road Bridge, longest suspension bridge in Europe and fourth largest in the world, is a major engineering achievement in itself. It will open up Fife to tourism and industry, and end, for thousands of motorists, the frustrations of a ferry service grown inadequate for modern traffic.

Into its construction has gone not only 210,000 tons of concrete and 35,000 tons of steel, but also the engineering skill of a nation. Two leading firms of civil engineers collaborated to produce the final design – which contrasts strikingly with the relatively ponderous cantilever railway bridge, completed in 1890, which runs alongside it.

Three great engineering companies joined forces to form the consortium which built the superstructure. The two main towers stand some 500 feet above the water, and between them, 200 ft. above the water is the main span – as long as Edinburgh's Princes Street. The overall length of the bridge is 8529 feet and it carries two carriageways each 24 feet wide, two cycle tracks nine feet wide, and two footpaths six feet wide.

Supporting it are the main cables, nearly 24 inches in diameter, each with a breaking strength of 100 tons per square inch. Each cable was made up on 11,618 parallel wires of galvanised high tensile steel one fifth of an inch in diameter, spun by a method never before used outside the United States. While the spinning was going on men were stationed at intervals of 400 feet along the catwalks to ensure that the wires had the same span. So vital was this that no one was allowed to leave his post during his shift, even for meals.

Gales and bitter cold during the cablespinning were responsible for delays in the construction of the bridge, which in its early stages had gone well. Work began on September 1, 1958, but initial

operations were preparatory and unspectacular, so there was no official ceremony until November 21, when Mr John Maclay, then Secretary of State for Scotland, opened a steam valve which drove the first pile for the bridge into the river bed.

The first phase included the foundations for the main piers in the Forth – one of them on a submerged reef known as Mackintosh Rock – and the anchorages for the main cables. The latter involved the construction of large tunnels some 200 feet into the living rock.

The side towers, like huge concrete triumphal arches, were also built at this stage and were the first permanent structure to be seen, and an indication of the scale of the operations to follow. In June 1960, a month ahead of schedule, the first section of one of the main towers was erected on one of the two main piers. Gradually the towers rose to their full height, completely dwarfing the side towers and half as high again as the Forth Railway Bridge.

Then came the first spanning of the bridge – with catwalks stretching from the anchorages and over the tops of the towers. Cable spinning followed. The final part of the bridge's construction was the building of the river, each new section being connected by wire rope suspenders to the main cables.

The spans were joined on December 20, 1963. Roadway and footpath decking, surfacing and lighting followed. The finishing touches were made yesterday just in time for today's official opening by the Queen.

Her Majesty the Queen Elizabeth II, pictured above with First Minister Nicola Sturgeon, officially opening the Queensferry Crossing on Monday 4th September, 2017.

The technological development seen in the 20th century is probably the greatest in mankind's history, massively fuelled by the wars and the prime directive of trying to find better ways of destroying your enemies before they destroyed you. In war terms this meant that in the space of just thirty-odd years we went from using horses and spears to charge the enemy to jet engines, radar and nuclear weapons. The end of World War Two did not mean the end of that intense quest for knowledge, but it was another war, the Cold War, that probably produced mankind's greatest showpiece achievement. With the USSR and America desperate to outdo each other in the space race it was America who put men on the moon.

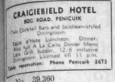

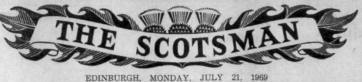

THE SCOTSMAN

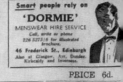

No. 39,360 EDINBURGH, MONDAY, JULY 21, 1969 3 a.m. news PRICE 6d.

Apollo's spacecraft at rest in Moon crater

Earlier lunar walk planned as Armstrong and Aldrin cut rest period

HOUSTON, Sunday.–Astronauts Neil Armstrong and Edwin Aldrin today flew their fragile moonship Eagle to a gentle touchdown on the Moon. The landing was so perfect that they decided to shorten their rest period and step on to the Moon earlier than scheduled.

Mission control gave the historic touchdown time as 21.17 (BST)—102 hours 45 minutes and 40 seconds into the Moon mission. As the landing—four miles from the scheduled landing spot—was confirmed the ground controller was heard to say: "We got a bunch of guys on the ground about to turn blue. We're breathing again."

The final touchdown on the lunar crust came after a tense 12 minutes as Eagle dropped swiftly from lunar orbit past the 40,000 feet, 20,000 feet marks and slowed as it came through 1500 feet. The astronauts' calm voices, matched by coolness and enthusiasm at mission control for the way the flight was going, ticked off the descent figures.

At one point in the conversation shortly after landing, mission control referred to Eagle as "Tranquillity Base"—man's first space station on the Moon's Sea of Tranquillity.

Ten minutes after landing Aldrin radioed: "We'll get to the details of what's around here. But it looks like a collection of every variety of shape, angularity, granularity, a collection of just about every kind of rock.

"Colour depends on what angle you're looking at . . . rocks and boulders look as though they're going to have some interesting colours."

Eagle had cast off from the mother ship Columbia, piloted in Moon orbit by Michael Collins, in a perfect manoeuvre which brought her down on to the Moon's surface for a gentle landing at the end of her 240,000-mile journey from Earth and 13 revolutions round the Moon. The landing time was a bare 83 seconds ahead of flight schedule.

Module's systems 'good'

At one point, as ground control was congratulating Armstrong and Aldrin on their landing performance, Michael Collins, orbiting above in the main ship Columbia, butted in to say: "Don't forget one up here."

Collins asked that Eagle be told to switch to an open antenna that would enable him to hear their talk, "or I'll miss all the action." Armstrong radioed to Collins: "Just keep that orbiting base ready for us."

Ground control reported that preliminary information indicated the lunar module's systems "looked pretty good after that landing."

Armstrong said he was not sure of the precise landing spot because the myriad tasks before landing had kept him from observing well-known lunar landmarks.

"Roger, Tranquillity," the ground replied. "No sweat. We'll figure it out."

Armstrong said they had no trouble going from a weightless condition to the one-sixth gravity of the Moon. "It seemed really natural." He also said that "at one-sixth G its (Eagle) just like an airplane."

He went on to say there were a large number of craters measuring about 5 to 50 feet in diameter and "literally thousands" of little craters in the area.

He reported some angular blocks about two feet in size with sharp edges. He said a hill was in view straight ahead, about half a mile to a mile.

'Ashen grey'

Ground control told the astronauts they had landed a little north or south of their planned landing site, but that they were within the east and west limits.

Armstrong reported that something had gone wrong

said Eagle was at an agle of 4½ degrees, well inside the range for take-off again.

Information from a biomedical harness strapped to Armstrong's body showed that, at the time of descent and landing, the mission commander's heart rate was 156 beats a minute. After the landing it dropped into the 90s. There was no information on Aldrin.

Explaining why he had taken over manual control to dodge a too rugged area, before making the touchdown, Armstrong said that going down on the target "would have taken us right into a football field sized crater with a large number of big boulders and rocks for about a 100 feet around it.

"So we flew manually over the rock field to find a reasonably good area."

Dr Charles Berry, medical director of the space agency, said the decision to leave the Eagle earlier than planned was agreed to because the astronauts had slept well last night.

"We have a crew that is rested and they are certainly as excited as we all are," he said.

The control team said they had no idea why the Eagle was four miles from the touch-down point. "There are a lot of people looking at this very heavily."

The control team said there were several alarms as the Eagle descended, but none were serious.

One series of alarms came from the on-board computer. The alarms, called the "bail-out alarm," was a signal that the computer thought it was being overworked at the moment and rejected new data to concentrate on navigation.

First lunar meal

As long as it did not happen repeatedly, agency officials said, there was no problem. The Eagle was guided down without the data the computer rejected.

Another alarm was on the fuel consumption. The Eagle used 65 seconds beyond the alarm point, or half of the remaining fuel in the descent stage. As the descent stage is left on the Moon, that would have no effect on the rest of the mission.

After satisfying themselves and mission control that their spacecraft was in good order following the landing, Armstrong and Aldrin relaxed for a moment and had their first meal on the lunar surface.

On the menu were bacon squares, peaches, sugar cookies, biscuits and fruit drink.

Prior to venturing out on to the lunar surface, the astronauts "powered down" the Eagle. This meant they switched off some machinery not immediately required and left other equipment merely "ticking over."

Editorial—Page 8

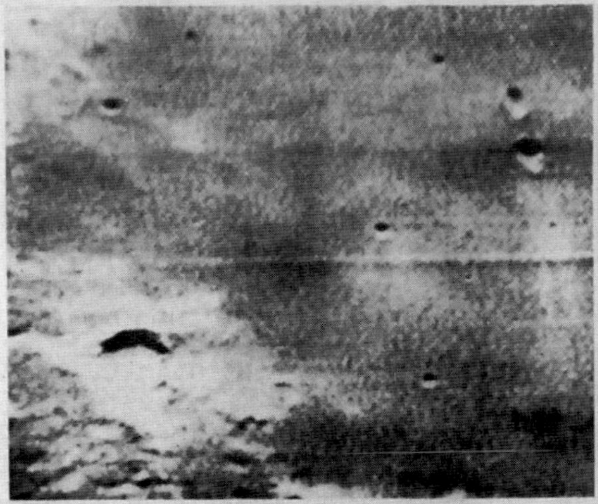

GOING DOWN: The Moon landing site viewed from Apollo-11.

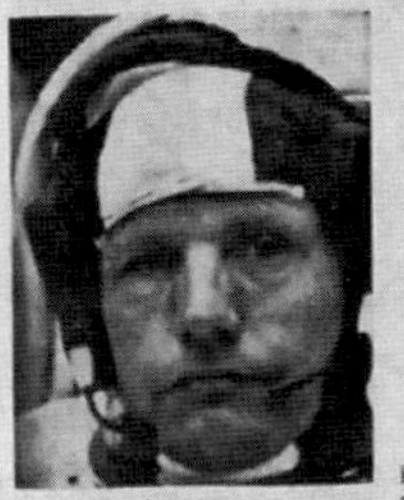

Armstrong

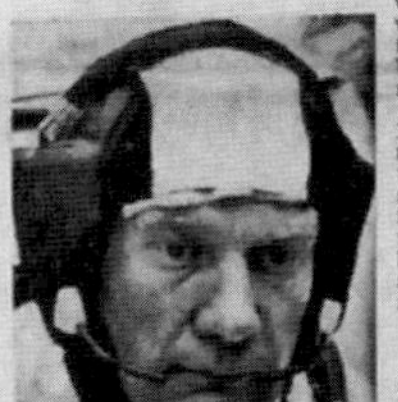

Aldrin

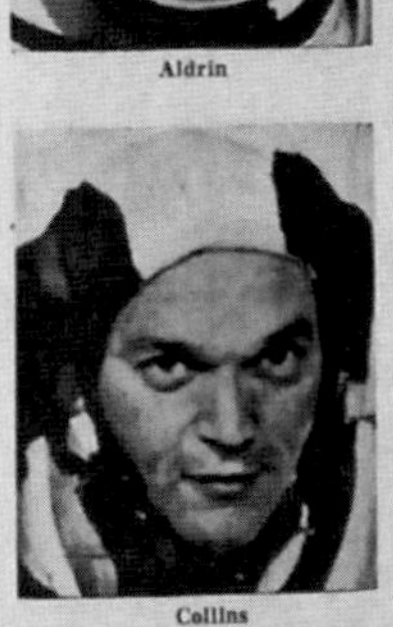

Collins

Luna-15 swoops to within ten miles of lunar surface

The past possibility that Luna-15 would forestall Apollo-11 in landing on the Moon to collect rock samples disappeared just after eight o'clock last night.

It disappeared as the Moon went below the horizon of the vast space communications centre from which the Russians have been transmitting the control messages.

Those messages brought Luna-15 down yesterday to about ten miles from the Moon's surface, the sort of orbit in which the U S spacecraft was travelling before its final descent manoeuvre. But no more control could presumably be exercised until the Moon rose again and was within range of radio communications.

FAINT CHANCE

There remained the faint chance that the landing operation had already been carried out during one of the changes of Luna-15's orbit yesterday or earlier.

A small capsule might conceivably have been ejected, and its descent controlled during one of the bursts of radio-communications activity from Luna-15.

If that has happened then Luna-15 has presumably been left in what seems an extremely close —and vulnerable — orbit to the Moon so that it can rendezvous with the capsule on its return with the minimum expenditure of energy.

It could still be that today would see the beginning of the return of Luna-15 from the Moon.

The change in Luna's orbit was announced in a brief statement issued in Moscow by the official news agency, Tass, which said Luna-15 was continuing "scientific exploration in near-lunar space," but gave no indication whether it would attempt to land on the Moon or not.

Tass said the flight path correction had been carried out at 3.16 p.m. (BST) and had brought the craft into an elliptical orbit ranging from ten miles to 68 miles above the surface, at an angle of 127 degrees to the plane of the lunar equator.

Luna-15 was circling the Moon once every one hour and 54 minutes.

Scientists at the Jodrell Bank radio-telescope station in Cheshire received another short burst of signals before Luna-15 went below the horizon last night.

Prof. John Davies, one of the experts at the station, said the spacecraft could not be left in its present orbit all night.

He thought the Russians would have either to land the spacecraft or pull it out.

Sir Bernard Lovell, Jodrell Bank's director, said: "One has to be extremely careful what interpretation one places on this, but the Luna-15 appears to be moving closer to the lunar surface."

He said: "It is rather strange that a simple orbiter should be placed up there compared with this colossal Apollo programme."

'WIDELY APART'

Asked if he thought Luna-15 and Apollo-11 were near each other, he said: "I think that they are widely apart in time in their orbits."

Moonwalk special

A special late edition of "The Scotsman" will be on sale later this morning giving fuller details of the moonwalk.

LATEST NEWS

ALDRIN'S MESSAGE

Edwin Aldrin interrup
his work inside the lu
landing craft on the Moo
surface to ask people throu
out the world to pause a
consider the events of
past few hours.

The 39-year-old Air Fo
colonel radioed to the grou
control at the manned spa
craft centre at Houst
Texas: "This is the lu
module pilot. I'd just like
ask that everyone around
world who might be listen
pause and consider the eve
of the past few hours.
like to ask everyone to c
template these events each
his own way."

In hour before the as
nauts landed safely on
Moon President Ni

watched television and sai
was "one of the grea
moments of our time."

President told Secretary
State William P. Rogers: "
success of this operation
have an immediate favoura
reaction around the world
will bring people of the w
closer together. This re
sents another great step in
whole history of man."

Outside the mission con
centre at Houston, 50 pe
gathered on a pathway
vigil to remind the worl
America's poor. They
members of the Wel
Rights Association in Hous

Armstrong was due to s
his walk at 3.10 a.m., a
40 minutes behind the
expected earlier.

Just before 3 a.m. the a

nauts were given permis
to go. The lunar module
being depressurised to a
them to do so.

As he donned his space
helmet, Aldrin comme
"Sure wish I'd shaved
night."

Astronauts voices h
saying "pretty well finish
checks before leaving Ea

Just to continue the theme of childhood reminiscences, which I will hopefully contain to this chapter, I remember my dad calling me down from bed to watch history in the making live on television.

MONDAY, 21 JULY, 1969

Apollo's spacecraft at rest in Moon crater

EARLIER LUNAR WALK PLANNED AS ARMSTRONG AND ALDRIN CUT REST PERIOD

HOUSTON, Sunday

Astronauts Neil Armstrong and Edwin Aldrin today flew their fragile moonship Eagle to a gentle touchdown on the Moon.

The landing was so perfect that they decided to shorten their rest period and step on to the Moon earlier than scheduled.

Mission control gave the historic touchdown time as 21.17 (BST) – 102 hours 45 minutes and 40 seconds into the Moon mission. As the landing – four miles from the scheduled landing spot – was confirmed the ground controller was heard to say: "We got a bunch of guys on the ground about to turn blue. We're breathing again."

The final touchdown on the lunar crust came after a tense 12 minutes as Eagle dropped swiftly from lunar orbit past the 40,000 feet, 20,000 feet marks and slowed as it came through 1,500 feet. The astronauts' calm voices, matched by coolness and enthusiasm at mission control for the way the flight was going, ticked off the descent figures.

At one point in the conversation shortly after landing, mission control referred to Eagle as "Tranquillity Base" – man's first space station on the Moon's Sea of Tranquillity. Ten minutes after landing Aldrin radioed: "We'll get to the details of what's around here. But it looks like a collection of every variety of shape, angularity, granularity, a collection of just about every kind of rock. Colour depends on what angle you're looking at… rocks and boulders look as though they're going to have some interesting colours."

Eagle had cast off from the mother ship Columbia, piloted in Moon orbit by Michael Collins, in a perfect manoeuvre which brought her down on to the Moon's surface for a gentle landing at the end of her 240,000-mile journey from Earth and 13 revolutions round the Moon. The landing time was a bare 83 seconds ahead of flight schedule.

At one point, as ground control was congratulating Armstrong and Aldrin on their landing performance, Michael Collins, orbiting above in the main ship Columbia, butted in to say: "Don't forget one up here."

Collins asked that Eagle be told to switch to an open antenna that would enable him to hear their talk, "or I'll miss all the action." Armstrong radioed to Collins: "Just keep that orbiting base ready for us."

Ground control reported that preliminary information indicated the lunar module's systems "looked pretty good after that landing."

Armstrong said he was not sure of the precise landing spot because the myriad tasks before landing had kept him from observing well-known lunar landmarks. "Roger, Tranquillity," the ground replied. "No sweat. We'll figure it out."

Armstrong said they had no trouble going from a weightless condition to the onesixth gravity of the Moon. "It seemed really natural."

He also said that "at one-sixth G its (Eagle) just like an airplane." He went on to say there were a large number of craters measuring about five to 50 feet in diameter and "literally thousands" of little craters in the area.

He reported some angular blocks about two feet in size with sharp edges. He said a hill was in view straight ahead, about half a mile to a mile. After satisfying themselves and mission control that their spacecraft was in good order following the landing, Armstrong and Aldrin relaxed for a moment and had their first meal on the lunar surface. On the menu were bacon squares, peaches, sugar cookies, biscuits and fruit drink.

Prior to venturing out on to the lunar surface, the astronauts "powered down" the Eagle. This meant they switched off some machinery not immediately required and left other equipment merely "ticking over".

Chapter thirteen

Delivering the news

Of course that massive technological change that has been seen in the time of the paper's existence has also driven huge change in the way that news is both gathered and delivered, and the pace of change in that does not seem to be slackening but seems to be increasing as we move emphatically in to the digital age. As *The Scotsman* has grown and developed as a newspaper and as a business some of the technical innovations employed by the paper seem at this distance to be nothing short of comedic.

The paper had early offices in Edinburgh's Royal Mile, but in 1862 it moved to purpose-built offices in Cockburn Street, and at the time these were state-of-the-art, and included a pigeon loft for the fleet used to get news to the paper. To aid communication within the building there were speaker tubes that linked departments similar to the ones used to allow captains to speak to the engine room on a ship.

And the delivery of the news changed models around this time too as railways became more plentiful, and this opened up new markets for the owners of *The Scotsman*. In the early days the economics of sending by rail to far-flung places meant that papers had to be sold at prices much greater than their marked cover price, which did not endear them to their readers, but in 1865 the owners of *The Scotsman* came up with an innovative plan that they would cover the costs of carriage, and soon circulation was growing all over the country. The papers continued to grow and by the turn of the century it was obvious that new and bigger premises were absolutely necessary. The widening of North Bridge gave the proprietors a suitable site for a new suite of purpose-built offices, and these were to be the home of the papers for almost a century. It was from these offices in 1988 that the newest member of *The Scotsman* stable was launched, *Scotland on Sunday*. A sister paper aimed at the quality Sunday market.

The North Bridge offices were large and in some parts lavishly fitted out, it was reported at the time that the 13-storey building was "the largest building ever erected by public enterprise in Edinburgh". This building was built to harness the power of electricity and included telephones instead of speaker tubes. The next decades saw huge changes in the technology used to produce newspapers up to and including the computer age. But by the end of the 20th century the building could be adapted no more for the changing life of newspapers. It had become a warren laced with cabling and ducts for obsolete systems, printing was done off site, again, it was clear new premises were needed. So, under the ownership of billionaires Sir David and Sir Frederick Barclay and the watchful eye of editor-in-chief Andrew Neil new, 21st century offices were planned. A site was identified at the foot of Holyrood Road where the old industrial world of the breweries was being re-developed. At first there were fears that moving from the centre of town might mean the paper losing its news edge. But then in what must be one of the happiest of coincidences the decision was taken to build the new Scottish Parliament almost directly opposite the new building, creating a new political and media centre for the city. With the changing economic fortunes of the newspaper industry and changes in news gathering and production those offices became too large, and the papers moved to offices on the top floors of Orchard Brae House close to the West End in Edinburgh in 2014.

The Walnut Hall of *The Scotsman* offices in North Bridge, Edinburgh.

The Advertisement Office, pictured in 1905.

Ornate staircase at *The Scotsman*. Below is the doorway to the *Dispatch* and *Weekly Scotsman* offices. The door upstairs leads to the Advertisement Office.

Lord Provost Weatherstone opens *The Scotsman's* newly reconstructed front office.

Boardroom meeting at *The Scotsman*.

Britain's very first Monarch teletypesetter in action at *The Scotsman*.

A copytaker receiving 'live' copy from a reporter at the scene of a story.

Scotsman Foundry Lino Room.

The Wire Room.

Front office bchind the counter at the Scotsman Publications HQ in Edinburgh 1967.

Working at the linotype machine in North Bridge caseroom.

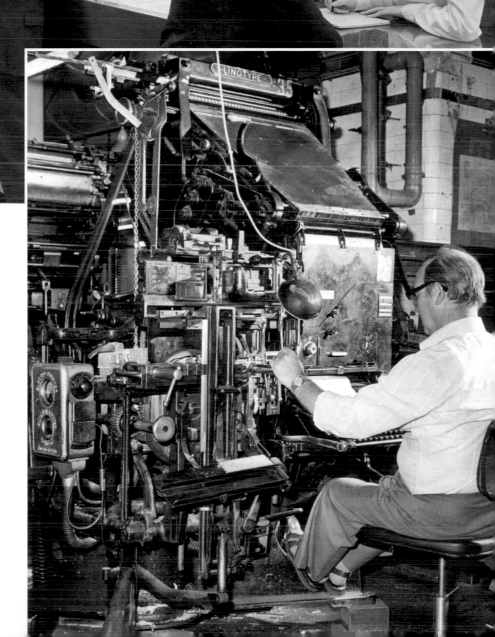

Workers at Waverley Station in Edinburgh load *The Scotsman* newspapers onto the company's own LNER carriage.

The Scotsman stand at the Highland Show.

Scotsman mobile dark room and wire room parked up outside Hampden football ground, 8th March 1960.

The new *Scotsman* delivery van and scooters outside the gates of Holyrood Palace, Edinburgh in December 1965.

Composing and linotype room. 1961.

Scotsman building printing press.

Journalists and sub-editors at work in *The Scotsman* editorial department, around 1948.

The Scotsman desks at Orchard Brae House, January 2017.

Mr Alastair Dunnett, the editor of *The Scotsman* from 1956 to 1972.

Eric B Mackay, editor of *The Scotsman* newspaper, in his office at North Bridge Edinburgh in June 1981.

Barclay House was officially opened by the Queen in 1999.

Writer and broadcaster Jim Naughtie, then a Scotsman Publications journalist, won the Scottish Press Awards Writer of the Year trophy in May 1983.

Andrew Marr, when business and political reporter with *The Scotsman* newspaper in September 1988.

Mr Roy Thomson, proprietor of Scotsman Publications, at the door of the office on North Bridge.

Opposite: First front page of *The Scotsman* with news. Previously the front page had been devoted to advertisements. April 17th 1957.

THE SCOTSMAN

No. 35,534   EDINBURGH, WEDNESDAY, APRIL 17, 1957   PRICE 3d.

NETS DESTROYED BY RUSSIANS

Protection demanded by East Anglian herring fleet

£2000 DAMAGE CAUSED

BY OUR OWN REPORTER

Demands for protection from the actions of larger Russian fishing boats were made by skippers of East Anglian herring drifters when they returned to Aberdeen yesterday from the Norwegian fishing grounds. The skippers and their crews alleged that the Russians had deliberately shot their nets over those of the drifters, causing damage amounting to well over £2000.

Dozens of nets, valued at £20 each, were reported to have been destroyed or badly damaged. Some of the East Anglian drifters known to have suffered are the Ocean Surf, Ocean Starlight, Kindred Star, Ocean Sunlight, Peace, and the George Spashett. A number of others still at sea are also believed to have had nets damaged.

An Admiralty spokesman said later last night: "Protection of British interests arising out of any incident of this nature is reported to the senior naval officer of the Fishery Protection Squadron, who decides what steps are considered necessary. In this case, it is possible that a fishery protection vessel will be sent."

The trouble took place at the week-end while the fleet was fishing for the first time this season about 40 miles off the Norwegian coast. The George Spashett, of Lowestoft, had 42 nets either damaged or destroyed, and its skipper, Robert Wadlow (42), said soon after berthing in Aberdeen that he had been forced to curtail his trip to get new gear.

The Russian fleet, he explained, numbered about 60 and the boats were much larger than the 113-ft. drifter, the British drifters, the Russians' practice was to shoot their nets during the night. "They wait until a shoal of herring is located and then go for it regardless of what is in the way," he said.

That was what happened on Saturday night. The damage was caused by the ropes attaching the Russian nets to their buoys slicing through ours to their part. The Russian nets do not suffer because they are much lower in the water than the British type.

"DELIBERATE ACTION"

Signal Ignored

Skipper Wadlow said they had no contact with the Russian vessels, but he managed to make a note of what he took to be the registration—CP.Z. 4039 —of the boat which destroyed his nets. After that incident, he steamed ten miles to avoid the Russians, but when he shot his nets a second time Russian boats came up and shot over them again.

"I don't think they have any real idea of how to work drift nets," he said. "They deliberately shot in among a fleet of our boats in the darkness and boats which have already shot have no chance of taking avoiding action.

"We cannot go back to the Norwegian fishing grounds where there are unless we get protection because we cannot stand the loss of gear. A fishery cruiser should be sent out to see there is fair play. We are not suggesting the Russians should be chased off the fishing ground, but we want them to play clear of us."

Mr J. S. Hewitt, skipper of the Ocean Starlight, from Great Yarmouth, said fifty of his nets had been destroyed on Saturday night. They had seen the Russian boats, but kept miles away from them. "About eight o'clock, the Russians shot their nets, and came right across those of our boats, fouling many of them," he said. "I signalled to the Russians, but they took no notice and carried on."

"OUT OF LUCK"

Fouled own nets

Mr A. Keable, skipper of the Lowestoft drifter, Kindred Star, who lost 48 nets, thought there was no doubt that the Russians were doing the damage deliberately. He saw one Russian boat come round the Ocean Surf and start shooting his nets. "The Russian was out of luck, however, for he finished up with his own nets in his propeller, and the last I saw of him he was signalling for assistance," said skipper Keable.

The skippers reported their losses to the local fishery officer at Aberdeen on arrival yesterday, and at the East Anglian ports. The owners of the drifters were also taking up the matter.

KING HUSSEIN CONFIDENT OF ARMY'S SUPPORT

Threat from Syria checked

BY OUR DIPLOMATIC CORRESPONDENT

According to despatches received in London, King Hussein seems to be fairly confident of the support of the Jordan Army. The former Chief of Staff, Major-General Abu Nuwar, has been given so-called "leave" for two weeks, which is taken to be a euphemism for dismissal.

It looks as if the military threat from Syria, which has about 3000 troops in Jordan has also been checked. The hope is that a friendly arrangement will be come to with the Syrian Government to have the troops withdrawn.

But this depends on whether King Hussein is able to be firmly on his throne, and Jordan is likely to become more stable. This would make the position of Chief of the Cabinet Kuwatly of Syria stronger against his Communist and pro-Nasser opponents and induce him to take more decisive steps to meet the threats from those quarters.

The new Jordanian Government, with its assembly of elder statesmen, is a marked improvement on the old as is the new Chief of Staff. It remains in power for the next few weeks it is likely to attempt American economic help for the United States Government would naturally be anxious to bring another Arab State...

Maj.-Gen. Nuwar

into the fold and further away from Syria and Egypt.

What has not yet emerged is how far Hussein can co-operate with the Syrian Government to maintain its hands of Jordanian neutrality and Arab unity and induce him to the prevention of rioting by the mob.

A decision on General Nuwar's future is to be announced later by the Cabinet. Reuter reports from Amman Government sources said the Cabinet was considering his "formal resignation."

Arab sources outside Jordan have described General Nuwar as the leader of a military revolt crushed by King Hussein on Sunday. Nuwar arrived in Damascus, the Syrian capital, on Sunday night.

King Hussein called on the Cabinet during its meeting yesterday. Leaving afterwards, he was welcomed with cheers from the Ministers, the King had earlier received a Royal salute from a guard outside Government House, crowds waited in the street. Later he offered to the palace to compensate for the crisis, and to express their loyalty.

A statement by the new Government policy is expected from Dr Khalidi, the new Independent Premier, who will try to steady the country, provided that these can be completed at the end of the academic year, ending July 31 during which the student benefits.

FRENCH RAILMEN TO STRIKE

Airline ground staff, too

PARIS, Tuesday.—Unions representing ground staff of the airline Air France decided to-day to begin a 24-hour token strike on Thursday in support of wage demands.

The decision came on the eve of a 48-hour strike by French railwaymen due to start at midnight to-night which is expected to tail all passenger and freight rail services, upsetting travel plans for Easter holidaymakers.

The Government to-day announced a further increase of 1.5 per cent. in railwaymen's wages. This, added to the one per cent. increase decided in February, gives railwaymen a total increase of 2.5 per cent.

The liner Queen Mary is due to sail for New York from Cherbourg on Thursday, and the Cunard company announced here to-day that because of the rail strike, buses will leave Paris on Thursday morning to convey passengers to Cherbourg.

Passengers for the Cunard ship Ivernia, due to sail from Le Havre to-morrow, will also be taken to the port by bus.

A British European Airways official said B.E.A. would be able to fly normal services to and from Le Bourget Airport which is not affected by the strike decision of Air France ground staff.—Reuter.

MORE CALL-UP DEFERMENT

Technicians now included

PART-TIME STUDENTS

It was announced yesterday that the Government have decided to extend deferment of call-up to cover more students and apprentices, including men being trained as technicians.

Mr Macleod, Minister of Labour, said in a written Parliamentary reply that he had decided on the extension within the framework of the present policy, to cover certain classes of young men who had not hitherto been eligible.

About 80,000 apprentices, learners, pupils, and students are deferred than each age class under present arrangements. It is estimated that the new concessions will affect only a few thousand young men.

The new arrangements will include:— Apprentices or learners not covered by existing recognised schemes of apprenticeship or training.

PART-TIME STUDY

Men who are being trained as technicians. These have not been previously covered, and will gain deferment on the basis that practical training on the job is combined with parttime study for an approved examination. The employer must be prepared to grant day release for study of not less than an average of eight hours a week.

Part-time students: These will be included provided that their course of study has a vocational bearing on the framework of the present policy, to cover certain classes of young men who had not hitherto been eligible.

Craft apprentices: Those who have completed their apprenticeship may have an entire deferment of one year if they wish to continue part-time study for qualifications not essential to their occupations but of use in their career prospects.

FULL-TIME STUDENTS

Full-time students: Present arrangements which allow deferment for courses depend on approval of the career; a man proposes to follow are to be extended to cover full-time studies at other courses, provided that these can be completed at the end of the academic year, ending July 31, during which the student benefits.

SIR ANTHONY EDEN'S "RESTLESS" DAY

BOSTON, Tuesday. — Sir Anthony Eden had a restless day to-day, but his general condition is satisfactory and remains unchanged, the doctors said in a bulletin to-night.

A bulletin issued earlier to-day said the former Prime Minister was up in a chair today after a comfortable night. He was operated on last Saturday to eliminate a bile duct ailment.—Reuter.

MLLE. SAGAN MAKING PROGRESS

PARIS, Tuesday.—Francoise Sagan (21), the French novelist, seriously injured in a car accident on Sunday, passed a "satisfactory night" and has continued to make progress, hospital officials stated.—Reuter.

"THE SCOTSMAN" MAKES FRONT-PAGE NEWS

Waverley Station bookstall displaying placards announcing that to-day's edition of "The Scotsman" is carrying news on the front page.

LABOUR M.P.'s ATTACK ON MR DRIBERG

Hypocrisy over H-bomb

FROM OUR PARLIAMENTARY CORRESPONDENT

WESTMINSTER, Tuesday

An attack on "hypocritical" criticisms of the Government's determination to carry on testing the hydrogen bomb was made in the Commons to-day by Mr Fred Bellenger (Lab., Bassetlaw.) He particularly attacked Mr Tom Driberg, his party's vice-chairman, for articles written in the "Moscow News."

Mr Bellenger speaking in the debate on the Defence White Paper, recalled that Mr Khrushchev warned Britain at the time of Suez that it might be necessary to use ballistic missiles on "this country to stop us, as Mr Khrushchev put it, waging war in Suez."

"There might be other circumstances where that gentleman, like Hitler would know no limits, and use this deterrent on us for our own protection would be any counter to that threat, I say we have got to have it."

Mr Bellenger said he would agree to Britain stopping tests for a limited period, but he would not agree if he thought that this would precipitate in so far as Russia was concerned.

Russia was carrying out tests "almost every week." In that respect the whole of the statements made around, of not hypocritical, to avoid the ghost.

"MOSCOW NEWS" ARTICLE

"My Tom Driberg, the vice-chairman of my own party's executive, has been writing, according to the "Times" this morning, in the "Moscow News," of all papers.

He writes that if this time is short, that the exact date is correct, but that the facts—that is our tests and that the Russians—may take a little, and that it may be possible by diplomatic and domestic pressure to revise the British Government's attitude to the Soviet suggestion that, at least tests be suspended at once for an agreed period."

"I hope Mr Driberg will accept the British suggestion, the suggestion of his own party, and not use the platform of a Russian newspaper for airing these things which he believes to be correct."

To-morrow, Mr Iain Macleod, Minister of Labour, will describe the machinery for effecting the proposed reduction of the Forces pending the abolition of National Service after 1960. Meanwhile, the House has it from Mr Sandys that the Government favours the idea of reducing the two-year period of National Service to the interim.

He justified this decision on the ground that, while the numbers of servicemen and their families would be reduced, all would be right to aid them to the increasing strain on their engagements, in losing the best part of a man's service, when he was the greatest value.

Debate—Page 8

TURKEY WARNS GREECE

Don't exaggerate to Makarios

"UNFRIENDLY ACT"

Turkey has warned Greece in a diplomatic démarche that if the welcome to Archbishop Makarios to-day in Athens is given an exaggerated and markedly official form, Turkey will regard it as an affront and an unfriendly act against her.

This was learned in Athens last night from an authoritative source. The warning has been stated seriously between Greek Government circles. Mr Averoff, Foreign Minister on Monday saw Opposition leaders and urged them to exercise restraint on the Cyprus issue.

This was to avoid rousing further Turkish resentment against it. If possible that the decision of Mr Karamanlis, Prime Minister, not to go to Athens Airport to-day to give to a wish to reduce the official nature of the welcome, following the Turkish warning.

On the eve of the Archbishop's arrival, which he saw fit in a Nairobi sermon to compare to the entry of Our Lord into Jerusalem, there is some apprehension in moderate Government circles. It is over what is to follow the "national welcome."

NEXT MOVE

When the flag-waving, addresses of welcome, and ceremonies of Orthodox Easter are over, Mr Karamanlis and his colleagues will have extended discussions with the Archbishop and members of the Ethnarchy on the next move in the Cyprus affair.

Some Greek Cypriots are not a little apprehensive about Archbishop Makarios's arrival in Athens. It reported from Nicosia. They fear he may be carried away by the enthusiastic welcome and be led to make rash statements.

The Archbishop left Nairobi to-day at last night on his way to Athens.—"Daily Telegraph" and "The Scotsman" News Service.

ARCHBISHOP COMING TO BRITAIN

Probably next month

From Our Commonwealth Correspondent

LONDON, Tuesday

Archbishop Makarios will probably arrive here about the middle of May. He is not coming at the invitation of the Government, however, but of his own volition. As a British subject he is perfectly free to do so.

It is unlikely that the Archbishop will be received by the Colonial Secretary, Mr Lennox-Boyd, for talks on a settlement of the Cyprus situation. The Government attitude is that the Archbishop would be unacceptable in discussions as one of a delegation from Cyprus but not as the sole spokesman for the whole of the Cypriot people.

AZIKIWE'S ESCAPE

Man with dagger foiled

LAGOS (Nigeria), Thursday. — An apparent attempt was made here to-day on the life of Dr Nnamdi Azikiwe, Premier of Eastern Nigeria. He escaped unhurt, but a Nigerian has been charged with attempted murder.

The attempt was made as Dr Azikiwe was driving into the courtyard of Government House for a meeting with the other two Regional Premiers on matters to be raised at the May constitutional conference in London.

A glance was thrown at the car, broke a window, and a man then emerged from the crowd carrying a dagger. As he was apparently making his way towards Dr Azikiwe, the man was intercepted by a Nigerian police inspector, Moses Chukwuma, who was helped by a British police superintendent, H. E.

ATTEMPTED MURDER CHARGE

Later, in the Magistrate's Court, the man, named as Pius Kaine, was charged with an attempt to murder Dr Azikiwe. No plea was taken, and Kaine was remanded in custody until April 24 for medical observation.

Kaine, who is married with five children, recently returned from England, where he spent three years studying law.

Dr Azikiwe, who is 52, is leader of the National Council of Nigeria and the Cameroons, which came to power in the Eastern Region in 1954. He was reappointed Premier last month after elections, in which his party won increased majority over a slightly reduced majority.—"Daily Telegraph" and "The Scotsman" Correspondent and Reuter.

5 PER CENT RISE FOR DOCTORS

No negotiation or arbitration, say B.M.A.

COUNCIL TO CONSIDER ACTION TO-DAY

An interim increase in doctors' pay announced in the House of Commons yesterday by the Prime Minister, was described last night by the British Medical Association as being "simply an arbitrary figure decided by the Government." There had been no negotiation or arbitration.

Mr Macmillan said the Government had decided to increase the basic remuneration of senior hospital medical and dental staff, including consultants and specialists, and all dentists engaged in general dental services, by 5 per cent from May 1. Five per cent would be added to the aggregate net remuneration of general practitioners.

"I know now that all concerned will turn their thoughts to the task of working out a satisfactory basis for future remuneration and for keeping it under review," said Mr Macmillan, who recalled that he had said previously that the appointment of the Royal Commission did not preclude an interim adjustment.

In their statement last night the B.M.A. said the Prime Minister's announcement would be reported to their council to-day in London and "the council will no doubt then decide what the profession should be advised to do about it."

The increase announced by the Prime Minister, writes our political correspondent, will give the doctors a net average pay of £2325. This is 146 per cent above the average net income earned before the war.

A consultant's maximum salary will rise by £155 to £3255, and those with the highest distinction award will receive £5455 a year. The maximum salary of a senior hospital medical or dental officer will be increased by about £100 to roughly £2125 a year.

COST OF INCREASES

£6 millions yearly

The estimated cost of the adjustments for England, Wales and Scotland is £6 millions a year.

On the basis of their interpretation of the Spens report, the medical pro...

(Turn to page 8)

(Turn to page 8)

PREMIER FOR GERMANY

To discuss closer union with Europe

The Prime Minister is to visit Germany next month. It will be the first time a British Premier has done so since the Federal German Republic was formed.

An announcement to-day by the Federal German Government Chancellor, Dr Adenauer, has invited the Prime Minister, Mr Harold Macmillan, to visit Germany from May 7 to 9 as the guest of the Federal German Government. The Prime Minister has gladly accepted the invitation. He will be accompanied by the Secretary of State for Foreign Affairs, Mr Selwyn Lloyd, who will already be in Bonn for the meeting of the North Atlantic Council.

For some time an invitation to the Prime Minister to visit Germany has been discussed, and it has not been previously possible for him to accept. He will be accompanied by his wife, writes our diplomatic correspondent.

His visit to the continent comes at a time when he has had during the last two months with Mr Mollet, the French Prime Minister, and President Eisenhower.

No agenda has been fixed for the talks in Germany, but matters of interest to both countries will be discussed, including closer association of Britain with Europe.

A Foreign Ministry spokesman in Bonn, quoted by Reuter, said Mr Macmillan was expected to discuss general political and military matters with Dr Adenauer.

ROYAL COMMISSION'S ANNOUNCEMENT

The Royal Commission on doctors' and dentists' remuneration announced last night that it is "now in a position to receive evidence from interested persons and organisations."

"Any person or organisation wishing to submit evidence," the announcement adds, "is invited to send a statement as soon as possible to the Secretary, Royal Commission on Doctors' and Dentists' Remuneration, 10 Carlton House Terrace, London, S.W.1."

MORE SCOTS VOTE FOR WITHDRAWAL

The Perth branch of the British Medical Association announced yesterday that it will press for practitioners in Perth and Kinross to agree to withdraw from the National Health Service if so advised by the General Medical Services Committee.

LATEST NEWS

MARTIAL LAW THREAT TO ASHANTIS

Accra, Tuesday.—Martial law would be introduced in the Ashanti region—stronghold of the opposition—if this was in the interests of the people, Mr Kwame Nkrumah, Ghana's Minister without Portfolio, told his constituents today. The Ashanti Minister was visiting his constituency for the first time in two and a half years.

Before Ghana achieved independence last month there was considerable unrest in Ashanti, where the opposition National Liberation Movement (N.L.M.) has strong support.

The N.L.M. demanded adequate safeguards for the Ashanti people in the new constitution, and threatened to support the secession of Ashanti and the Northern territories if their demands were not met.

But after the visit of Mr Lennox-Boyd, the Colonial Secretary, in January, the party expressed its satisfaction with the new constitutional proposals negotiated during his visit.—Reuter.

2 AUSTRALIAN FLIGHTS DESPITE PILOTS' STRIKE

SYDNEY, Tuesday. — Qantas Empire Airways announced to-day that airline staff pilots would man two operating flights from here to-morrow as the strike by Qantas pilots and other air crew entered its sixth day with no sign of a settlement.

One of the flights will be to London, the other to San Francisco.—Reuter.

MAYFLOWER II's SAILING TRIALS

The Mayflower II, viewed from the air, under full sail during trials at Torbay yesterday evening.

EDITORIAL

ON OTHER PAGES

	Page
Agriculture	4
The Corporation	6
Finance and Commerce, 2, 3,	4
Pictures	10
Scotsman's Log	6
Sport	11
TV and Radio	3
Theatres	6
To-day's Events	7
Towards an Industrial Philosophy	8
Weather	14
Women's Features	5
World News	9

ADVERTISING

CLASSIFIED INDEX

	Page
Births, Marriages and Deaths	14
Country Quarters	14
Farm Stock	12
General Notices	14
Hotels and Hydros	14
Personal	14
Property	12
Sales by Auction	12
Situations Vacant and Wanted	12
Shipping	11
Specific Articles	12
Theatres, Cinemas	6
Motors	12

THE SCOTSMAN
No. 37,595
EDINBURGH, SATURDAY, NOVEMBER 23, 1963
PRIC

PRESIDENT KENNEDY ASSASSINATEI

A security man stands on the bumper of the Presidential car as Mrs Kennedy bends over her husband, who is slumped down in the back seat, after the fatal shot.

MAN SAW RIFLE AT A WINDOW

President Johnson arrived by air at Andrews Air Force Base in Washington, last night, accompanying the body of Mr Kennedy. A guard of honour carried the coffin from the Air Force jet plane as a mourning nation watched on television screens.

Mr Johnson said: "This is a sad time for all people. We have suffered a loss that cannot be weighed . . . I will do my best—that is all I can do. I ask for your help and God's."

The White House announced that the body would "lie in repose" in the White House beginning today, from 10 a.m. to 6 p.m. The Senate had suspended its sittings even before the news of Mr Kennedy's death had reached it (Reuter reports).

President Kennedy's funeral service will be held in Washington's St Matthew's Cathedral on Monday. Cardinal Richard Cushing, Archbishop of Boston, will conduct a pontifical Requiem Mass.

A Press photographer reported in Dallas that he had seen the shooting, and even glimpsed the rifle used from the window of a nearby building.

He was riding in a car behind the President's. He gave this account: "There were five of us in the car. When we heard the first shot, the President had already turned the corner. We had not made the corner yet. Then we heard two more shots.

"As far as I know, three shots were all I heard. I just instinctively looked that way. First, somebody joked about it being a firecracker.

"Then since I was facing the building where the shots were coming from, I just glanced up and saw two Coloured men in a window straining to look at a window up above them.

"As I looked up to the window above, I saw a rifle being pulled back in the window. It might have been resting on the window sill. I didn't see a man; I didn't even see if it had a scope (telescopic sight) on it.

"It was the second floor down from the top of the building and it was the end window facing Elm Street, the corner window. The President's car was about half-way between Houston Street and the underpass. We were beginning to turn the corner. He (gunman) had about a 45-degree angle from the building to the President's car."

Katherine Wood quotes her friend, Marilyn Coco (26), of the "Dallas Times-Herald," as saying in a Transatlantic telephone call from Dallas: "People are just standing about not saying anything—in shocked, stunned groups."

"It's just dreadful. I am stunned," she repeated in her deep Southern accent.

Marilyn watched the President, and his wife smiling and gaily dressed in bright pink, pass by in his car seconds before she heard that he had been shot.

"My first reaction when a man came into the hotel and told us, was just not to believe him. I thought he was joking until it was announced on a television set in the room. The idea that I'd just seen him . . .

"We thought that he had just been wounded and little prayers started to run through my head.

"We didn't know till an hour afterwards that he was dead. Everyone in Dallas feels deeply sorry that if it had happened it happened here."

Marilyn could give no news about Mrs Kennedy. "She was crying as she held his head in her lap on the way to the hospital. Then they put her in a room, and we haven't heard anything more," she said.

"The ironic thing was the weather," she went on. It was very rainy here all morning, then just before the plane landed the sun broke through, and everyone said what a wonderful day for the President's visit. But they took the bullet-proof bubble off his car, so it contributed to his death."

SHOT BY DALLAS SNIPER

Struck down as he travels in open car with wife

GOVERNOR OF TEXAS IS SERIOUSLY INJURED

PRESIDENT KENNEDY OF THE UNITED STATES WAS ASSASSINATED IN DALLAS, TEXAS, YESTERDAY.

The 46-year-old President was riding in a procession of cars with his wife, Jacqueline, when three shots were fired, and he was hit in the head. He was rushed to hospital and given a blood transfusion, but he died shortly afterwards.

Governor John Connally, of Texas, who was with them in the car, was also hit by bullets. He was later operated on, and hospital authorities said that his condition was "very, very serious."

Mr Edgar Hoover, chief of the F.B.I., ordered an all-out man-hunt for the assassin or assassins. Police were reported to have taken possession of a rifle soon after the shooting.

The rifle had a telescopic sight and was found near a corner window of the building from where the shots were fired. Three empty cartridge cases were on the floor.

Later police arrested Lee Harvey Oswald (24), a Texan who defected to Russia in 1959 but returned to the U.S. last year. He was being questioned in connection with the assassination.

Harvey, who had a pistol, was hauled screaming from a cinema and charged with the murder of a policeman who was shot soon after the Kennedy assassination. He was said to have worked in the building from which the assassination shots were fired.

MR LYNDON B. JOHNSON IS SWORN IN

Lyndon B. Johnson was sworn in as President of the United States at about 2.39 p.m. (20.39 G.M.T.) yesterday. The oath was administered by U.S. District Judge Sarah Hughes. Mr Johnson took the oath aboard the Presidential plane at Dallas, as he was preparing to fly to Washington.

National Broadcasting Company television reports said Oswald had been identified as chairman of the "Fair Play for Cuba Committee," a pro-Castro group.

The President was shot down as his open car passed near an intersection in the main business area of the city. As the shots rang out, Mr Kennedy fell face down in the back of the car. Mrs Kennedy cried "Oh, no" and tried to hold up his head. Police rushed the car to a nearby hospital.

The President, concerned about his unpopularity in the South over his Civil Rights Bill, arrived in Texas on Thursday with Mrs Kennedy, to win support and close the divided ranks of the Texas Democrats. Dallas is a centre of conservative politics.

A reporter, speaking by Transatlantic telephone from Dallas, said that it had rained all morning. Then just before the Presidential plane landed, the sun broke through, and people said it was going to be a wonderful day. Because of this, the bullet-proof bubble was removed from the President's car.

Reporters saw the President lying flat on his face in the car. The President was reported to have been carried into the hospital unconscious and bleeding. He was given a blood transfusion and later the last rites of the Roman Catholic Church. He died 25 minutes after the shooting.

Doctors at Parkland Hospital later said the President died of wounds in the neck and head. They were possibly caused by the same bullet, but there may have been two bullets.

Dr Malcolm Perry, the hospital surgeon who attended President Kennedy, said: "When the President arrived in the emergency ward I realised he was in a critical condition with a wound of the neck and head."

Immediate emergency measures were taken and Dr Kemp Clark, chief of neuro-surgery, was called as well as other members of the hospital staff. "They arrived immediately but at this point the President's condition was critical and moribund," Dr Perry said.—Reuter and A.P.

GOLDWATER'S PROSPECT MAY BE AFFECTED

Political upheaval possible

President Kennedy's death will undoubtedly transform the p scene in the U.S. There was no doubt in the mind of any p observer in the country that he would have been the Democratic date again in next November's election.

He would also have been a strong favourite to win again, despite the fact that he had lost ground recently over his Administration's stand on civil rights.

Whether his death will open up a battle in the Democratic Party for the Presidential nomination remains to be seen. Much will depend on the leadership shown by President Johnson.

The President's death could also have a tremendous impact on the choice of a Republican candidate. His assassination in Texas—a hotbed of Right-wing sentiment—may adversely affect the chances of Senator Barry Goldwater.

RIGHT-WINGERS BLAMED

Without knowing the full facts of the President's death, people on the streets in Washington were already disposed to blame "those crazy Right-wingers." In such an atmosphere Senator Goldwater, who has been the darling of the Conservative wing of the Republican Party and has been ahead in all the public opinion polls, could suffer.

The comments to be heard in Washington were bitter and outspoken. Many blamed the "Birchites"—members of the ultra-patriotic Right-wing John Birch Society.

Representative Hale Boggs, the Democratic Party Whip, declared to reporters: "Those Birchite bastards ought to be happy. They pulled the trigger."

Even before Mr Kennedy's death there were many thoughtful Republicans who were disturbed over the possibility of a clash between the Right and Liberal Wings.

In these circumstances it seems possible—some observers said likely—that demands will grow f re-emergence of President Ke opponent in 1960 — forme President Richard Nixon, w been in political retirement s made an unsuccessful co attempt in 1962.—Reuter.

LATEST NEW

POSTAGE
Inland, 4½d; Overseas, 6½d.

POIGNANT MOMENT, SAYS PRIME MINISTER

"Gay and brave statesman"

Everything in one cried out in protest at the news that President Kennedy had died at the hand of an assassin, the Prime Minister, Sir Alec Douglas-Home, said last night on B.B.C. Television. Sir Alec spoke of "this gay and brave statesman, killed in the full vigour of his manhood, when he bore on his shoulders all the cares and hopes of the world."

He went on: "You will be glad to know that Her Majesty the Queen has sent to message to Mrs Kennedy and the people of the United States on behalf of you all, and I now do so on behalf of Her Majesty's Government—and I know that all in both Houses of Parliament will allow me, as they are not sitting, to do so on behalf of them, too.

"MAN OF PEACE"

"This moment is the more poignant because only a few weeks ago I was walking with President Kennedy in the grounds of the White House, and he was telling me of his plans to guard and keep the peace of the world.

"And as I recall his vivid presence, he lives in my mind as a man who, first of all, was a man of peace and a man with a deep religious faith dedicated to healing the divisions between men, and then, as a man of physical courage.

"And then again, I recall him as a just man, a man who hated bigotry, who believed all men were equal in the sight of God and acted on that belief, and a man who, as a husband and a father, was tolerant an human, and as politician was a statesman who grasped all the opportunities that he had, and looked forward with an imagination rare in a man of his years.

"In three short years of his Presidency, he left an indelible mark on his country and on the world, and for us in Britain his loss is a deep and sad one because he was a most loyal and faithful ally."

DEDICATION

The Prime Minister concluded: "Tonight I fear there is no comfort that I can bring to the American people, nor indeed to ourselves, nor indeed to men anywhere who care for tolerance and liberty and justice and peace, unless it be this: that this dreadful deed should shock us all to dedicate ourselves anew to those things which he liked, which he loved, and for which he worked during his life.

"And if we can help to bring to men the liberty, justice and peace for which he did so much, then we shall be doing something to serve the causes in the service of which he himself died."

"NEW PURPOSE" INSTILLED

Mr Wilson praises fight for rights

Mr Harold Wilson, speaking after the Prime Minister on television, said that what the President achieved was to bring a new sense of purpose to the American people. "He did wake America and get them moving in the economic sense. He got a sense of purpose into the social field and the field of education.

"Above all he will be remembered by us for his great and courageous fight for human rights, his great fight which once begun had to go on to the end, for ending racial conflict in the United States."

NOTHING SLIPSHOD

Mr Wilson said that others would pay tribute to President Kennedy's administrative work. "At any rate one can feel that when decisions had to be taken, because of his keen brain, his keen sense of administration, that decision was taken in the full light of all the knowledge. Nothing ever went through in a slipshod way.

"He made many mistakes because every person fails, but every decision was taken with courage and certainty."

ABOUT THE MAN

A series of pictures of President Kennedy illustrating many sides of his life and character, together with his obituary, is on Page 8.

On Page 6 there is an article on the problems facing the new President, and another by Our Own Correspondent on Lyndon Johnson's long political experience.

World-wide reaction and the President's last speech are on page 7.

THE CRADLE OF THE 'FORTY-FIVE

Local tales of the area where Prince Charlie landed for the '45, now to be opened up by the new Kinlochmoidart - Kinlochailort road, are recalled in an illustrated article in the Week-end Magazine by "North Argyll," an authority on the lore of the West Highlands. John Steel describes the famed Spanish Court Riding School at the former Imperial Palace of the Hapsburgs in Vienna. For full details of the contents see Page One of the Magazine.

FARMING SCENE

Robert Urquhart reports a major drive by leaders of the National Farmers' Union of Scotland to put forward union views on vital problems, and urges rank-and-file members to acknowledge this strong

"MONSTROUS ACT," SAYS SIR WINSTON

Britain was thunderstruck last night by the assassination of President Kennedy.

Tributes from the leaders of the country and the man-in-the-street began after the news was broken on

by the assassination of President Kennedy. He was greatly admired and loved by us all. I extend to you our assurance of friendship and support in the heavy burdens which have devolved upon you."

tressed to learn of the tragic death of President Kennedy. My husband joins me in sending our heartfelt and sincere sympathy to you and to your family."

It was announced from ...

The sailors at the American Polaris submarine base at the Holy Loch learned of the President's death from the radio. Lieut. Glen Pecor, squadron duty officer on the depot ship Hunley

THE SCOTSMAN

No. 38,959 EDINBURGH, MONDAY, APRIL 8, 1968 PRICE 6d.

NEW VIOLENCE FEARED IN MEMPHIS

Memorial march today

ne thousand National Guard troops were being flown to his, Tennessee, yesterday to join 4000 Guardsmen already amid growing fears that today's planned massive memorial for Dr Martin Luther King would result in a new wave of action in the city.

bout 4000 mourners from all parts of the country are ted to parade for six hours through the streets of Memphis, where Dr King was assassinated on Thursday.

Dr King, an apostle of non-violence, would probably have viewed with sorrow the irony of the march—through streets which will be lined with the bayonets and guns of steel-helmeted troops.

Although there were reports of fresh looting yesterday from some cities, the situation generally was one of uneasy calm in troubled areas after three days of violent disturbances.

Local and federal authorities believed that the parade would be peaceful, but they feared that widespread disorders might occur as the marchers dispersed to Negro areas, where sporadic looting and fire-raising were continuing.

A Negro hotel doorman said in Memphis: "Some of my people who are coming here from other parts of the country may cut loose after dark and it'll be like Washington and Chicago."

PRAYERS

President Johnson, flanked by a heavy security guard, led the nation in prayer yesterday for Dr King. He drove to Mass at St Dominic's Roman Catholic Church in a former Washington slum area which has been rehabilitated. The church is just over a mile from one of the ghettoes where, only a few hours earlier, Negroes were rioting.

Mr Johnson had proclaimed yesterday a day of national mourning for Dr King.

Churches throughout Memphis offered prayers for Dr King's widow and family. An open-air meeting organised by civic, religious and business leaders was being held in a stadium later in the day.

More than 100 telephone calls were received by the police in Memphis on Saturday, each claiming to have clues to the identity and whereabouts of the "long-nosed white man" who booked a room at the hotel from where Dr King was shot.

A police spokesman said: "Many people are being lured to make a stab in the dark because of the size of the reward (about £41,600) that is being offered for the arrest and conviction of the killer."—Reuter.

Uneasy calm—Page 7

UBLICANS IN EDINBURGH FEAR BEER SHORTAGE

e Edinburgh publicans are they may run out of beer week because of a work to and overtime ban by about lorry-drivers employed by h & Newcastle Breweries.

rewery spokesman said last that, although they were d with deliveries, it was not that any public-houses d run dry. He added: "We robably have to look at the from the point of view r own pubs. We will have e how we can share the ties out, but everybody is to get their beer."

"FURTHER TALKS"

spokesman added that ement representatives had he unions and further meet- would take place this week. is an unofficial overtime nd the men evidently feel e are taking too long about

drivers want a £22 a week in lieu of overtime and payments and the Scottish ercial Motormen's Union failed to reach an agree- over the dispute with the ement.

PRISON HUNGER STRIKE GOES ON

Enters second week

The hunger strike by 20 prisoners in the top security wing of Durham Prison entered its second week last night, the prison's deputy governor, Mr John Beaumont, said.

"We are continuing to make food available. That is as much as we can do," he said, adding that there was no apparent sign of the hunger strike ending.

The prisoners, who are being seen daily by a medical officer, are protesting against the system of serving food, introduced as a result of punishments for disturbances five weeks ago. They say the new system is too slow, and under it, the food deteriorates.

TWO BOB A JOB?

Boy Scouts' annual "bob-a-job" weeks are the latest casualty of rising prices, the Scout Association said today. Some jobs, they say, are big enough to warrant a "larger reward" and a new name is being sought for next year's scheme.

AMBLER'S BRAIN OPERATION OFF

Father's statement

eucotomy operation, planned day in an effort to end the pulsive gambling" of Mr Wills (21), of Warrington, shire, will not take place, ther said last night.

r visiting his son in hos- Mr Kenneth Wills said his d told him they were not ahead. His son, he added, d to have the operation as s possible.

chief consultant psychia- at the hospital, Dr Harry ng, refused to comment last about the operation. He was a "medical matter."

The crumpled wreckage of Jim Clark's racing car after the fatal crash yesterday at Hockenheim.

JIM CLARK DIES IN CRASH AT 170 m.p.h.

Body will be flown home today

Jim Clark (32), the Scottish farmer who twice became world champion racing driver, was killed yesterday when his car skidded off the track and somersaulted into a wood at Hockenheim, West Germany.

His white Lotus-Cosworth car, screaming out of a bend at about 170 m.p.h., zig-zagged along the track, then somersaulted away and crashed broadside into the trees.

The shocked crowd of spectators rose to their feet in spontaneous tribute when told over loudspeakers of Clark's death. Then the flags of the ten nations in the race were lowered to half-mast.

A chartered jet aircraft will fly Clark's body home to Scotland today, his agent in London said.

The aircraft is expected to land in mid or late afternoon at Turnhouse Airport, Edinburgh, where a hearse will be waiting to take the body to his home. The funeral is expected to take place at Chirnside Parish Church on Wednesday.

The race in which Clark died was the Deutschland Trophy, first of 11 races in this season's unofficial European Formula Two championships.

It was Clark's first race on the fast Hockenheim circuit, which still showed wet patches from a morning shower when the race started. Just before the crash, Clark had been lying only eighth, and was evidently unhappy, according to a race official.

The rear wheels failed to hold the road as he was coming out of a fast right-hand bend to enter the long back straight on the sixth lap.

"Clark must have been travelling at 170 miles an hour," said an official who saw him crash.

Somersaults

He fought to keep the car on the road as it weaved 500 yards along the track and grass safety strip. A policeman said the car somersaulted three or four times before smashing broadside into the trees.

Clark is believed to have died almost at once from severe multiple injuries, including a broken neck and a fractured skull. He was taken to hospital but was dead on arrival.

Graham Hill, Clark's team-mate, and the other British former world champion in the race, withdrew his Lotus-Cosworth at the end of the first 20-lap heat after trailing well down the field.

The crash happened well out of sight of the public enclosures and the crowd of 80,000 people did not hear of Clark's death for more than two hours. "We did not announce it earlier because we did not want the crowd to panic," an official said.

An official investigation of the crash has been ordered (cables Reuter).

Jim Clark's father, Mr James Clark (73), said last night: "Racing was his life. His mother never wanted him to take up the career; I was never very keen, but we had to accept it and we were proud of him."

The tributes to Jim Clark were summed up in a message from Mr Wilfred Andrew, chairman of the R.A.C., who said: "British motor racing has never suffered a more severe blow. Jim Clark may well have been the greatest driver of all time in terms of Grand Prix racing. No one, not even the legendary Fangio, was his equal.

Drivers weep

At Monte Carlo, Louis Chiron, director of the Monaco Grand Prix and former world and European motor racing champion, said: "With Jim Clark has gone the great driver of modern times. It is an irreparable loss for motor sport."

At Monza, several drivers, including Jonathan Williams, of Britain, competing in a race there, wept on hearing of Clark's death.

Graham Hill said Clark's death "leaves a hell of a gap in the racing scene." He added: "For me it means the loss of a friend as well as for thousands of others."

Enzo Ferrari (70), the magnate of Italian car racing, said at Modena he was too moved to make any comment on Clark's death. Only last week Ferrari had called Clark "a perfect driver."

Today at Fords factory at Halewood the flag will fly at half-mast as a mark of respect for Clark. A Halewood spokesman said: "If any man individually succeeded in advancing Britain's achievements throughout the world, it was Jim Clark."

Obituary—Page 9

R.A.F. pilot charged

An R.A.F. pilot has been charged in connection with an unauthorised flight over London on Friday, a Ministry of Defence spokesman said yesterday.

He is Flight-Lieutenant Alan Richard Pollock (32), of R.A.F., West Raynham, Norfolk.

The spokesman said that Flt.-Lt. Pollock had been released from close arrest. Normal inquiries were continuing.

On Friday, a Hunter jet fighter, reported to have come from R.A.F., West Raynham, was flown between the roadway and top structure of Tower Bridge, London.

Mother and son died after drink of cocoa

Carlisle police yesterday were investigating the death of a mother and her son and the serious illness of six more of her children.

Mrs Eunice Shepherd (38), was found dead at her home in Madam Banks Road, Dalston, Carlisle, on Saturday night. Her son, Mark (3), died later in Cumberland Infirmary, Carlisle.

SENT FOR TESTS

A police spokesman said the family had been drinking cocoa. Articles of crockery had been sent to Preston Forensic Science Laboratory for tests.

The dead woman's six other children, aged from three to 14, were said by a Cumberland Infirmary spokesman to be "all out of danger."

Mr William Shepherd, husband of the dead woman, was out at the time.

LATEST NEWS

VIET-NAM COMMAND

Washington, Sunday. — President Johnson has chosen Gen. Westmoreland's successor as Field Commander Viet-Nam. Will name him soon, White House sources said tonight.—Reuter.

POSTAGE
Inland, 3d; Overseas, 9½d.

Tory policy document amounts to 'war' on incomes policy

By OUR POLITICAL CORRESPONDENT

Signs in plenty of clashes to come between the two major parties over compulsory wage restraint and wider aspects of industrial policy are contained in an important new Conservative policy document published today.

Called "Fair Deal at Work," it comes out strongly against legal powers to hold down wages and asserts that if continued these would destroy free collective bargaining.

The Conservatives call for the Prices and Incomes Board to be changed into a new Productivity Board with its principal aim to encourage a "high productivity by earnings" economy. Its powers should include authority to investigate restrictive practices, or working methods, thought to be harmful to the economy or socially unjustified.

Under the Tory plan, strikes to enforce a "closed shop," those resulting from inter-union disputes and "sympathy" strikes would no longer be protected against civil actions for damages.

COINCIDENCE

It is a coincidence that the Conservative policy statement should come out on a day when Mrs Barbara Castle is settling into her new responsibilities as Secretary of State for Employment and Productivity. It still amounts, however, to a declaration of total war against the Prices and Incomes policies for which she has been made responsible in Parliament.

Conservative leaders were against compulsory wage restraint. Now that they have declared a full policy on industrial relations—following a three-year study—they will challenge Mrs Castle strongly. It looks as though she has been moved from the tough Transport Bill battle to face an even sterner Parliamentary fight piloting the Government's new wage-curb Bill through the House.

In a bid to rally the Labour back benches, Mrs Castle will play hard on the fears of trade unionists that the Conservative policy will limit their freedom to strike.

Plan for Incomes Board—Page 9

CAR DRIVER SOUGHT

Stirling Police are investigating an accident on Saturday night, in which William Reynolds (63), roadman, of 34 Park Crescent, Bannockburn, was knocked down and injured in King's Park Road, Stirling, by a car, which failed to stop. The car is believed to have been a black Ford Consul or Zephyr.

'RELIGIOUS MURDER' THEORY

A young woman, whose torso was found in one suitcase and her legs in another, may have been the victim of a religious murder. This is the theory of Det.-Supt. Roy Yorke, of New Scotland Yard murder squad.

The legs, found in a suitcase recovered from a river, came from the same body as the torso found in another suitcase on a Euston-Wolverhampton train on Thursday night.

ANOTHER SECT

The head and neck of the woman, believed to be of Indian or Pakistani descent, aged between 20 and 30 and about 5 ft. 1 in. tall, is still missing.

"This girl may have misbehaved in some way, or associated with a member of another sect. She may even have disobeyed her husband and been killed.

"We are inquiring at mosques and Hindu temples all over the country, and particularly in Bradford, Yorkshire, and Southall, Middlesex, where there are big Pakistani populations."

"MOHICAN" CUT

A man is believed to have travelled in the same compartment as that in which the suitcase containing the torso was found. Police have asked for a white man with a "Mohican hairstyle" to come forward to help them in their inquiries.

Meanwhile, police are checking railway and bus stations for another suitcase which may contain the head and neck.

Round-Moon spacecraft launched by Russians

MOSCOW, Sunday.—The Soviet Union today blasted off a rocket capsule which could be intended to make history by circling the Moon and returning to Earth.

The instrument-packed capsule, Luna-14, was the first probe in more than 15 months in Soviet scientists' nine-year-old programme to land a man on the lunar surface.

The Luna-14 capsule—its existence revealed by the official Tass news agency six hours after launching — should reach the vicinity of the Moon on Wednesday night, according to unofficial calculations.

PICTURE-TAKING

The official announcement said the spacecraft would make more scientific studies of near-lunar space, wording which suggested that it would not attempt a soft-landing on the Moon like its predecessor, Luna-13, in December 1966.

There was immediate speculation that Soviet scientists might be attempting their long-awaited feat of sending a capsule round the Moon on a picture-taking journey and then returning to Earth.—Reuter.

Ins and outs of Wilson Cabinet 'Mk. 2'

By OUR POLITICAL CORRESPONDENT

Mr Wilson's "Mark 2" Cabinet are expected to meet for the first time tomorrow. As Ministers settle down round the large Cabinet table they are bound to exchange speculative glances and to wonder how the new regime will affect not only their own future but that of the Prime Minister and of the very Government itself.

As well as promoting Mrs Barbara Castle and Mr Richard Crossman to new and important responsibilities, Mr Wilson had decided that the large and cumbersome Cabinet meetings have been taking place too often. These gatherings have become almost twice weekly occurrences.

MAGIC CIRCLE

Now the Prime Minister intends ... tasks will be to look towards the next election.

Inevitably, this new group could become known as the inner Cabinet or the "magic circle." Tensions could be created between the "insiders" on this committee and the Ministers remaining outside. Mr George Brown's resignation hints at a devaluing of Cabinet government are too recent to be forgotten.

Much, therefore, will depend on how the Prime Minister uses the new body. He will want to avoid any suggestion of first and second class Ministers. Mr Wilson can expect a public outcry from Scotland if Mr William Ross, the Scottish Secretary, is not included ... Parliamentary ...

Mr Wilson has dropped completely the presidential style of premiership which marked his early years in office—the period when every Government move was proudly announced by himself while the departmental Minister responsible sat glumly by. Since devaluation, Mr Wilson has contented himself with more of a background role. He has sought to switch the spotlight away from Downing Street and towards the Ministries.

It is questionable how much the Government reshuffle and this change of emphasis has been Mr Wilson's own choice. The result has been that the Prime Minister has surrounded himself with powerful and ambitious personalities emerging as his deputy. This could explain the surprising reappointment of Mr Michael Stewart as Foreign Secretary following Mr Brown's resignation.

UNCERTAINTY

Mr Stewart ranks number two in the Cabinet but he could not be regarded as a serious challenger for the premiership. It is a reflection of the uncertainty of politics that Mr James Callaghan, the Home Secretary, who last autumn seemed set as heir-apparent now finds himself ranking number seven in the Cabinet just above the formidable Mr Denis Healey, the Defence Secretary.

The Prime Minister intends to ensure that the strings of power remain firmly in his own hands. Perhaps the real change is that he will not be seen so clearly to manipulate them.

EGYPT MAY BUILD SUEZ OIL PIPELINE

CAIRO, Sunday.—The United Arab Republic is studying the feasibility of an oil pipeline linking the Gulf of Suez with the Mediterranean, the newspaper Al-gomhouria," said today, quoting the Minister of Industry and Petroleum, Mr Aziz Sidky.

The pipeline would have an annual capacity of 50 million ... —Reuter.

THE SCOTSMAN

No. 39,814 EDINBURGH, MONDAY, JANUARY 4, 1971 3 a.m. news PRICE 9d.

Ibrox disaster raises five vital questions on safety at matches

Leaving Glasgow City Mortuary yesterday are Chief Constable Sir James Robertson (left), with Mr Alick Buchanan-Smith (Scottish Under-Secretary for Home Affairs) and Lord Provost Sir Donald Liddle.

BY OUR OWN REPORTERS

EDITORIAL Page 6
JOHN RAFFERTY, MORE PICTURES Page 7

A full-scale police inquiry into the Ibrox Stadium disaster was ordered by the Lord Advocate, Mr Norman Wylie, as the full horror of the Glasgow tragedy, with 66 deaths and nearly 200 injured, became clear yesterday.

Faced with the worst disaster in British football history, at a spot where tragedy has struck twice before, the inquiry must find, and a shocked public will demand, answers to five key questions.

Is the steep slope of the Cairnlea Drive exit inherently dangerous? It has 100 steps and three short landings and supporters can walk up to six abreast between each of six handrails.

Are two exits at the East End of the stadium sufficient for more than 20,000 spectators.

Are the concrete-filled steel barriers which divide the staircase strong enough and placed in the best position, or should they have been staggered to prevent a "tidal wave" of spectators tumbling unobstructed down the 100-foot slope?

Could removal of fencing and better crowd control at the top of the terracing have prevented the disaster?

Did the safety factor of the exit rebuilt to specified standards on the instructions of insurance experts and passed at the beginning of the season, take into account the human element of football fervour raised to fever pitch in the heat of a photo-finish Old Firm derby?

Called to talks

Mr Eldon Griffiths, Minister responsible for sport, has called Sir John Lang, principal Government adviser on sports, and Mr Walter Winterbottom, director of the Sports Council, to his Ministry in London today. They will be discussing safety at football grounds (see Page 7).

Sir John is the author of the recent report on hooliganism and crowd control at football matches.

In view of the large death roll at Ibrox, the normal procedure of a fatal accident inquiry is almost certainly in question. This was confirmed last night by the Secretary of State for Scotland, Mr Gordon Campbell, when he said, after visiting both the scene of the disaster and victims in the Victoria Infirmary, Glasgow, that an announcement on the exact form of the inquiry would be made within the next few days.

He added that if it was felt a fatal accident inquiry would limit the scope, they would consider a wider form of inquiry. He would make a report to the Prime Minister today.

Asked if he would be making any recommendations in that report, Mr Campbell said he would simply be detailing what had happened. "I do not know of any simple panacea which can avoid this kind of unintentional accident. I feel that it is tragic that this should happen when supporters themselves had been very good and had enjoyed a good match, and in no way caused any kind of trouble."

He emphasised that the results of the inquiry could be of great importance in the future, not only for Scotland but for England and countries abroad. "Clearly such a report could have implications beyond the borders of Scotland. If we come up with wise recommendations, they could benefit communities furth of Scotland."

The safety implications alone for dozens of other football clubs and perhaps for all mass-audience public entertainment, could merit a full-scale Government commission of inquiry.

Valencia Football Club yesterday offered to play a charity match against Rangers, at any convenient date, to raise funds for bereaved families.

The Spanish side were to have played a friendly against Rangers there on Wednesday, but the Glasgow club asked for the game to be cancelled because of the disaster.—Reuter.

Unbelievable

Disaster struck swiftly, indiscriminately, unbelievably in the dying seconds of the most sporting and happy duel between the two great Glasgow rivals in recent years, on the staircase where two people died in 1961 and where 24 people were injured on January 2, 1969.

It struck in a dusky mist and many of the 80,000 spectators knew nothing of the tragic drama unfolding over the rim of the stadium.

As quickly as it struck, emergency procedures swung into smooth operation that belied the size of the operation.

Within hours, messages of sympathy poured into the Lord Provost Sir Donald Liddle's office as the news was flashed round the world.

Donations for the Ibrox Disaster Fund followed and some were even pledged before the Lord Provost opened the fund officially.

Rescue workers arrived within seconds and as darkness fell many broke down as they tried desperately but in vain to resuscitate children pulled from the broken heap of supporters who had cheerfully left the field such a short time before.

A full major-incident alert went out from Glasgow police headquarters, calling in every available ambulance in the city, seven fire tenders and reinforcements to help the 300 policemen already on duty in the ground.

The rescue operation involved emergency disaster procedures at the Southern General Hospital, and as the death and injury totals mounted, at the Victoria Infirmary also.

Medical teams of two doctors and two nursing sisters were sent from both hospitals and in the ground a row of stretchers was laid out from the corner flag to the goalmouth.

A fleet of 18 ambulances began a shuttle service to both hospitals. One-way traffic was imposed on the track to speed the operation.

Dozens of people with slight injuries were treated on the spot by some of the 100 volunteer St Andrew's Ambulance staff on duty for the match and were not taken to hospital.

A total of 150 injured were removed to hospital within an hour of the disaster.

Volunteers help

Players, ground staff, club officials, supporters and volunteer first-aid teams helped to bring aid to the injured alongside police, firemen and ambulancemen.

Sir James Robertson, Chief Constable of Glasgow, who was attending the game, took charge of the rescue operation within minutes, and despite the vast crowd flooding out of the ground from other exits causing traffic chaos, rescue vehicles were on hand as the first injured were brought from the stairway.

Edmiston Drive was closed to normal traffic during the first two hours of the disaster.

Opposite the staircase Mrs Elizabeth McKim was watching from her third-storey lounge window at 12 Cairnlea Drive. She said: "I always look out ... tried to get back up. Suddenly the whole mass of people began swaying. I could hardly watch because I had seen it before and I knew what was going to happen. Within seconds people were tumbling down the stairway. All you could see was arms and legs.

"I could see that the barriers had been twisted and bent. Some of my neighbours ran down to the park and there were people screaming. I could hear them from here."

A Celtic supporter, Mr George Connor (37), dealer, 334 Albert Drive, was at the match with his son, Anthony (9). He said: "Because I had my little boy with me, I decided to walk around the terracing to the Rangers' end in the hope that the crowd would have cleared there when I reached the exit. Suddenly I realised there was something wrong. I couldn't describe the scene when I looked over the top of the terracing.

"I have had some first-aid training and a policeman asked me to help. I went from one to another. They were all dead. I could not find any injured in that particular part of the staircase.

"I then went to the gym where the bodies were being laid out and I realised just how bad it was."

Money offered

Soon after the midnight announcement by the Lord Provost of an appeal fund for the dependants of the victims, a message was received from a Manchester firm promising 100gns.

Mr William Balshaw, chairman of the William Hill organisation, said in Glasgow that they would give 500gns to any relief fund.

As news of the tragedy spread through the city there were many spontaneous expressions of sympathy, some of them anticipating the Lord Provost's appeal. In one public-house near Ibrox more than £500 was raised in under an hour. The first donation came from a Celtic supporter, who contributed £10.

Last night, the Lord Provost announced that a memorial service for the victims would be held next Saturday in Glasgow Cathedral.

At his Press conference earlier in the day, the Secretary of State for Scotland described the disaster as one of appalling dimensions.

He thanked Glasgow police and those who had taken part in the rescue operations, including members of the Salvation Army. In talks with survivors and relatives, all had praised Glasgow police for their quick, efficient response.

Appalling as the tragedy had been, it would have been worse if the police had not been able to hold off many of the spectators crowding in on the scene and siphon them away elsewhere.

Sir Donald Liddle announced that all flags on public buildings in Glasgow would be flown at half-mast today.

Relatives of the dead will be visited by social workers over the next few days, both in Glasgow and outwith the city.

Broken and twisted barriers on the east terracing stairway are inspected by officials yesterday.

Five Markinch schoolboys among the dead

A sad, steady procession of relatives was the grim aftermath of the disaster as they made their way to the mortuary to identify the victims.

They came from all over central Scotland and the tragedy struck particularly cruelly at the small Fife burgh of Markinch, home of five of the youngest dead, all schoolboys, who lived within a few hundred yards of each other.

The boys, Mason Phillips (15), Peter Easton (13), Bryan Todd (14), Richard Douglas Morrison (14), all of Park View, and David Patton (14), of Googe Street, were ardent football fans.

They played for the same under-age football team and Auchmuty Secondary School, attended the same school, Glenrothes.

They had travelled in a Glenrothes Rangers supporters' bus to the game, and when they did not turn up for the return journey it was thought they had lost their way.

Provost Jack Mackie said the first indication that the boys might be involved in the disaster was when Bryan Todd's parents, on holiday in England, asked him to make inquiries.

"I thought at first just one boy was missing, but I was deeply distressed to learn later that five young lives had been lost."

ONLY WOMAN

The only woman victim, Margaret Ferguson (18), was a keen Rangers supporter, who made a doll for the baby daughter of Ranger's centre forward Colin Stein at Christmas and delivered it personally to his home.

Stein's equaliser on Saturday came seconds before the disaster. Margaret, a factory worker, of Craigend Drive, Maddiston, near Falkirk, had been teased by her father on New Year's Day after Falkirk had beaten Rangers 3-1.

She died only seconds after another Maddiston supporter, Mr Jim Hynds (25), on holiday from Nottingham, let go of her arm when he felt himself falling.

Mr Hynds, of Steely Road, Nottingham, said yesterday: "I shouted to her to keep going but just as I hit the ground I heard her screaming: 'Buff, help me.'"

Mr Hynds, nicknamed "Buff" by his friends, never saw her again. Margaret would have been 19 next month.

One of three Edinburgh victims, Mr James Sibbald (28), of 5/6 Lochend House, Restalrig, Edinburgh, a prison officer, was to have attended his son's birthday party after the game.

A relative said: "His son, Leslie, was five on Saturday. His wife had prepared a birthday party. James only went to the matches now and again, but he had just joined the Rangers' Supporters' Club. He always phoned to say when he would be home, and his wife realised there was something wrong when he had not phoned by after six o'clock."

The youngest victim was eight-year-old Nigel McPherson who died with his father, Donald. They had returned to Scotland from Edmonton, Alberta, to spend Christmas and New Year with Mr McPherson's parents at 2 Greenfield Street, Glasgow.

A keen Rangers supporter, Mr McPherson had decided that he should take his son to see his first Old Firm game. They were officially identified yesterday among the 66 dead.

LAST IDENTIFIED

Throughout the day groups of anxious relatives called at police station in Glasgow

Journalists' peace formula

"Daily Mirror" and "Sun" journalists were last night recommended by their strike leaders to resume normal working — and to suspend strike action.

But in Glasgow "Daily Record" journalists went home claiming that they had been "locked out." They are to meet again at 10 a.m. today.

After five hours of talks with Mr Vic Feather, general secretary of the TUC, National Union of Journalists' officials proposed talks "on the definition or clarification of areas where ... action," said Mr Bryn Jones, chapel father.

After the talks at the TUC, a meeting of the "Daily Mirror" Chapel ended with a recommendation that they should work normally, a chapel spokesman said.

NO VICTIMISATION

Mr Feather said last night: "The NUJ have proposed to the NPA that there should be discussions as quickly as possible on the definition or clarification of areas where discussions can take place domestically.

"The NPA agreed to meet the NUJ for this purpose tomorrow.

"The representatives of the two ...

IPC Newspapers said last night that the management and chapel officials had exchanged assurances that there would be no victimisation of journalists who had joined the strike, or victimisation or harassment of executives who had continued to produce the newspaper.

Earlier, "Daily Record" journalists in Glasgow—who had come out on unofficial strike on Friday in support of their "Daily Mirror" colleagues — agreed to return to work but Mr Stewart MacLachlan, chapel father, claimed they were "locked out" by the management.

He said the Glasgow journa-

Group want end to charter flight curbs

Irksome rules hampering cheaper air charter flights should be scrapped, a consumer research group said at the weekend.

People wanting to visit friends and relatives in many parts of the world are faced with unreasonable difficulties and hazards when they seek cheaper flights, says the British Consumer Group of the Zurich Air Fares Conference.

At present groups chartering cheaper flights must have a purpose other than travel and passengers must belong to the group for six months and have attended at least six meetings.

Full-scale alert for Biggs

A full-scale police alert w[...] mounted in Dublin last night af[...] a civil servant reported that [...] man resembling Ronald Biggs [...] escaped train robber, had visit[...] his premises in search of acco[...] modation for himself, his wife a[...] two children.

Police have ordered a rou[...] the-clock watch on all sea and [...] exits.

Earlier railway police search[...] the London to Glasgow express [...] Crewe after receiving a rep[...] that Biggs was on board.

A police spokesman said, "[...] did interview a man. We [...] perfectly satisfied Biggs wasn't [...] the train."

Over the weekend there w[...] nearly 100 reports of sighti[...] of Biggs after Scotland Yard [...] closed that he may be in Brita[...]

Biggs escaped with three ot[...] men from Wandsworth Prison [...] London in 1965. He had ser[...] only 14 months of a 30-[...] sentence.

His "cut" in the robbery [...] reputed to be £120,000. Mos[...] the £2.6 million haul is [...] missing.

Dentists have been asked [...] try to trace Biggs since [...] Yard believe he may [...] dental treatment after a [...] crash in Australia more tha[...] year ago.

LATEST NEW[S]

POSTAGE
Inland, 4d; Overseas, 3d.

THE Scotsman

Clelland Brown
FOR PLATINUM GC & DIAMONDS
131 Rose Street, Edinburgh EH2 3DT
031-226 4292

No. 45,194   ★   Friday, July 8, 1988   Price 30p

Death of Piper Alpha

ig blow ealt to K oil utput

By FRANK FRAZER

TAIN lost up to 14 per cent. North Sea oil production erday when six oilfields shut down by the cas ons which devastated the Alpha platform.

e impact of the blast, could cost insurers £1 caused a sharp rise in oil worldwide, with North eds adding more than £1 15.70 a barrel.

t with predictions that it d take some years to repair ge and restart the fields, K's balance of payments be put under more strain further deficit of between illion and £5 million a day ming from lost oil produc-

e Government will suffer estimated at £300 million 400 million a year as a t of reduced tax revenue the Piper field, one of the est and most profitable of Sea discoveries.

ch of the insurance for the orm was arranged by the on insurance broker, Willis where an official con- d last night "This is prob- going to be the largest loss North Sea."

ough the offshore industry eviously a good insurance d, some analysts thought in the long run, oil com- would have to pay the for the disaster by facing r insurance costs for oil- operations. "It will en off the competition and p premiums in oil and said Mr Chris tain, an insurance analyst he stockbrokers, County est Woodmac.

disaster had an immedi- pact on shares in the US Occidental Petroleum, led the consortium of ers in the Piper field.

e company's shares fell cents, to $26.25 dollars, in York Stock Exchange after official at Occidental's Los t night. Occidental's chair- Dr Armand Hammer, for he was leaving edlately for Aberdeen to vise the setting up of a force to help families of dental employees.

HER PAGES

Gas leak blamed as blast kills 164

By BRIAN PENDREIGH and DAVID STEWART

THE HUGE explosion which destroyed the Piper Alpha platform and claimed the lives of more than 160 men may have been caused by a gas leak directly under the on-board living quarters.

Early inquiries by the platform operators, Occidental Oil, suggest that the initial blast occurred in a compression chamber on the side of the platform which housed the crew's accommodation area. That section, more than half the platform, has been obliterated.

Of the 229 crew on board, only 68 survivors have so far been picked up by rescuers and the remainder are almost certainly dead. By last night, 16 bodies had been recovered but 148 people remained unaccounted for in what has become the worst disaster in the history of the North Sea oil industry.

The original explosion which began the process of destruction on the giant platform 120 miles north- east of Aberdeen happened just before 10 pm on Wednesday. The fierce fire which followed gave rise to a series of other explosions, rip- ping apart most of the super-structure, and leaving only a burned-out, shrunken shell standing above the waterline.

Yesterday survivors, who were forced to leap hundreds of feet into the sea to escape, told of the horror of watching workmates die in the inferno. "It was fry or jump," said one man who made it to safety.

Pilots approaching the area in the early stages of the drama painted a graphic picture of conditions. Flt Lt Steve Hodgson, pilot of the first land-based helicopter to reach the scene, said he could see the platform burning 25 miles away. "We were flying at 2000ft and when we got down the flames were going above us."

The fire-fighting barge Tharos poured huge quantities of water on to make much impression or prevent virtually the total destruction of the platform.

The flames had died down by yes- terday morning, but several well- heads on the shattered platform still burned intermittently.

Specialists may be brought in from the United States to ensure the fire is extinguished, but a company spokesman said that aspect of the operation was not seen as a major problem. He did not believe there was a danger of further explosions.

The drama produced many tales of bravery and tragedy. Mr Iain Let- ham (27), of Muir of Ord, was on a small rescue boat when the second big explosion happened and he and the others in the boat were thrown into the sea.

"Flames were going everywhere and my hard hat and lifejacket melted. I thought I was going to die."

He managed to swim to a supply vessel, but there is no news of the two other men who crewed the rescue boat with him.

Mr John Maxwell watched from the Tharos as an explosion blew up the Piper Alpha's helipad, on which men were waiting to be rescued.

He said they were hit by a massive ball of flame and he never saw them again.

"We all felt helpless. We were not terrified. We were angry that there was nothing we could do."

Tragically, the catering crew for the platform was on its first tour of duty, the company concerned having won the contract from July 1.

The rescue teams and medical crews won widespread praise for their efforts in difficult conditions. The Energy Minister, Mr Peter Morrison, flew to Aberdeen early in the morning, and later flew to the Tharos to view the smouldering remains of the platform. He described the events of Wednesday night as horrific.

Mr John Brading, head of Occidental's operations in Britain, said investigations were under way by the Department of Energy, as well as by the company itself. A police team also flew to the location yesterday.

Mr Brading said some eye-witnesses suggested the explosion had originated in a gas compression module, but others suggested its origin was in an adjacent module housing production facilities.

Grampian's chief constable, Mr Alistair Lynn, said there was absolutely no question of terrorism or sabotage involved.

There have been two other much less serious explosions in the North Sea oil industry in the last week, both connected with gas compression. One was at Sullom Voe in Shetland

two other men who crewed the rescue boat with him.

and the other on the Brent Field, and investigations into those incidents are continuing.

Mr Brading confirmed that in March 1984 there had been an explosion on the Piper Alpha platform.

Mrs Thatcher is expected in Aber- deen today, after the announcement in the Commons that a far-reaching public inquiry is to be held.

A police spokesman said it was not expected that any names of sur- vivors, deceased, or those missing, would be released until today. The majority of personnel on the plat- form were British.

○ There was some confusion last night about the precise number of victims. The total of 164 dead have been published is based on figures from Occidental Oil which, they say, include 16 bodies which have been recovered and 148 people still miss- ing. They say there are 68 sur- vivors.

Grampian police say there are 17 bodies, 150 people missing and 67 survivors, but that their figures were based on information given to them early yesterday by Occidental.

- **Full reports and pictures — Pages 2,3,4** ● **Editorial — Page 14** ● **End of a chapter — Page 15**

Parkinson promises full inquiry into disaster

By PETER HANNAM, Chief Political Correspondent

THE Energy Secretary, Mr Cecil Parkinson, yesterday promised the fullest possible public inquiry into the Piper Alpha explosion.

Giving a subdued Commons detail of the destruction of the platform, Mr Parkinson stress- ed that safety was the top priority for the Government and the North Sea operators. He said there was no common link among recent North Sea incidents.

As MPs from all parties un- ited in sympathy for the injured and bereaved and in praise for the rescue and emergency services, Mr Parkinson rejected claims that safety standards had been allowed to fall. He said Piper Alpha had been inspected and given the all-clear at the end of last month.

The Queen expressed her shock at the "dreadful disaster" and sent her sympathy to the victims and their families. She expressed admiration for the "gallant efforts of the fire-fight- ing, rescue and medical services in preventing even greater loss of life."

Mrs Thatcher, who was told of the disaster late on Wednes- day evening, and the Labour leader, Mr Neil Kinnock, voiced their sympathy and praise. She

report on the inferno, told MPs: "The Government is deter- mined to establish urgently the cause of the explosion and the lessons to be learned. Nearly 30,000 people work in the UK sector of the North Sea. They and their families have the right to expect the fullest possible investigation."

Later he promised that no time would be lost in conveying any lessons of the inquiry to other operators. He added that the success of the emergency arrangements was the only plus.

The Shadow Energy Secre- tary, Mr John Prescott, welcomed the public inquiry and said it should cover the increasing number of North Sea accidents, the reductions in health and safety inspections— and the issue of no-fault com- pensation. He said the tragedy highlighted the conflict of inter-

est within Mr Parkinson's department which was respon- sible for both safety and produc- tion.

Mr Parkinson said his depart- ment's safety procedures, oper- ated under an agency agree- ment with the Health and Safety Commission, were regarded world-wide as the best. He also insisted the number of serious accidents in the sector was fall- ing — from 101 in 1986 to 59 in 1987.

Piper Alpha had been sub- jected to a week-long annual inspection which ended on June 20. It had found there was no- thing seriously amiss with safety.

The Shadow Scottish Secre- tary, Mr Donald Dewar, said: "It is a terrible tragedy, traumatic and dreadful for the men and families involved, and a vivid reminder of the risks

and dangers of the offshore industry.

"I believe safety standards are maintained and the industry does have a good record but every effort must be made to build on this to ensure this kind of disaster is made an impossi- bility in the future."

Mrs Margaret Ewing, for the SNP, said the tragedy showed the human cost of extracting the wealth of the North Sea. "I trust the Government, which has received the vast benefits of this wealth, will be as generous as possible to the families." Mr Parkinson said he would bear her calls in mind.

The Scottish Secretary, Mr Malcolm Rifkind, said the disas- ter had brought home to people the risks borne by those employed in the North Sea oil industry, whose work was often taken for granted.

"On behalf of the people of Scotland I express my deepest sympathy and concern to those who have been injured and to the families of those who are missing and where life has been lost."

The Moderator of the General Assembly of the Church of Scot- land, the Rt Rev Prof James Whyte, said the country held in

THE SCOTSMAN

Helpless in the face of disaster

JOHN COUTTS

![main photo]

A disaster unfolds: The Liberian-registered tanker Braer, carrying 84,000 tonnes of crude oil, starts to leak as she lies grounded on the rocks in Quendale Bay, Shetland, around noon yesterday lashed by heavy seas whipped up by a Force 9 gale

Shetland's oil nightmare comes true

By Frank Urquhart and Allan McLean

SHETLAND last night stood on the brink of an ecological disaster, powerless to prevent catastrophic contamination of its coastline and marine environment by 84,000 tonnes of oil spewing from a wrecked tanker.

Emergency teams and the local population could only stand by and watch helplessly, praying for the atrocious weather to abate enough to allow a massive clean-up to begin.

In potentially one of the world's worst ecological disasters, slicks spread oily black tentacles from the deadly 19-million-gallon cargo aboard the Liberian-registered Braer, which was carrying twice as much oil as was spilt from the Exxon Valdez four years ago.

The Braer's crew of 34 were all winched off safely by helicopter rescue crews who risked their lives in appalling conditions. Desperate efforts to get lines on to the tanker from a tug failed.

The tanker, badly holed below the water line, was battered by mountainous waves which thumped her under Garth's Ness, the rocky headland in southern Shetland near where she was grounded.

Last night, there were unconfirmed reports that the vessel was beginning to break up under the constant pounding of the waves.

"It is going to be a catastrophe — there are no two questions about it. One can only hope the weather will improve before all its tanks are ruptured," Capt George Sutherland, the director of marine operations with Shetland Islands Council, told a press conference at Sumburgh.

He said that the environmental threat facing the islands was unquestionably as serious as that posed by the Exxon Valdez to Alaska in 1989.

He went on: "Eighty-four thousand tonnes of crude oil is serious on anybody's coastline and it has to be borne in mind that not all the cargo of the Exxon Valdez was released.

"At the moment, the weather conditions are so adverse, it is impossible to get anywhere near the vessel. There is considerable danger of it breaking up."

Oil-covered birds and seals were washed ashore in Quendale Bay amid fears that there could be large-scale destruction of wildlife in one of the most environmentally sensitive areas in Europe.

A flotilla of pollution control vessels and a squadron of oil dispersal planes were on standby. But winds gusting from violent storm Force 11 to hurricane Force 12 and the grounded tanker's position made it impossible to stop the spillage.

Oil spurted from the Braer when she ran aground about 11:20am after the ship had drifted out of control for ten miles. Her engine had failed, apparently because sea water had got into the fuel.

The weather, which was worsening last night, meant that it was not possible to bring another tanker alongside to take off much of the cargo, as was done when the Exxon Valdez ran aground off Alaska in a calm sea.

The Braer was driven ashore almost six hours after a desperate battle to stop the rogue tanker had begun.

Coastguards on Shetland — who said later that they had been given no time to mount a meaningful rescue operation — were alerted about 5:30am by the Greek master that the tanker, en route from Norway to Canada, had lost all power and was drifting ten miles south of Sumburgh Head.

In a last desperate attempt to stop the vessel being driven on the shore after the crew had been rescued, a four-man salvage team was winched aboard.

Members narrowly escaped death when the vessel was driven ashore by huge waves as they tried to get a line on board. They were airlifted to safety as the Braer began to break apart on the rocks.

Members of the Shetland council emergency response team and specialists from the marine pollution control unit of the Department of Transport were last night laying plans for a huge operation to deal with the pollution.

As darkness fell last night, it was apparent that most of the oil from the tanker was being contained within the small bay at Garth's Ness but the heavy swell was also dispersing huge quantities of oil to bays on either side.

Pollution-control specialists said the only mitigating factor was the fact that they were dealing with a spill of light rather than heavy crude oil. Light crude can be more easily dispersed in heavy seas and 30 per cent of the oil evaporates within a short period of time.

However, the Braer is also carrying 500 tonnes of fuel oil on board which could pose major environmental problems if it leaks into the sea.

Capt Sutherland said that the emergency services were in the hands of the wind and the tide. If the wind were to turn to the north-west then the worst of the pollution could be blown away from the beach.

"If the wind goes north-west, there is every chance that a fair big proportion of it would actually go past."

He went on: "I think it is fair to say this is the worst scenario we have expected to see around here.

"We have been gearing ourselves up for this particular circumstance over a great many years but in the full knowledge that if something like this happened in extreme weather conditions on an iron bound coast like this there is very little that can be done immediately to wave a magic wand and clean it up overnight."

Dave Okill, the environmental services director with the Shetland council, said that had the vessel run aground in the summer, the scale of the disaster would have been between 20 and 100 times worse because the rare populations of puffins and guillemots were at sea in winter.

> 'I think it is fair to say this is the worst scenario we have ever expected to see around here.'
> Capt George Sutherland

The questions that must be answered

- Why was a high-risk cargo being transported in high-risk conditions close to an environmentally important area when gale-force conditions had been forecast?
- Why did tugs not reach it in time?
- Why was there an alleged two-hour delay between the emergency signal going out from the tanker and the first tug being dispatched from Lerwick?
- Why were warnings from unions about an "inevitable" oil pollution disaster ignored?
- Are single-hulled tankers such as the Braer, which was built in 1975, too old to remain in operation?
- Is there a need to speed up the upgrading of tankers which don't have double hulls?

Full report, Page 3

SHETLAND

ATLANTIC OCEAN

Lerwick

OIL DISASTER
At 11.20am yesterday the oil tanker Braer ran aground in Quendale Bay, despite a desperate six-hour battle by the ship's crew and tug boats. The vessel, battered by Force 9 winds, was caught in a vicious "tide race" off Sumburgh Head.

FAIR ISLE

ORKNEY

Kirkwall

Graphic by KATIE MURRAY

'Sickening smell of a wounded ship'

By Tom Morton

THE SMELL is sickening, overwhelming: the smell of a ship mortally wounded. Rocking gently, huddled into the rocky shore of Garth's Ness, the Braer bleeds stinking, oily death into Quendale Bay.

As Shetland's afternoon twilight fell yesterday on the promontory, the tiny grinding movements of the broken vessel opened ever bigger holes in the for'ard and stern oil tanks.

crude oil spread through one of Britain's unspoilt natural habitats.

The brooding mass of Fitful Head with its 200 ft cliffs shadowed the scene, lurking above the tragedy like some giant voyeur. Up its slopes climbed a few determined onlookers, forbidden by police from driving to the old Ministry of Defence buildings at Garth's Ness.

Other local residents were too upset to speak much about what they had seen, and

Councillor Magnus Flaws watched the tanker's death agonies with mounting fears for the shoreline of his home area. "It was terrible to watch. Really terrible. It's an environmental disaster."

Seals and birdlife along the southern part of the Shetland mainland had already begun to suffer, he went on. "The gulls are already diving into the polluted water."

Sheep droppings, mud, a vicious rain and the unrelenting wind made it almost impossible to stand on the grassy

seemed to snuggle into the shore in its last moments of fading life.

The dirty orange funnel, bearing an M on a black and red painted flag, stood sad and proud over the bits of battered superstructure visible from the only safe vantage point, some 50 yards down wind.

Nearby one of Shetland's finest beaches was feeling the first effects of the accident. Oiled seals were being found, and the immaculate sand of Quendale was turning brown

CONTENTS

Arts	9
Business	13-16
Crosswords	4, 22
Education	17
Farming	16
Foreign	7
Gazette	12
Home	2-6
Letters	10
Lifestyle	8
Sport	19, 20, 21

INSIDE

- Defences left powerless — 2
- The ecological tragedy — 2
- Government under fire — 2
- The losing battle at sea — 3
- Questions after disaster — 3
- Catalogue of

THE SCOTSMAN

• SCOTLAND'S NATIONAL NEWSPAPER •

THURSDAY 14 MARCH 1996   PRICE 42p

THE DUNBLANE PRIMARY SCHOOL TRAGEDY: A town devastated and a nation numbed after the murder of 16 children and their teacher

Gunman who brought horror to the classroom

JOHN SMITH, STEPHEN BREEN, JIM McBETH and JAMES ROUGVIE

The man who shot dead 16 children along with their teacher in a Dunblane primary school believed he had been the victim of a smear campaign and allegations of child sex abuse.

Thomas Hamilton, 43, from Stirling, a gun club member holding firearms certificates, also wounded a further 12 children and two other teachers before turning one of his four guns on himself.

It has emerged that Hamilton, who also ran youth clubs and summer camps, had been investigated by four Scottish police forces over a number of years after allegations of inappropriate sexual behaviour, but was never prosecuted. He was known to think himself a victim of smear campaigns and resent what he saw as harassment.

The 29 five-year-old children in class P1 were in the gymnasium at Dunblane Primary,

Perthshire, when Hamilton – who police say had no history of mental illness – burst in at about 9:15am and opened fire.

Fifteen children died in the hail of bullets. Another died in hospital. Only one child escaped injury which police described as "sheer luck". Two children were off sick.

Last night, the injured children and teachers were being treated in hospitals in Stirling, Falkirk and Glasgow.

Ambulancemen who were among the first on the scene told how they found teachers trying to help and protect the injured children. "They were lying over the children and I got the impression they were trying to gather them in when they were shot," said John McEwen, the divisional manager of the Forth Valley Scottish Ambulance Service.

"We found them embracing and comforting, nursing individual children, some of whom were in a very poor way and doing their best with school first aid kits and bits and pieces.

"They were kneeling on the floor, covered in blood and cradling the heads and bodies of these wee souls with bullet holes in them. It wasn't so much the dying, it was five-year-old children looking unbelievingly at bullet holes in their arms and legs and who couldn't comprehend what was happening to them."

The class teacher, Gwen Mayor, 44, was also killed. The two other teachers, Mary Blake and Eileen Harild, were understood to have been injured as

Hamilton went to the gym. A third adult was injured but later released from hospital.

News of the shooting spread rapidly through the town, which has a population of about 7,300 and parents rushed to the school in Old Doune Road.

Police had sealed off the school and faced the awful task of giving the news to the parents of the children who had died and allowing others to take their children home. Last night, grieving families were receiving counselling.

The Scottish Secretary, Michael Forsyth, whose Stirling constituency includes Dunblane, and his Labour shadow, George Robertson, whose home is in Dunblane and whose children went to the school, visited the town.

Mr Forsyth said: "I cannot find words to express the horror at what has happened in Dunblane here today." Mr Robertson said: "We saw parents in grief and I think that's the abiding impression ... and I don't think I'll ever forget it."

Hamilton, who had no convictions for any sexual offences, was cautioned by Lothian and

Borders Police 18 months ago. Officers had spotted him with his trousers down in a compromising position with a young man in Edinburgh's Calton Hill area.

Last night, a spokesman for the procurator-fiscal service would not comment on reports that police investigations into Hamilton had not proceeded to court.

The incident brought messages of sympathy from all over the world and again raised the issues of school security and gun control.

The Queen, in a message to Mr Forsyth, said: "I was deeply shocked by the appalling news from Dunblane. In asking you to pass my deepest and most heartfelt sympathy to the families of all those who were killed or injured, and to the injured themselves, I am sure I share in the grief and horror of the whole country."

The Prime Minister, John Major, who was informed of the incident as he attended the anti-terrorism summit in Egypt, de-

scribed the massacre as a "mad and evil act", and added: "It is beyond belief that so many young lives can have been so brutally ended in this way."

The Labour leader, Tony Blair, said: "These are little children who at the weekend would have been playing with their brothers and sisters and mothers and fathers. They went to school today with the whole of their lives in front of them – now, nothing."

Alex Salmond, the leader of the Scottish National Party, said: "For so many young lives to have been ended in such a cruel and senseless manner is horrific and deeply shocking. Words cannot convey the deep horror that everyone will feel."

The Liberal Democrat leader, Paddy Ashdown, said: "At times like this, it is impossible to find words to express how you feel."

The Moderator of the General Assembly of the Church of Scotland, the Rt Rev James Harkness, said the slaughter left all civilised people "numbed and bewildered".

Hamilton, who lived in Stirling, about four miles from Dunblane, was a member of one local gun club and, only a month ago, was told he was not fit to join Callander Rifle and Pistol Club because his behaviour had been dangerous at a trial for would-be members. The club secretary, Raymond Reid, said: "He was not safe with a gun."

Just five days ago, Hamilton wrote to Buckingham Palace accusing the Scout Association of mounting a campaign to sully his reputation.

He had been forced to resign as a Scout leader more than 20 years ago after allegations of improper behaviour – and it also emerged yesterday that he had taken photographs of semi-naked boys.

No fewer than four police forces investigated Hamilton after allegations from parents about bullying by Hamilton at clubs he ran in Dunblane, Falkirk, Linlithgow and Alva.

Hamilton: Investigated by four police forces

Profile of a lone killer, Page 2

Chronicle of the shootings, Page 3

Caution over school security, Page 4

The arms control debate, Page 5

Editorial comment, Page 12

The place we call home, Page 13

'It's a massacre, a massacre ... we'll never get over it'

IAN COCHRANE

... accounts, after rumours of a ... was drowned by anguished ... and the wails of ... relatives. For the Primary 5 parents the news of their ... see the gymnasium where the atrocity occurred. "You ... The streets emptied as the dark day went on, except for ... A few yards up the road next to Dunblane's ancient cathedral local people ... Bill Saichney. "We are devastated. It all started off so quietly this morning. It ...

3am special

PRICE 35

THE SCOTSMAN

WEDNESDAY 12 SEPTEMBER 2001 ◆ SCOTLAND'S NATIONAL NEWSPAPER ◆ www.scotsman.co

A date which will live in infamy

Smoke billowing across the New York skyline yesterday after the famous twin towers of the World Trade Centre collapsed. The terrorist attack on the busy office blocks has been condemned around the world.

Picture: Hubert Michael Bo

Alastair McKay

WE HAVE seen this sort of thing before, in *King Kong*, in *Godzilla*, in *Independence Day*. But this was not the popcorn logic of Hollywood.

This horror was real. These were real lives, and real deaths – at least 10,000 of them – unrolling in real time, on live television. Yesterday's events at a calamitous rush-hour in New York and Washington resembled a disaster movie, but there were no comfortable moments of resolution or redemption.

This was a bad day, one of the worst. It was the most deadly attack on the United States since Pearl Harbour, and it leaves that country in the same uncertain state. It was a day in which the world changed, and uncertainty began to rule. It was terrorism as theatre. The US, and the West, were hit at their symbolic heart.

The twin towers were collapsing, the jagged deco peaks of New York were wreathed in smoke. This fantastic landscape, so familiar from celluloid, was under attack. The richest corner of the richest country in the world was collapsing. Steel melted. Oil prices rose. The FTSE 100 fell by 6 per cent.

The eyes of the world were fixed on TV images of the streets of lower Manhattan, the gateway to America for generations of immigrants, filled with bliz-

banks ran dry. On television, a man called Arthur Angel was talking about how he escaped the explosion. There was talk of Armageddon, and of a strange calm on the streets. Yet the US was closed, isolated, at war.

President George Bush flew to Washington to address the American people, who were struggling to come to terms with a day in which government buildings were evacuated, planes were grounded and airports closed.

Fighter aircraft patrolled the skies over Washington. US military forces around the world were put on a Delta footing, the code for imminent threat. Guards armed with automatic weapons patrolled the White House grounds.

Within hours, long lines of blood donors were queuing outside hospitals.

A stark eyewitness account of one of the hijacks came from CNN newsreader Barbara Olson, who called her husband, Solicitor-General Ted Olson, on a mobile phone seconds before the aircraft crashed into the Pentagon.

Locked in the plane's toilet, she told her husband the passengers and crew had been ordered to the back of the plane. She whispered: "What do I tell the pilot to do?"

Not since John F Kennedy faced the Cuban missile crisis

PRESIDENT Bush's address to the nation:

"Today, our fellow citizens, our way of life, our very freedom came under attack in a series of deliberate and deadly terrorist acts. The victims were in airplanes or in their offices. Secretaries, business men and women, military and federal workers. Moms and dads. Friends and neighbours.

"Thousands of lives were suddenly ended by evil, despicable acts of terror.

"The pictures of airplanes flying into buildings, fires burning, huge structures collapsing, have filled us with disbelief, terrible sadness and a quiet, unyielding anger. These acts of mass murder were intended to frighten our nation into chaos and retreat. But they have failed. Our country is strong. A great people has been moved to defend a great nation.

"Terrorist attacks can shake the foundations of our biggest buildings, but they cannot touch the foundation of America. These acts shatter steel, but they cannot dent the steel of American resolve. America was targeted for attack because we're the brightest beacon for freedom and opportunity in the world. And no-one will keep that light from shining.

"Today, our nation saw evil, the very worst of human nature, and we responded

with the best of America, with the daring of our rescue workers, with the caring for strangers and neighbours who came to give blood and help in any way they could. Immediately following the first attack, I implemented our government's emergency response plans. Our military is powerful, and it's prepared. Our emergency teams are working in New York City and Washington, D.C., to help with local rescue efforts.

"Our first priority is to get help to those who have been injured and to take every precaution to protect our citizens at home and around the world from further attacks. The functions of our government continue without interruption. Federal agencies in Washington, which had to be evacuated today, are reopening for essential personnel tonight and will be open for business tomorrow.

"Our financial institutions remain strong, and the American economy will be open for business as well.

"The search is under way for those who are behind these evil acts. I've directed the full resources of our intelligence and law enforcement communities to find those responsible and bring them to justice. We will make no distinction between the terrorists who committed these acts and

those who harbour them.

"I appreciate so very much the members of Congress who have joined me in strongly condemning these attacks. "And on behalf of the American people, I thank the many world leaders who have called to offer their condolences and assistance. America and our friends and allies join with all those who want peace and security in the world and we stand together to win the war against terrorism.

"Tonight I ask for your prayers for all those who grieve, for the children whose worlds have been shattered, for all whose sense of safety and security has been threatened. And I pray they will be comforted by a power greater than any of us spoken through the ages in Psalm 23. 'Even though I walk through the valley of the shadow of death, I fear no evil for you are with me.'

"This is a day when all Americans from every walk of life unite in our resolve for justice and peace. America has stood down enemies before, and we will do so this time.

"None of us will ever forget this day, yet we go forward to defend freedom and all that is good and just in our world.

"**Thank you. Good night and God bless America.**"

we, the democracies of this world, are going to have to come together to fight it together and eradicate this evil."

The Prime Minister then travelled to London to chair a meeting of the Cabinet's emergency Cobra committee.

NATO ambassadors were summoned to an emergency meeting in Brussels, after which the Secretary-General, Lord Robertson, pledged the support of his organisation. "NATO solidarity remains the essence of our alliance," he said. "Our message to the people of the United States is that we are with you."

But words of support can do nothing to take away from the enormity of what has happened. On the ground, in Manhattan, emergency workers didn't dare estimate the number of fatalities, but is likely to run into thousands. Up to 40,000 people were thought to have been in the towers when the planes crashed.

The facts are bare enough. Between 8:45 and 9:05am, the twin towers were hit by two hijacked American Airlines planes. The buildings, which had survived a car bomb attack in 1993, which killed six people and injured more than 1,000 others, burst into flames.

Just before 9:30am, President Bush, in Florida, made a statement saying the US would hunt down the perpetrators.

Minutes later, the Pentagon was hit by a United Airlines

Airlines plane crashed Pittsburgh. It is believe plane was flying towards David when it was forced ground by US air force je

The fallout from yest events is impossible to late. Financial trading American markets is like affected for several days, the concentration of fi businesses in and arou World Trade Centre.

The US Federal Reserve man, Alan Greenspan, but returned to a secret l in Switzerland. Analys gested that the event push the US econom recession.

American sources ha renegade Saudi terroris bin Laden as the lead row as the sentencing o Bin Laden associate for in the 1998 bombing embassy in Tanzania. tencing was scheduled place at a court near the Trade Centre.

Explosions rock Afghan capital Kabul night, but a former US Secretary said it was u be a US reprisal attack.

Thousands of Pale celebrated in the We town of Nablus, but th were condemned b Arafat. "We are co shocked. It's unbeliev Arafat told reporters.

At Pearl Harbour,

ently unaware of the terrorist activity which must have taken extensive planning, and failed to protect the air space around the Pentagon. A defiant President Bush told the National Security Council: "We will find these people and they will suffer the consequences. Nobody will diminish the spirit of this coun-

warning, he said: "First things first, his concern is with the health and security of the American people and with the families of those who have lost their lives. There will come an appropriate time to do all appropriate lookbacks."

Public opinion usually rallies behind the president during

would meet with Yasser Arafat at the UN next month, but it is now far from clear whether that visit will take place.

The US Secretary of State, Colin Powell, told a meeting of the Organisation of American States in Lima, Peru, that a "terrible, terrible tragedy" had befallen the US.

ing display of national unity by singing *God Bless America* on the steps of Capitol Hill.

Democrats and Republicans, normally at each other's throats, burst into song after observing a moment's silence for the victims of the attacks.

Tony Blair, the Prime Minister, had cancelled a keynote

NEWSPAPER OF THE YEAR

THE SCOTSMAN

SCOTLAND'S NATIONAL NEWSPAPER   £1 SUBSCRIPTION PRICE: 75p   WWW.SCOTSMAN.COM

AY 3 AUGUST 2012

The Greatest

- **Tears on podium as Hoy powers to fifth gold medal**
- **Scot becomes Britain's most successful Olympian**
- **World record smashed on glory night at velodrome**

PAGES 3-5, PLUS 12-PAGE PULL-OUT

OSSWORDS AND GAMES 2 & 46, TELEVISION & RADIO 44-45, LETTERS 32-33, WEATHER 47, ANNOUNCEMENTS 42, SUDOKU 46

Chapter fourteen:

Books and writers

Literature has always been important to *The Scotsman*. Right at the outset this was reflected in the name, which to give it its full title was *The Scotsman or Edinburgh Political and Literary Journal*. In 1817, the year of the paper's birth, it published a review of Sir Walter Scott's novel *Rob Roy*.

In the early days only literary advertising was accepted.

The close relationship with literature has endured throughout the years, and the paper is now the publisher of the longest running serial novel in the world thanks to author Alexander McCall Smith.

The award-winning author best known for *The No1 Ladies Detective Agency* series of books began his *44 Scotland Street* series, a novel about the residents of a street in Edinburgh's New Town, in 2004 when it was published daily in *The Scotsman*, a return to an honoured tradition in newspapers of publishing daily novels.

It has appeared over a period of three months every year since then, netting it the global title.

Also in 2004 Edinburgh was granted the status of the first ever UNESCO City of Literature, and there is a very close connection to *The Scotsman* in that.

Up until then UNESCO had no cities of literature, but four book lovers in Edinburgh were determined to persuade the organisation that they should have, as a means of promoting literature and forming a global partnership of creative cities – and that Edinburgh should be the first.

Those four enthusiasts were James Boyle, former controller of BBC Radio 4 and a former chair of the Scottish Arts Council, Jenny Brown, one of the UK's leading literary agents, Lorraine Fannin, director of the Scottish Publishers' Association and Catherine Lockerbie, who had been the Literary Editor for *The Scotsman* and a leader writer for the paper. She had gone on to be the director of the Edinburgh International Book Festival.

There is even a *Scotsman* connection to Edinburgh-born Arthur Conan Doyle and the creation of one of his most enduring characters: Dr Watson.

A 20-year-old Conan Doyle broke off his medical studies at Edinburgh University to fill the post of surgeon on a whaler, the Hope, out of Peterhead.

While on the ship one of the highlights for him were the copies of *The Scotsman* his mother used to send him. His diaries confirm: "The mail steamer St Magnus came in with a letter from home and one from Letty and also a week's Scotsmen. Satisfactory news."

Later in the voyage he describes reading about the Battle of Maiwand in *The Scotsman*: "Lighthouse keeper came off with last week's weekly Scotsman by which we learn of the defeat in Afghanistan. Terrible news."

That news was to stay with him and when his character Dr John Watson is narrating the first Sherlock Holmes story, a Study in Scarlet, the former army surgeon reveals: "I was removed from my brigade and attached to the Berkshires, with whom I served at the fatal battle of Maiwand. There I was struck on the shoulder by a Jezail bullet."

Conan Doyle also wrote a letter to *The Scotsman*, correcting a reader's erroneous identification of a killer whale. Conan Doyle had seen many of these creatures, in those days also known as

Sherlock Holmes (r) and Dr. John H. Watson.
Illustration by Sidney Paget from the Sherlock Holmes story The Greek Interpreter.

Arthur Conan Doyle. Walter Benington

swordfish, and there are drawings of them in his diaries.

His letter states: "That frightful creature the swordfish, the scourge of the northern seas, is a very different fish to the poor 'lang-nebbit' brute which TG confuses it with."

But Edinburgh is a city that even in modern times is associated with literary greats. There can be no doubt that JK Rowling is one of the most successful authors of all time, she is the UK's best-selling living author, her *Harry Potter* books can rightly be called a phenomenon.

That success has brought the author wealth, she is currently thought to be worth £650m, but she is also noted for her philanthropy and work for charities.

Now her rags to riches story is well-known, in fact the author has seemed to want to shift away from it in recent years, but in this article from *The Scotsman's* archives from the year that the first *Harry Potter* book was published Ms Rowling talks openly about the poverty she faced and how she hoped she would be an inspiration to other women. And she is also referred to as Joanne, again something that seems a little odd today.

Coffee in one hand, baby in another: a recipe for success

By JUDITH WOODS

A woman sat in the corner of the busy cafe, pen in one hand, espresso in the other and baby in a pram by her side. Around her plates clattered, waiters tripped backwards and forwards in their starched white aprons and the customers chattered over pains au chocolat. The woman didn't seem to notice the chaos in the large wooden-floored space. She was writing a children's book and the only place she could find which was warm – and for the price of a 90p espresso would let her sit quietly all day – was Nicolson's cafe on Edinburgh's South Bridge.

When children's author Joanne Rowling recalls her darkest days, there is a shiver in her voice. But the poverty, the depression and the clammy chill of her one-bedroomed Edinburgh flat where the single mother who had fallen on hard times sought to keep her baby daughter warm, pall in comparison to the looming loss of her identity. "The feeling of who I was was badly damaged by suddenly finding myself a single parent on benefits," says Rowling. "So I wrote to protect my sanity. I have always written and so it was a way of continuing to be me, despite all the ghastly circumstances."

There is no romance to the starving-artist in-a-garret existence at the best of times. With a baby to feed and clothe and fret over, it possibly constitutes the worst of times. "There were times when Jessica ate and I didn't. I feel like it's a case of 'cue the Hovis music' when I say that, but it's true, however it sounds.

"When I fetched up in Edinburgh I was pretty much penniless and it was a complete shock to my system." Her marriage to a Portuguese TV journalist had disintegrated when their daughter Jessica was just three and a half months old and she had moved to Edinburgh to be with her sister.

Rowling, 32, has just picked up a prestigious literary award, the Nestle Smarties Book Prize, for her children's book Harry Potter and the Philosopher's Stone. It is the latest success in a string of events which have seen her rocketed into the league of high-earning professionals, with rival companies bidding for the film rights and a massive six-figure advance.

Nursing a single cup of coffee, she sits in a cafe for hours, and, as her baby daughter sleeps, in laborious long-hand she feverishly writes a children's story about a lonely little boy, Harry Potter, who escapes his Dickensian misery by becoming a wizard. The magic is catching. When she sends off the manuscript, to an agent, it is admittedly more in hope than expectation, but a fairy tale ending is in store: a £100,000 US publishing deal for the first of seven books, and four companies, two of them Hollywood studios – tussling for the movie rights. Yet if this rags-to-riches tale of real-life smacks, unavoidably, of cliche, the resulting fiction has been hailed as inventive storytelling at its best. Potter, a little orphan boy, is persecuted by his nagging relatives until at 11 he boards the train for Hogwarts School of Wizardry and Witchcraft, after which his life will never be the same again. The same can justifiably be said about Rowling herself. Still based in Edinburgh, the city she "instantly fell in love with", her living conditions are a far cry from her first dank city-centre flat. But her experience of the rough end of life has been a salutary one and she remembers the little kindnesses rendered to her in times of need. "It is an escapist book and by writing it I was escaping into it. I would go to Nicolson's cafe, because the staff were so nice and so patient there and allowed me to order one espresso and sit there for hours, writing until Jessica woke up. You can get a hell of a lot of writing done in two hours if you know that's the only chance you are going to get." For its part, the cafe staff was quite happy to let inspiration take its course.

"We all know Joanne and Jessica," says general manager Roland Thomson. "They would come in almost every day, and the wee girl would sleep while her mother wrote. It was really sweet." Rowling says her sympathies go out to single parents in a similar position, while acknowledging that her good fortune is not the kind of thing everyone in the poverty-trap can realistically emulate.

"When Harry Potter was published there seemed to be an aura of amazement that a single mother could produce anything worthwhile, which is pretty offensive.

"I would hope that other women would see what I've done as inspirational, but on the other hand I know I was very lucky.

"I had a 'saleable talent', to put it crudely, and I also had an education, so even if I hadn't written the book I would have had the raw materials to rebuild my life."

The staff at Nicolson's make no secret of their pride at Rowling's success. She is still one of their most regular customers, but in one respect at least fame has changed her: now she can afford to eat lunch.

JK Rowling at the Edinburgh International Book Festival in 2004.

Chapter fifteen:

Independence and a' that

In recent years there is absolutely no doubt that the political environment of Scotland has been dominated by the independence issue. Now almost every political shift in the UK and abroad is seen in Scotland through the prism of the constitutional question.

And that has been the case for probably longer than most people think. The argument for home rule for Scotland raged for decades, and the Labour party had been in favour of devolution, although there was much impassioned debate within the party on what devolution might bring.

In 1977 the much respected Labour maverick Tam Dalyell, who described devolution as "a motorway to independence with no exits" wrote a book entitled *Devolution: The End of Britain?*

And in it he wrote: "And the tragedy is that it could well be brought about by well-meaning politicians who fail to realise the full implications of what they are doing in their feverish - and quite unnecessary - anxiety to appease small yet vociferous nationalist minorities in Scotland and Wales."

But Dalyell was something of a rebel within the Labour party, and there were those closer to the heart of the party who passionately believed that devolution would satisfy the Scottish appetite for going its own way. They thought that people would no longer see the need for full independence if they had control of certain key areas like health and education.

George Robertson said in 1995, when he was shadow Scottish Secretary, that "devolution will kill nationalism stone dead."

So when Tony Blair swept to power in 1997 with his landslide victory the Labour party had made a manifesto commitment for a devolution referendum in Scotland, and only four months later the Scottish people were asked to vote on whether they wanted a Scottish parliament, and whether that parliament should have tax raising powers.

The Scotsman was firmly in favour of a Yes Yes vote. The victory marked a watershed in Scottish politics and *The Scotsman*, like the country, was conscious of the historic nature of the decision. So when it came to reporting the opening of the first Scottish parliament for almost 300 years, it did not stint itself in its coverage. Award-winning journalist Ian Bell gave this considered and intelligent insight in the edition of *The Scotsman* published on the day of the opening ceremony.

And now it begins

ONCE THE FLAGS HAVE BEEN FOLDED AND PUT AWAY, THE SPEECHES ARE DONE AND THE CELEBRITIES HAVE GONE HOME … THEN THE HARD WORK MUST BE STARTED

By IAN BELL

Anyone can make a parliament. All you need to do is hold an election, book a hall, invite a head of state, stage a procession and make few speeches. The hard part comes when you try to make a good parliament.

There was nothing inevitable about the creation of a devolved parliament for Scotland under a semi-proportional voting system and a constitution whose central principle works against the sharing of power.

Most Conservatives did not want it, believing it would break Britain on a point of constitutional logic. Most Nationalists did not want it, seeing it either as inadequate to the needs of the nation or as a trap designed to snare them. Most Liberals, keen on the philosophy, would nevertheless have preferred to see it created as part of a coherent federal system. And Labour? Old habits die hard. Enthusiasm for devolution is not yet universal within the People's Party. Some were early converts to home rule, some late, and some – though we are no longer supposed to say so – have never been reconciled.

For those last, in particular, the first taste of a measure of PR has not served to gladden hearts. But here, today, we have it: the official opening of a new European legislature that is not, in its design, precisely what anyone wanted.

Optimists will regard that as the beginnings of healthy and civilised compromise. The politicians, who talk constantly of making the parliament work, will understand better the different demands about to be made on each of the parties if this electoral and constitutional novelty is to succeed.

But the people? The people in whose name and so forth and so on all this is being done?

In Edinburgh, at least, the word history is beginning to hang a little heavy over a town that has more than its share of the stuff. The citizens who saw their cars towed away by the dozen from city centre streets a couple of nights ago for the sake of the rehearsal for today's proceedings will probably not regard their trip to the pound as particularly historic.

The rest of us, meanwhile, have perhaps enjoyed (or endured) quite enough epoch-making moments to be going on with lately, what with a historic referendum, historic elections, and a historic reconvening of parliamentarians, to be entirely roused. In the capital, the inevitable disruption caused by today's events will certainly lose a few commuting hearts and minds, at least for now. There is, in any case, a touch of disenchantment in the air and a slight sense of anti-climax.

YES 74% FOR A SCOTTISH PARLIAMENT YES 63% FOR TAX-VARYING POWER

A nation again

war hails 'great' as voters give ssive support home rule

acMAHON
litical Editor

e have spoken. Em-
and unequivocally it
es to a Scottish par-
th tax-varying pow-

rds of the late John
eated so often in the
eeks, were proved to

ule is the settled will
tish nation. The un-
usiness will be fin-

was claimed in the
rs by Donald Dewar,
tish Secretary, for
result was a personal
The devolution refer-
Government had in-
before it would leg-
eturn a parliament to
h after nearly 300
produced the man-
e feared the people
t deliver.

g the end of the long,
ne-rule road on which
avelled for more than

Mr Dewar declared:
great day for Scotland,
e most important days
ountry's long history.
ple have seized the

the ill-fated referen-
1979, Scotland was
its support for the
of devolution. From
and Galloway in the
-west to Orkney and
, in the north the people
s to the first question on
ciple with only a few
ecting the proposition
parliament should have
ers.

43am the final result
Highlands put a seal on
ric night with 72 per
ng Yes for a parliament
per cent for tax pow-

Blair, who was roundly
ed when he insisted
referendum as leader of
osition, welcomed the
Prime Minister said:
osolutely delighted that

reforms, including of the House
of Lords, to follow. The Prime
Minister said: "A new modern
constitution is an essential part
of the new politics and the new
Britain we want to build."

The Scottish Secretary
claimed victory after just two
results when it became clear
that the Scots had voted by
three-to-one for the principle of
a devolved parliament and by a
comfortable majority to give it
tax-varying powers with a respectable turnout of about 60
per cent. Just over 2.4 million
people voted.

Legislation will now be introduced in Westminster in the
autumn and a devolved Scottish
parliament seems certain to be
sitting in Edinburgh by the new
millennium.

The Scottish Office minister
Brian Wilson said: "It's not just
a victory, it's not just Yes, Yes, it's
a moral authority and the settled will of the Scottish people
has been established.

"That is important to the parliamentary process in the short
term and the authority of the
constitutional settlement."

Mr Dewar said: "The people
recognised the moment, we
have done the business."

He said that they had en-
dorsed the Government's proposals for a Scottish parliament
with real powers. It was, he
added, a proud day for him,
especially after the decision in
the 1979 referendum and the
following 18 years of Tory
government.

The Scottish Office would today, he promised, begin to put
together the Scotland Act and
that the parliament would be up
and running by the year 2000.

"For the people of Scotland
that will be our celebration. A
new Scotland for a new millennium."

As the trickle of results from
the 32 councils across Scotland
became a torrent, the Tories
and the No.No Think Twice
campaign admitted defeat.

A former Tory minister, Lord
Mackay of Ardbrecknish, ad-

wiped out at the general election the Scottish Tory deputy
chairman, Annabel Goldie, reflected on a further election set-
back: "By any standards it is a
historic moment for Scotland. It
is really quite breathtaking."

conflict between London and
Edinburgh.

Andrew Hunter, the Tory MP
for Basingstoke, told The Scotsman: "The people have spoken –
damn the people."

As only the second result
came in from South Lanark-

a journey and the end of this
journey will be independence.

"For the first time in 300
years we are going to have a
parliament in Scotland. Scotland has done it with a bang and
not whimper." However, he denied that independence would
necessarily follow swiftly on the
heels of a Scottish parliament.

At 12:45am, Clackmannan-
shire became the first council to
declare a result, delivering a
resounding Yes to both questions. By 3:37am the Yes vote
had achieved a majority of the
total votes on the first question
as the total passed the 1.2 million with the declaration from
Fife. At 4:07am a clear majority
emerged for the question which
the opponents said would never

powers but reversing the anti-
devolution result in the isles in
1979.

The final turnout figure was
seen as effectively spiking the
guns of the opponents of devolution who had counted on
basing their opposition to home
rule on a lack of a mandate
from a low turnout.

Before the campaign proper
began, Mr Dewar had privately
expressed the hope that the
turnout would be above 60 per
cent in order to demonstrate
that devolution had the clear
support of the Scottish people.

A turnout which exceeded 60
per cent with a Yes,Yes result
will be seen as delivering a clear
mandate to the Government to
press ahead and legislate for

Scottish Secretary Donald Dewar hears the first declaration – overwhelming support for Yes, Yes – with Chief Secretary to the Treasury, Alistair Darling.   Picture: l

Big margins across the nation, Page 2
Glasgow's support for tax power, Page 3
New dawn is just the beginning, Page 4
Normal service is resumed, Page 5
The Wee County leads the country, Page 6
It's time to make a difference, Page 7
Blair faces federal demands, Page 9
Vigil ends and the party begins, Page 26

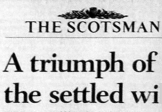

THE SCOTSMAN

A triumph of the settled wi

THE turn-out could have been a little better, perh
but not by much. The result itself, the swee
triumph for reform, could scarcely have been
passed.

The consequences of defeat yesterday wer

THE SCOTSMAN

FRIDAY 2 JULY 1999   ♦ SCOTLAND'S NATIONAL NEWSPAPER ♦   PRICE 45p

A moment anchored in Scotland's history

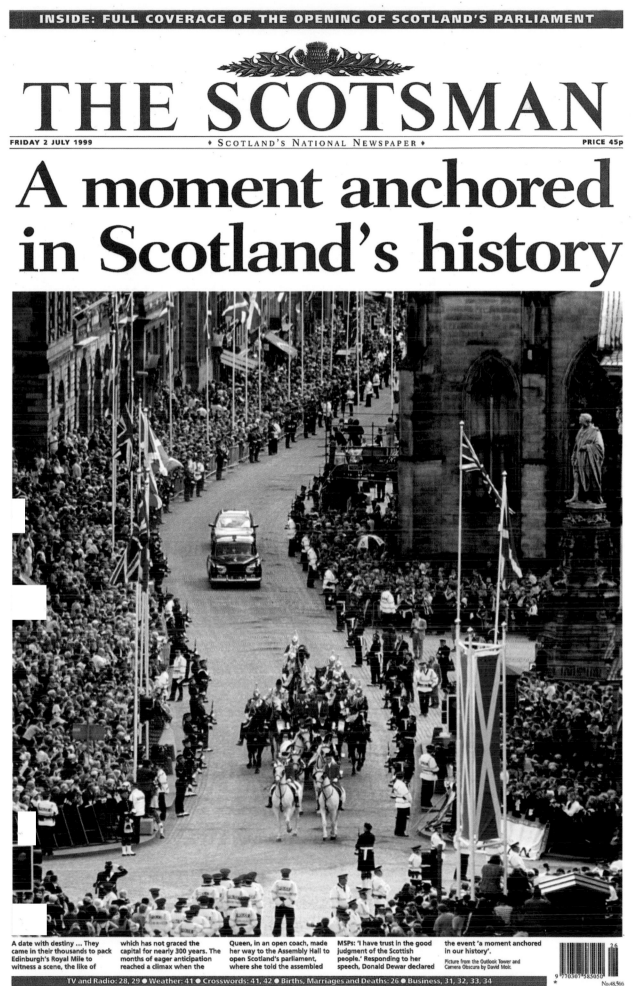

A date with destiny ... They came in their thousands to pack Edinburgh's Royal Mile to witness a scene, the like of which has not graced the capital for nearly 300 years. The months of eager anticipation reached a climax when the Queen, in an open coach, made her way to the Assembly Hall to open Scotland's parliament, where she told the assembled MSPs: 'I have trust in the good judgment of the Scottish people.' Responding to her speech, Donald Dewar declared the event 'a moment anchored in our history'.

Picture from the Outlook Tower and Camera Obscura by David Moir.

No.48,566

And the next day he gave this very personal description of the events of the day.

FRIDAY, 2 JULY, 1999

Celebration for the great, the good and the rest

By IAN BELL

Sunshine on Leith. Sunshine folding over New Town and Old, sunshine bent over every northern vista in Edinburgh, poured in warm streams northwards to the expanse of the Forth and south to the green Border. Sunshine with a fleck of white cloud here and there, making the architecture, turning the morning grey into soft browns and yellows. Sunshine on faces. A good morning, a good day. The worst you could say of 1 July, 1999, is that no-one had the wit or the will to declare a public holiday.

People who decide such things wanted a big day for Scotland but not – on balance, you understand? – too big a day. Some might have got ideas. In consequence all the children who ought to have been freed from the last, lazy, pointless hours of the school term were not permitted, through official wisdom, to glimpse their own future. Their heritage is video tape. A pity.

It took a morning, for all that, to complete the formalities of the final devolution of power from Westminster to a Scottish parliament housed in temporary quarters on the Mound.

We had MSPs in procession, a fragment of Windsor pomp, pipe bands and a thundering fly-past from Concorde escorted by the Red Arrows. We had a man in a kilt at our elbows muttering about "Alba" and a Spanish tourist who said "fiesta" in an amused voice.

Children in push-chairs wanted to be held up to see what could be seen and the students massed with banners on George IV Bridge wanted the government to know what it could do, constitutional innovations notwithstanding, with tuition fees.

They were having a good time. Even the police were having a good time. Not everything was new or fun or reassuring, of course. As the clock struck nine, the Duke of Hamilton, Scotland's senior peer, claiming the right and given the rite, for reasons unexplained, marched out of the Great Hall of Edinburgh Castle carrying all four bejewelled pounds of the Crown of Scotland.

For escort he had feudal gibberish: the Rothesay Herald of Arms, the Ross Herald of Arms, the Lord Lyon, King of Arms. With merely one pair of arms the duke signed a receipt for his cargo: "Honours, Scotland, in transit" or some such.

Down in the streets of the Old Town beneath the Castle, where the mob once raged to prevent an incorporating union between Scotland and England, tourists and natives waved their little paper Saltires.

Opposite Parliament Square and the entrance to St Giles, the people responsible for raising a new parliament's home had hung a banner from their office windows promising that Holyrood would be ready by 2001.

THE QUEEN MAKES HER WAY DOWN THE HIGH STREET FOLLOWED BY THE HOUSEHOLD CAVALRY. PICTURE SHOWS RIDER FALLEN FROM HORSE IN FRONT OF CAR
Scottish Parliament 1999 Opening Ceremony.

Donald Dewar and the Queen at the opening ceremony of the Scottish Parliament in 1999.

The Duke of Hamilton presents the Queen with the Scottish crown.

The Red Arrows and Concorde fly over Princes Street.

Sean Connery with his wife Micheline and SNP leader Alex Salmond in the crowd.

In 2006 I had lunch with Alex Salmond at Duck's Restaurant in Edinburgh's New Town. Lunches with senior politicians were a regular thing, and he had phoned up and invited me, so along I went. What was quite unusual was that it was just the two of us, he did not have a PR minder, adviser or bag carrier. He just turned up on his own.

During that lunch he talked me through how he saw the future of Scotland and the future of the Scottish National Party, and how closely the two were tied.

He said that the SNP would win the Holyrood elections in 2007 and form a government. He said it would be the SNP's aim to show the Scottish public that they were a steady hand on the tiller, they would avoid the scandals that had beset Labour, and would build confidence in their ability to govern.

At the same time they would point out wherever relevant where the powers of devolution were wanting when it came to meeting the needs of the Scottish people. He said this would be more fertile ground if there was a Tory government in Westminster.

And he emphasised that this would be a long period, a lengthy process but would in time convince more and more Scots of the SNP's ability to run the country in the best interests of the Scottish people, and convince them of the benefits of independence.

He is a man who is not short of confidence, but back in 2006 it seemed to me then he was being somewhat over optimistic.

But he got almost everything right. The only part that he did not foresee was just how successful they would be (helped by the implosion of the Labour party of course) he did not expect the Scottish National Party getting an overall majority in the Scottish Parliament in 2011. Given the way the parliament was set up and the voting system used, an overall majority for anyone was supposed to be impossible in practical terms. Not so much.

And that meant that a bill for a referendum on Scottish independence would get through the Scottish Parliament. I got the impression this had come a little early for the SNP's grand strategy, but by then it couldn't be stopped.

So the referendum on independence was to dominate Scottish politics until the vote in 2014. Everything was seen in that context. It was a debate that inspired passion, and that split the country, sometimes in the most acrimonious way.

My view as editor of *The Scotsman* was that we had to be fair, balanced and accurate in our news reporting and that we would give as broad a spectrum of opinion as possible. We wanted to have voices from all parts of the political spectrum, and many of them. For me this was the biggest debate in Scotland for centuries and it was the job of the newspaper to ensure that debate was had, that debate was public and it was as thorough as it possibly could be. We had to give our readers the information they needed to make an informed choice. We had to ask questions of all. And we encouraged non-political organisations to have a say in the debate, to make their feelings known, because it was about the country and went beyond politics. Some did, many Scottish organisations, conscious of the bitterness of the divide and wary of consequences either from the public or from a vengeful government, did not.

I say we achieved those aims in our coverage, although I know I will not convince everyone that was the case. But I am confident that reasonable opinion backs me up, and here is why.

Because *The Scotsman* had urged others to get involved, and because organisations and individuals had, bravely in some cases, made their views known, I felt that we had to do the same.

We had discussions among the senior journalists in the office, and the very practical risks in terms of how circulation and advertising revenue might be impacted were considered. But in my view the reputational damage to *The Scotsman* for not declaring an opinion on the most important decision Scotland had faced for centuries far outweighed the risks. For me it was incumbent upon a newspaper such as ours to do so.

I also thought it was incumbent upon me to write it. So I went in to the office at 6am for three mornings to get the peace needed, and I wrote *The Scotsman's* leading article on the referendum for independence.

On the night we were going to press with our article I received a phone call from the First Minister's office and his adviser said that they had heard we were going to declare and could I tell him in advance which way we were going to go?

For me that phone call is a convincing indication that we had fulfilled our aims, and that our coverage had been balanced and broad and shown no obvious favour. I take great pride in that.

But I said I would not tell them, they would have to wait until the morning. This is what they read.

THURSDAY, SEPTEMBER 11, 2014

Scotland's decision

We have been given a historic opportunity. We have a say in a decision that will have a fundamental and far-reaching impact on all our lives, our country and its future. We will all make that decision on where we believe the best interests of Scotland and the Scottish people lie. We will make that decision from a position of pride in our country and belief in ourselves.

One of the questions at the heart of the referendum debate has been: "Could Scotland be a successful independent country?" There is only one answer to that: of course it could. We are a nation of innovative and hard-working people, with a culture of altruism and egalitarianism. We can stand alongside any country in the world, large or small, and hold our own. Scotland could be a successful independent country, but next week's question is: "Should Scotland be an independent country?" What we then have to look at is whether this is where the greatest success will lie. As we approach this pivotal

moment in our history, there are issues to be weighed and measured.

There are some areas where straight answers are not clear, and they are not only worthy of examination but it is absolutely crucial that examination takes place. The debate has seen strong arguments on both sides and throughout we have endeavoured to air all arguments fairly and give a voice to as many shades of opinion as possible. That will continue regardless of the position we take on the referendum today.

Perhaps the first area to be examined is currency. The Scottish Government's preferred option is a formal currency union between an independent Scotland and the rest of the UK (rUK). The Scottish Government has accepted that our best economic interests lie with the pound. The Governor of the Bank of England, Mark Carney, said in a speech in Edinburgh that, for a formal currency union to be possible, an independent Scotland would

have to cede some sovereignty. He said this week that a currency union between rUK and an independent Scotland would be "incompatible with sovereignty" and both statements probably amount to the same thing; that some political power over factors that would have an impact on the currency would have to sit with the remainder of the UK. We don't know exactly how much sovereignty we would have to cede yet.

There are other problems with a formal currency union that would allow Scotland to continue operating under the UK economic mantle. The three main Westminster political parties have declared against it, saying they will not enter in to one. The First Minister has dismissed this as "bluff and bluster", saying that position will change after a Yes vote. To add pressure to bring about that change, the First Minister has said that if rUK won't share the Bank of England in a formal currency union then Scotland would not pay any share of the UK's accumulated £1.6 trillion of

First Minister Alex Salmond delivers his final message to the people of Scotland at the Perth Concert Hall on the eve of the Scottish Independence Referendum.

Gordon Brown speaks at Gilmerton Miners Welfare Club in Edinburgh before the Referendum.

SCOTLAND'S DECISION

With exactly a week to go before our historic referendum *The Scotsman* gives its verdict on the choice before us: we are better together

COMMENT

WE HAVE been given a historic opportunity. We have a say in a decision that will have a fundamental and far-reaching impact on all our lives, our country and its future. We will all make that decision on where we believe the best interests of Scotland and the Scottish people lie. We will make that decision from a position of pride in our country and belief in ourselves.

One of the questions at the heart of the referendum debate has been: "Could Scotland be a successful independent country?" There is only one answer to that: of course it could. We are a nation of innovative and hard-working people, with a culture of altruism and egalitarianism. We can stand alongside any country in the world, large or small, and hold our own.

Scotland could be a successful independent country, but next week's question is: "Should Scotland be an independent country?" What we then have to look at is whether this is where the greatest success will lie.

As we approach this pivotal moment in our history, there are issues to be weighed and measured. There are some areas where straight answers are not clear, and they are not only worthy of examination but it is absolutely crucial that examination takes place.

The debate has seen strong arguments on both sides and throughout we have endeavoured to air all arguments fairly and give a voice to as many shades of opinion as possible. That will continue regardless of the position we take on the referendum today.

Perhaps the first area to be examined is currency. The Scottish Government's preferred option is a formal currency union between an independent Scotland and the rest of the UK (rUK). The Scottish Government has accepted that our

CONTINUED ON PAGE 2

ROSSWORDS AND GAMES 4 & 46, **TELEVISION & RADIO** 44-45, **LETTERS** 34-35, **WEATHER** 47, **ANNOUNCEMENTS** 42, **SUDOKU** 46

debt. It is argued that Scotland would have no legal or moral obligation to pay that debt. What English politician would lay his people open to that financial cost, goes the argument. And although this rejection of formal currency union may be political posturing, because that's what politicians do, and of course pledges have been broken in the past, underlying a formal currency union is a political decision that would seem to be difficult to thole if you were an rUK politician. You would be asking the people of your country, with their savings and assets and taxes, to be the ultimate backing for a foreign country. A foreign country that has just decided to leave a union with you and set out on its own. And all this when the very real banking collapse is still a vivid memory with the effects still being felt. Those taxpayers are already unwittingly large stakeholders in the Royal Bank of Scotland. That has to be a difficult ask. And it may well be right, under the law, following a Treasury statement to reassure money markets, that Scotland has no legal responsibility for the UK's debts and the UK has taken full responsibility for them, but the assertion that Scotland has no moral obligation for part of that debt will sit awkwardly with a lot of Scots; Scotland had a part in running up that debt. Is it fair and right to walk away from that?

Is it the best way to start a new relationship with a country that is still going to be your closest partner and ally? Should the politicians all act as they have said they will, and refuse a formal currency union, the most likely fall-back position is sterlingisation – an informal currency union where we just keep the pound. But there are significant problems with an informal currency union without any political union. There are arguments over the effects of this and the cost of this, but regardless of them, political power over decisions that could affect Scotland's currency would sit in London with no input from Scotland.

It is clear that any currency union would leave some power residing outside Scotland. But we don't know how much. We also do not know what impact Scotland walking away from the UK debt would have – some say the markets would welcome a debt-free country which had the nous to get itself in to that position and it could then borrow at really good rates, others that would be regarded as untrustworthy defaulters. We just don't know.

And in the event of Scotland going its own way on a new currency, that would also probably have an impact on borrowing costs and interest rates. What can we take from all that? It seems highly likely that there will be a cost implication here, but we don't know what it is.

The issue with EU membership and what that brings is also a difficult one. It seems clear now that Scotland will not be automatically and immediately accepted as a member of the EU and that there will be some admission procedure to be gone through. We do currently fulfil many of the convergence criteria, but what we would have to do for membership is unclear. It may well be the case that common sense on the rest of Europe's part would be to accept Scotland in, and that we would be welcomed as a valuable member, but there is no certainty of that.

Possibly of greater consequence is doubt over some of the special agreements the UK has negotiated and enjoys over the euro, borders and rebates. This whole issue is, of course, complicated by the doubt over the UK's position in Europe, with the referendum on membership promised by David Cameron. But it is probably wise not to let that form a part in Scotland's decision, given there are fairly fundamental questions, not least whether Mr Cameron will still be in power in 2017 to deliver on his promise.

So, in tick-list terms then: Europe is generally seen as a good thing for Scotland, but the future for an independent Scotland in Europe is unclear. We just don't know what the terms of that would be.

Defence is another major issue. It is said that the primary responsibility of the state is the safety of its citizens. Some people will vote for independence just because it will come with a pledge to clear nuclear weapons from our country. Weapons of mass destruction are an emotive subject, there are deep and fundamental issues about their morality. There surely must be huge doubts about whether our society now would mandate their use in any circumstances, there are questions over their military value given the changing nature of the threats to our security, and there is the far more pragmatic question of their cost for their perceived benefit.

But those issues should be

separated from Scotland's constitutional future. The proposal, as things stand, is that an independent Scotland would become nuclear-free but would still be a member of Nato. How we can take the principled stance to free ourselves of nuclear weapons and then shelter under Nato's nuclear umbrella is difficult to reconcile. The bottom line is that, as a Nato member, we would be part of an organisation whose back-stop is nuclear strikes. All this assuming we were to be accepted as a Nato member on the terms we outline. Again, opinion is divided on the subject but we don't know for certain. It stands to reason we would be more secure as a member of a larger alliance, especially when it comes to intelligence sharing.

There are many other unknowns in many other fields, not least the actual cost of creating a separate Scotland and how that Scotland would be represented around the world and what relationships it would have with other countries. But unknowns are a part of all life, we all have to deal with them and plan for them as best we can. The benefits for an independent Scotland are posited as bringing decision-making vital to our creation of the society we want to see to the people best-suited to make them – the Scots. And that by doing so we will improve social justice in our society, making us fairer and more equal and reflecting and retaining our cultural values and sense of identity.

But we are already holders of many of the levers that allow us to create a society that reflects our desires and values. And more are on the way in the Scotland Act 2012, including greater control over taxes. And that's without any more powers which have been promised as part of this referendum battle. We are in complete control of education, which must be the surest way of shaping the future we want, we are in charge of health, which is the very practical delivery of how we care for people. The NHS has become an emotive topic in this debate, because it is close to us all for very practical reasons but also because it is the embodiment of the altruism and egalitarianism that forms a large part of our collective identity. But we can shape the NHS in Scotland as we choose.

We have our own unique legal system and we are predominantly in charge of the policing of our society. All these policies are formulated by the people we Scots vote for, with the decisions taken by our parliament in Scotland. We have already gone our own way and created a different country in many big areas, including no tuition fees, free care for the elderly and free prescriptions. The biggest factor in creating a prosperous and equal nation is the economy, and an independent Scotland would, of course, be able to stand on its own two feet, but under current proposals some of the levers needed would lie elsewhere and stability is under threat and that could come at a cost.

Next week, for many people, it will be independence at any cost. Others will weigh cost against benefits, risks against potential gains and losses. There are significant uncertainties with the proposals before us. There are some major parts of life that will be changed and we do not know what those changes are or what impact they will have, and at a cost we cannot calculate at present. It is clear there will be some constraints on what an independent Scotland can do. The political Union has helped to provide security and stability. And over the centuries Scots have played a large part in shaping that Union. Many, many Scots have benefited from opportunities it has afforded. We are a part of the fabric of the United Kingdom. We are a significant part of its history. Does the Union cast a dark shadow over us? It does not seem that way, Scotland is a prosperous, peaceful, successful country. We are confident in our national identity with our own distinctive society. We have our history and heritage. So, with the choices before us, the conclusion is that we are better together, that Scotland's best interests lie not in creating division but in continuing in the Union and using its strengths to help us continue in our success.

That is not a view taken because of fear, or lack of confidence, or lack of patriotism. It is the very opposite. It is not a view that simply does not want to take risk. It is a measured view that assesses risk against possible benefit and loss. It is seeing where the best interests of the Scottish people lie, understanding the benefits of working with the people in these islands in collaboration and partnership and seeing the opportunity to shape the strongest, most secure, fair and just society that we all want.

Former First Minister Alex Salmond, leaves Queensferry House at the Scottish Parliament, after handing over the job to Nicola Sturgeon. Accompanied by his wife Moira, he was clapped out by colleagues.

Of course I received the expected wave of protest and insult. I was called a traitor and a quisling, bought and sold for London gold, and by one man accused of editing *The Scotsman* "from my bungalow in Surrey". But I also received some support, including this from author Simon Schama, who I admit was an avid supporter of the Union. He tweeted: "Rigorous, level-headed front page essay in @TheScotsman – Adam Smith cheering from beyond, Hume from Old Carlton Burial Ground".

But of course the narrow result in September 2014 did not resolve the issue "for a generation" or anything like, but it continued to be the issue through which every political event and strategy was seen. Even the seismic shift of Brexit was in Scotland an independence issue.

Keep cool and carry on, we need to think this through

We know for sure that there will be consequences, but at the moment we have no way of knowing exactly what all the consequences will be. The vote on Thursday on the UK's continued membership of the EU has revealed a deeply divided Britain. The result will have huge ramifications for Scotland, and the United Kingdom, and Europe and knock on to the rest of the world.

Given the way that Scotland voted there can be little argument that this shows a massive difference in how Europe is viewed by the different sides of the Border. It can be no wonder that First Minister Nicola Sturgeon says it is "democratically unacceptable" and that a second Scottish independence referendum is now highly likely and is on the table. It was, after all, in the SNP's Holyrood manifesto.

The biggest consideration for Ms Sturgeon will be demonstrating there is public demand for a referendum and if there is, does that mean she will go on to win it? There has to be a doubt about how many people who voted No in the last independence referendum would put European membership above Union membership and change their vote in a second referendum. And it is worth pointing out that 38 per cent of Scots wanted to leave the EU, and they are getting what they wanted so presumably will not be seeking a reversal of that decision.

But using the EU result as the reason for a second referendum has some big practical difficulties. If it is all about giving the Scots their democratically expressed wish to stay in Europe, how can that be achieved? A close examination of Ms Sturgeon's words reveal she is aware of the potential pitfalls. She said: "I intend to take all possible steps and explore all possible options to give effect to how people in Scotland voted - in other words to secure our continuing place in the EU, and in the single market in particular."

She went on: "It is important that we take time to consider all steps and have the discussions, not least to assess the response of the European Union to the vote that Scotland expressed yesterday."

Given that at the last referendum the EU made it known there would be no automatic place in the EU for an independent Scotland, clearly she is hoping for change there. But that might not be a forlorn hope. There is already evidence of the tensions between the new UK regime and the European leaders. They have ripped up the deal agreed with David Cameron in February to protect London's financial markets, curb immigration and opt out of closer union. Perhaps those EU leaders are now wishing they had given Mr Cameron a little more in the way of reforms to take home to his rebellious electorate.

Boris Johnson wants time taken before the Brexit is triggered, the EU leaders want it to begin immediately. Mr Johnson wants to change immigration immediately regardless of treaties, the EU leaders say all treaties must be adhered to until the UK leaves the EU in two years' time. The tone of the relationship is already being set, and it is looking acrimonious.

Mr Cameron has said he will go, and the fact is that he had to. His hubris has brought us to this spectacular rift, when there was no need for us to be here at all. A cannier politician, or at least one that was not willing to take massive risks for his own personal legacy, would have realised the dangers, not courted them. His place in history will be very much different from how he envisaged it.

The division between Scotland and England is not the only one to be forced open by his reckless ambition. England is largely united against its capital as well as its political elite. Those splits will be difficult to heal, particularly in straitened economic times. And ironically, given that Mr Cameron's initial motivation in this was to unite his party, there is a deep rift in the Tories.

So who will take over from Mr Cameron and pilot the country through these complex and difficult changes? Both Michael Gove and Mr Johnson have been the faces of the Leave campaign but might they be seen as too partisan for the reconciliation that is to come? Has Theresa May distanced herself enough to step in as a neutral candidate, or has her stance been seen as too calculating? If indeed Mr Johnson does succeed Mr Cameron as prime minister, that must be worth at least another couple of percentage points to independence campaigners during a referendum campaign.

And of course Jeremy Corbyn's leadership of Labour is also under fire, although it is hard to remember a time now when it has not been.

His heart was never in the Remain campaign and that was obvious.

There has been much talk about the EU referendum result being about popular dissatisfaction with the political establishment and not so much about Europe, and there seems to be evidence for that view. But in many ways the motivations do not matter. The vote has been taken, the result has been given.

But now is a time for cool heads and consideration. There is much to be decided: it is complicated but of huge import to the society we are about to come. We are on the brink of momentous change, so everybody should take the time to open up the debates, and think actions through.

There is here a great opportunity to change society to better reflect people's altered desires and needs and aspirations, to heal the divides, so let's get it right.

And so Scotland's political future remains at the crossroads, and *The Scotsman* continues to report on the events of consequence for the nation and the world, as it has for the last 200 years.

I conclude with a final cutting from the archives which was published to mark the 200th anniversary of the founding of the paper. I wrote it. Editors like to have the last word.

WEDNESDAY, NOVEMBER 30, 2016

From such precarious beginnings was built a national newspaper which earned an international reputation, with its distinctive thistle-adorned masthead recognised the world over. We hope you enjoy this first taste of what is to come, and will join us on the exciting journey of celebration that lies before us. It is an honour and a privilege for me to continue the work of all the great journalists that have gone before, whose efforts, determination, skills and integrity have resulted in this newspaper becoming a part of the fabric of our nation, a position that I and my colleagues strive to maintain and enhance every day. It is right that we take this opportunity to celebrate our past, while looking very positively at our future as we continue to play what we see as a vital role in our country, Scotland.

THE SCOTSMAN

THURSDAY 24 JULY 2014　　SCOTLAND'S NATIONAL NEWSPAPER　　£1.30 SUBSCRIPTION PRICE: 97p　　WWW.SCOTSMAN.CO

Pure dead brilliant

2014 Games off to flying start with spectacular opening ceremony in Glasgow

The Games
Entry of the Gladiators

The Games Don't miss your 16-page daily supplement inside

PLUS Fantastic all-singing and dancing, and money-raising, night PAGES 2, 3, 4, 5, 6 & 7

CROSSWORDS AND GAMES 8 & 44, TELEVISION & RADIO 42-43, LETTERS 32-33, WEATHER 45, ANNOUNCEMENTS 40, SUDOKU

ESDAY 5 SEPTEMBER 2017
w.scotsman.com

£1.80
SUBSCRIPTION PRICE £1.28

THE SCOTSMAN

CELEBRATING 200 YEARS: SCOTLAND'S NATIONAL NEWSPA⬛⬛ NCE 1817

Sport: Malta win puts second place in Scotland's hands

Why our roads are now too dangerous too cycle on
AIDAN SMITH, PAGES 30-31

PICTURE LISA FERGUSON

cola Sturgeon joins the Queen for official opening of new bridge

Queensferry Crossing was officially opened by the Queen yesterday, 53 years to the day after she cut the ribbon to open the neighbouring Forth Road Bridge.
the weekend, 50,000 people were lucky enough to walk over the new structure, described as a 'once-in-a-lifetime' opportunity. **SEE PAGES 14, 15, 16 & 17**

Scotland slides in UK prosperity rankings

By **PARIS GOURTSOYANNIS**

Scotland has slipped in the UK's prosperity rankings despite a rise in average earnings, new research has suggested.

The study from Barclays Wealth and Investments found start-ups north of the Border are adding fewer jobs to the economy than in any other part of the UK.

London was again rated the most prosperous part of the UK, while Scotland fell by two places to ninth on the list.

Opposition parties last night blamed SNP policies that had made the nation "the highest-taxed part of the UK".

The Scottish Government said high earnings contributed to Scotland being one of the wealthiest parts of the UK.

FULL STORY, PAGE 6

H-bomb shows North Korea s 'begging for war', says US

NNIFER PELTZ
ARIA SANMINIATELLI

h Korea's leader is "begging for , the US ambassador to the Unitations told an emergency meetf the Security Council yesterday Kim Jong Un's latest nuclear test. kl Haley said the US would look at untries doing business withgyang and planned to circulate

● Calls for the United Nations to now impose 'strongest possible measures'

a resolution this week with the goal of getting it approved by next Monday.

The ambassador said: "Enough is enough. War is never something the United States wants. We don't want it now. But our country's patience is not unlimited.

"The United States will look at every country that does business with North Korea as a country that is giving aid to their reckless and dangerous nuclear intentions."

US president Donald Trump spoke by phone with his South Korean

counterpart Moon Jae-in and agreed that North Korea's hydrogen bomb test on Sunday was an "unprecedented" provocation.

South Korea is set to scrap a warhead weight limit on its own missiles and yesterday it carried out live-fire exercises, simulating an attack on Mr Kim's nuclear test site.

The emergency UN session came six

→ CONTINUED ON PAGE 4

Job fears as capital chiefs blow budget

Edinburgh Council chiefs are to make severe cuts after the city overspent its budget just three months into the financial year.

New figures are set to be presented to councillors today that reveal the authority is £11 million over budget in the first quarter of the year.

City officials have been warned that cutbacks will be to required over the next five years to correct the problem.

And there are also warnings that £140m in savings will be needed over the next five years.

Finance convener Alasdair Rankin warned more redundancies could be expected.

FULL STORY, PAGE 10

CROSSWORDS AND GAMES: 2&46 — TELEVISION & RADIO: 44-45 — LETTERS: 34-35 — WEATHER: 47 — ANNOUNCEMENTS: 42 — SUDOKU: 46

Subscriber list

D.M. Abbott
Nettie Adams
Dr James Aitken
William Alexander
Francis Alexander
Duncan Anderson
Malcolm Anderson
John Anderson
Sheila Anderson
Sandra Armor
Linda Armstrong
James Arnot
Ron Ashton
Christina Ashton
Dorothy Bartlett
James Bateman
Mr Leonard Bell
Roger Bing
David Binnie
Stewart Blair
Jaap Bossinade
Alan J C Brown
Iain R C Brown
Angus Brown
James Brown
James Thomas Brown
William George Rhind Brown
Elizabeth Lexie Brown Nee Mackay
Crystal LeAnn Bruce
Noreen Bryce
Denise Brydon
Neil Brydon
Neil D Buchanan
Joyce M Buchanan
Doreen Bunton
Alasdair John Burns
Gordon Burns
Robert Burns
The Team At Caledonia Public Affairs
David Cameron
Roderick Cameron
David R Campbell
John Campbell
Johnnie Campbell
Neil Campbell
Ronnie Campbell
John Cardownie
Anne Carle
Megan Carrie
Dennis Cassidy
Grant Cathro
Carlene Catramados
David Chalmers
Margaret Chambers
Eileen Cheyne
David Charles Clark
Terence J Coates
John Collington
James Musgrave Coltman
Andrew James Combe
William S Cooper

John D Cornwall
Ian Coxon, The Sunday Times
Alan Craig
Quentin Cramb
Jim Crosbie
Hazel M Cunningham
James Curren
Robert Dennis McDougall
Stevan Devine
Robert Donaldson
Colin Douglas
John T Drume
Agnes Christian McLean Bennett Duncan
Robert M. Dunn
Neil Dunning
Alex Duthie
Carltorpe Emslie
Elspeth Campbell Elgin Everett
Deirdre Jane Everett
Tina Evans
Georgia Anais Fallow
George Fallow
Stephen Farrell
James Fisher Employee 1952-2000
Lilian Flett
Paul M Flint
William Smith Forbes
Hannah Forshaw
Vincent George Franke
Josef Derek Franke
Ian Fraser
Peter B Freshwater
William Fulton
Katherine Gammie
Jan Garland
Caroline Gerard
Peter W M Gibb
David A Gibson
Frank S Gibson
Anne Ceres Gibson
Gilbert Gilbertson
John and Nancy Gilbertson
James Gilheany
Alastair Gillies
Elizabeth Gillies
Miss Dorothy Goate
Paul & Judy Goldfinch
Ian D Gow
David Gow
Maureen Gowans
Jardine Graham
Gerald M Graham
Norman A J Grant
William P Gray
Dr Rena Gray
Cathryn Gregor
Anne Gregor
Alister Greig
Gordon Greig
Alex Gunn
Jimmy Guthrie

Ewan Hamilton
Geoffrey Hamilton
John Hannah
David K Hardy
David Pinnock Harlow
Christina Harrison
John Harrison
Douglas Harrower
C M Hastie
Doug Hatch
Brian Hawkins
Lynne Hay
David Heggie
Meg Heggie
Andrew Scott Henderson
Carole Henderson Nee Mackie
Charles Ernest Henderson, D.S.O.1894-1946
David Henderson
Gordon Henderson
Douglas Henry
Sir John Herbecq
Lorraine Herbert
Ron Hill
Joseph Hobkirk
Ken Hogg
Elizabeth Honeyman
Emily Florence Hope
Madeleine Rose Hope
A Hope
Alistair & Karen Horn
Ian Horne
Rodger Horsfall
Leslie Dean Hough
Robert Stephan Iruin Houston
Donald Francis Iruin Houston
Janice Howell
David Hunt
Eric Hunter
Sally Hutton
Adam Hynd
Jennifer Hynd
Ben Ireland
Alexander Izitt
John Jackson
Kenneth NM Jamieson
Catherine & Yves Jarles
Alastair R Johnston
Derek C Johnstone
Glyn Jones
Dr Edward Jones
David O Jones
Petra Kalinowski
John & Kath Kesson
Michael G Kidd
Suzan W. King
Mary Kirkpatrick
Steven Knapp
Simon Knowles
Thelma Kropidlowska
George Laing
Eileen M Lapthorn

John Lauder
Peter T Laurie
P. C. D. Laverman
Ronnie Lawson
Doreen Keth Lee
Tom Lees
Robert Anderson Leslie
Linsay Leslie
Agnes Mary Anne Lind
William Andrew Locke
Seumas Lorimer
William Russell Love
David M. Low
The Luurtsema Family
Debbie Lyle
Jane Lyle
Richard Lyle
Kieth Lymn
Anne MacAskill
Calum MacDonald
David N Macdonald
Robert MacDonald
Jim MacDonald
Colin Macfarlane
Seumas MacInnes
K.D MacIntyre
Gordon & Nancy Macintyre
Bob MacKay
Bill MacKay
Hamish MacKay
Angus Mackenzie
John Stewart MacLellan
D.A.D. Macleod
Neil MacLeod
Sheila Macleod
Donald MacMillan
Pam MacMillan
Alasdair (Sandy) MacRae
Dr Malcolm MacRae
Alison Marr
David Masino
Joan Matthewson
Stephen McCrosson
Pat McCulloch
James J McDevitt
Aileen Margaret McFee
Stephen J. McGlashan
Jacqueline Ormiston McGovern
Andrew McGurk
Dominic McGurk
Dr Gordon McGurk
Dr Kenneth McGurk
Dr Simon McGurk
William Ernest McKeich
Paul McKelvey
Alexander McKenzie
Euan McLean
Argyll McLetchie
James McQueen
Henry W Melrose
Willie Millar
Derek Mills
Maggie Milne
Elizabeth Mitchell

Brian Morgan
John Ian Moore
Frances Morton
Graeme Morton
Douglas M Mottashaw
Miss Margaret Mouncey
Cameron A.M. Muir
John Mungall
Charles Murphy
Stuart Murray
Ian J Murray
Donald Murray
David S. R. Nangle
Donald Ness
Peter Ness
Richard Ness
Ronald Nugent
Alistair Ogg
John Cumming Pagan
Iain C.S. Parker
Simon Parnell
Liz Parnell
Colin S Paterson
Douglas Paton
Anne Patrick
Jean L Pearce
Dr Timothy H Perri
Alexander Phillip
Corinne de Popow
Mrs Geraldine Prentice
Sally Quinn
Mr Gareth Quinn
Robert Rae
William Redgrift
Jean Redmond
Rose Mary Reece
Ian Reekie
Guy Charles Barrington Reid
David Reid
Sandy Renwick
W.H.M Robson
C.P. Robson
Gillian F Ronaldson
Graham Rosie
Marcus Roskilly
Ken Ross
Kenny Ross
Franz-Joseph Rustemeier
Christl and Thomas Schlag
Douglas Schooler
Sheila Anne Scott
Mary Sear
Wing Commander C.A. Selkirk RAAF
Bernd Sengespeick
Bill Shade
W K Shearer
Neville H Shenton
Campbell Shillinglaw
George Shirriffs
Lewis Simpson
Alastair Sinclair
Syd Sinclair
Elizabeth Anne Sinclair
Jock Elliot Smith

Iain & Nancy Smith
James P. Smith OBE
Tom Sneddon
Michael Spence
James Spowart
Graham Stalker
F.J. Stephenson
Anna Stephenson
Robert Louis Stevenson
Ian M Stewart
Graham D Stewart
Robert E Stewart
Albert Still
Colin WJ Strathdee
Raymond P Strathdee
Richard R Strathdee
Eric Stratton
Denis Straughan
Ian Sutherland
Alan G Templeton
Christopher J Thomson
Colin S. Todd
Alex Tonner
Moyra Macpherson Traupe
Angus Tulloch
Fiona J Tweedie
Sue Urquart
Isobel Valentine
R Veitch
John B Waddell Snr
Mrs M F D Walker
Agnes Walker
Sarah Wallace
Andrew S Wallace
David Wallace
Jannette Wallace
James Warnock
John Waters
Imogen Olive Margaret Waugh
Jim Webster
Gail Welsh
Derek Whigham
Valerie White
Elaine K Wilson
Sheila Wilson
Brian Wilson
Stuart Wilson
Grace Winton
Alexander Wood
Hazel Woodsell
Peter D Wright
R.M Wyatt
George Wishart Young
Raj
Lesley
Irene & Brian
Pat & Keith
Allan & Evelyn
Douglas & Georgie & Isobel
Frances and Neil
Graeme
Bob
Tricia & Peter

WEDNESDAY 25 JANUARY 2017
www.scotsman.com

THE SCOTSMAN

SCOTLAND'S NATIONAL NEWSPAPER

SUBSCRIPTION PRICE

Some of the events covered by The Scotsman since it was founded in 1817, when its first edition reported on plans for the Union Canal and the death of author Jane Austen at the age of 41

200 years of news

● Special souvenir edition to mark bicentenary

By **MARTYN MCLAUGHLIN**

Tributes and messages of support have been flooding in to The Scotsman as the newspaper celebrates its bicentenary.

On a landmark day in the history of Scotland's national newspaper, key figures from across the nation's public life, led by the Queen, have joined in the celebration of 200 years of the newspaper.

They include political, religious and business leaders as well as leading lights in the worlds of the arts and sport.

The newspaper was founded by solicitor William Ritchie and customs official Charles Maclaren, under the guiding principles of "impartiality, firmness and independence", which to this day are printed at the head of its leader articles.

Its first edition was published on 25 January 1817, a year in which plans for the Union Canal were ratified, Jane Austen died at the age of 41 and George III was monarch.

Two centuries on, as the title marks its

→ CONTINUED ON PAGE 4

INSIDE YOUR SCOTSMAN TODAY

- A commemorative re-print of the historic first edition of The Scotsman from January 1817
- A 16-page pull-out looking at how The Scotsman has covered the news for the past 200 years
- New columnists and contributors in expanded Perspective and Business sections
- The start of bringing to life Scotland's past, present and future through the stories of 200 remarkable people

THE SCOTSMAN
SCOTS
Celebrating 200 years of Scotland's national newspaper, 1817-2017